MW00454574

SPORTING RHETORIC

PETER LANG
New York • Washington, D.C./Baltimore • Bern
Frankfurt am Main • Berlin • Brussels • Vienna • Oxford

SPORTING RHETORIC

Performance, Games, and Politics

EDITED BY BARRY BRUMMETT

PETER LANG
New York • Washington, D.C./Baltimore • Bern
Frankfurt am Main • Berlin • Brussels • Vienna • Oxford

Library of Congress Cataloging-in-Publication Data

Sporting rhetoric: performance, games, and politics /
edited by Barry Brummett.
p. cm.
Includes bibliographical references and index.
1. Sports—Social aspects. 2. Rhetoric--Social aspects.
I. Brummett, Barry.
GV706.5.S73899 306.4'83—dc22 2009025930
ISBN 978-1-4331-0427-5 (hardcover)
ISBN 978-1-4331-0428-2 (paperback)

Bibliographic information published by **Die Deutsche Bibliothek**.
Die Deutsche Bibliothek lists this publication in the "Deutsche
Nationalbibliografie"; detailed bibliographic data is available
on the Internet at http://dnb.ddb.de/.

Cover design by Sophie Boorsch Appel

The paper in this book meets the guidelines for permanence and durability
of the Committee on Production Guidelines for Book Longevity
of the Council of Library Resources.

© 2009 Peter Lang Publishing, Inc., New York
29 Broadway, 18th floor, New York, NY 10006
www.peterlang.com

All rights reserved.
Reprint or reproduction, even partially, in all forms such as microfilm,
xerography, microfiche, microcard, and offset strictly prohibited.

Printed in the United States of America

◻ To the graduate students in the Department of Communication Studies at the University of Texas at Austin—past, present, and future. They help to make the department a community of excellence and collegiality.

■ Contents

■ **Part Three: How Elements of Sports and Games
Are Taken up into Performance in the Wider Culture**

■ Foreword

Sport Communication Linked with Linguistics

□ Linda K. Fuller

As the field of sport communication works its way into many different disciplines, Barry Brummett's *Sporting Rhetoric* is an invaluable addition to the emerging genre examining the language of sport in our popular culture(s). Because he is first and foremost a rhetorician, it is particularly refreshing that Brummett encourages application of Burkean theories to popular culture and, as he does here, to the multifaceted arena of sport.

Elsewhere, after a discussion on the Neo-Aristotelian method, Brummett (2006: 149) has outlined seven schools of thought relative to rhetorical criticism of popular culture: (1) Marxist, (2) Visual, (3) Psychoanalysis, (4) Feminist, (5) Dramatistic/narrative, (6) Media-centered, and (7) Culture-centered. Here, his emphasis demonstrates how sport and games—that is to say, the performances around sport and games—can offer insights externally on audiences and sociocultural change as well as internally on performers' psyches. As such, contributors demonstrate how sports, while representing a microcosm of society, works to show the way societies of sporting performance are constantly occurring, and changing.

By way of example, chapters include topics such as advertisements promoting female athleticism, challenge matches invoking representations of masculinity, myth-making ("Super")heroes as well as myth-breaking scandals and controversies, nostalgia, pushing bodies to "perfection," iconographies and televised "reality" programming, naming and narrative restraints, mediated sport spectacles, the politics of stereotyping, weird competitions and contests, the feminist "gaze," music and media, spectator perspectives, the cult of celebrity and the indelibility of words both printed and spoken. By being so inclusive, Brummett is easily able to make his argument about the sociopolitical consequences of sport.

Performance, he maintains, is central to how sports and games in our popular culture are interpreted both by athletes and audiences. As in theatre, characters don uniforms and roles, ritualistic strategies and themes are followed, training and rehearsals are necessary, and productions vary depending on the day. "Performativity is not a singular 'act,'" Judith Butler (1993:12) reminds us, "for it is always a reiteration of a norm or set of norms, and to the extent that it acquires an act-like status in the present, it conceals or dissimulates the conventions of which it is a repetition." Small wonder that some athletes take what are called "performance-enhancing" drugs.

Games, we realize, are being enacted for consumers of sport. Analogies again can be made to theater, as people pay a price to participate in visual displays. Suspended judgments encourage spectators to see the athlete in action, perhaps discounting what s/he may know about off-the-field stories. Sporting games have heroes and heroines, villains and the victorious, underdogs and umbrage, triumph and trial, drama and denouement. But, basically, we all play to win, and to have fun. Tracing the history of games as a source of communal élan, Barbara Ehrenreich (2006: 227–228) has noted that, "Spectators began 'carnivalizing' sports events, coming in costume, engaging in collective rhythmic activities that went well beyond chants, adding their own music, dance, and feasting to the game."

Sports reporting, brought to us through a lens of corporate-constructed reality—whether through print or electronic means, on newspapers and magazines, via radio talk shows or 24-hour television networks, the Internet, sport Web logs, and/or on our phones, our pagers, even our iPods—is often rife with politics. A form of journalism that is about much more than games, athletes, and audiences, it investigates topics ranging from racism and sexism to steroid usage to gender equity and other sticky subjects. Politics, infused as it is in every profession, is clearly apparent in sport. Poulton and Roderick (2008) see sport as a metaphor for many areas of social life, such as our social identities, politics, consumerism, and violence. To their list, let us also add notions of nationalism, which permeate sport according to geocultural proclivities. And, taken to extremes, consider the implications of athletic warriors wanting to be on battlefields.

As an amazing demonstration of the multidisciplinary interest in sport, let me encourage you to read the "About the Contributors" section for this volume. There, you will see that their interests include the following: Argumentation and Persuasion, Communication Studies, Community Development, Cultural Studies, Debate, English, Film History, Gaming and Simulations, Gender Studies, History, International Relations, Media Criticism, Organizational Communication, Political Science, Popular Culture, Radio-TV-Film, Rhetoric and Language Studies, Social Movements, Sociology, Speech.

Whether personal and/or organizational, sport mass media, or servicing/supporting areas, sport communication is just now emerging as its own distinct discipline (Pedersen, Miloch, and Laucella, 2007). Offering numerous career options—advertising, advocacy, athletics, business, facilities, marketing/media, personnel, photography/videography, public relations, sports agency, sports journalism, statistics, team management, and more—the best part is learning critical, transferable skills.

"Without necessarily seeking to do so," Blackshaw and Crabbe (2004: 18) have noted, "social considerations of sport have tended to be framed by structure functionalist narratives…which emphasize what sport does *to* people and *for* 'society.'" For our purposes, examining linguistic attributes of the $200+ billion world of sport offers endless insights. So, the real value of Brummet's collection of essays lies in its excellent entwining of so many outstanding examples of rhetorical selections relative to performance, games, and politics.

References

Blackshaw, T. and Crabbe, T. (2004). *New perspectives on sport and "deviance": Consumption, performativity, and social control.* London: Routledge.

Brummett, B. (2006). *Rhetoric in popular culture, 2nd ed.* Thousand Oaks, CA: Sage.

Butler, J. (1993). *Bodies that matter: On the discursive limits of "sex."* New York: Routledge.

Ehrenreich, B. (2006). *Dancing in the streets: A history of collective joy.* New York: Metropolitan Books/Henry Holt and Company.

Pedersen, P. M., Miloch, K. S., and Laucella, P. C. (2007). *Strategic sport communication.* Human Kinetics.

Poulton, E. and Roderick, M. (Eds.) (2008). *Sport in films.* London: Routledge.

■ Acknowledgments

Any edited book is already the product of many hands. I want to thank all the chapter authors, who worked well and tirelessly to bring their chapters to perfection. Thanks to our editor, Mary Savigar, who invested her time, energy, and commitment in this book. We thank the anonymous reviewers, whose comments made us better. I especially want to thank Mr. Roger Gatchet, who undertook the editing of the book with regards to MLA style and did the most professional job of editing I have ever seen.

■ Introduction

Sports, Games, Rhetoric, Performance, and Politics

☐ Barry Brummett

The summer of 2008 brought to television and computer screens around the world the biennial spectacle of the Olympic Games. Beijing, China, played host to the festivities that year. Although every new Olympic Games is different, many people tune in to watch them because they know they will see some recurrent dramas. Certain themes will come up—you can count on it! The themes we are most concerned with in this book have to do with the way that performances in and around sports and games—as central components of popular culture today—have rhetorical impact on audiences, leading to social and political changes.

One theme is performance, a term that is often used to describe how athletes do in their events. An athlete will be described as having put in a star performance in the discus throw, for instance. Some performances begin even before the games, as when American gymnasts Paul and Morgan Hamm dramatically and emotionally withdrew from competition due to injuries. Four American cyclists inadvertently insulted their Chinese hosts by ostentatiously wearing pollution masks as they arrived in the airport. During the games, emotional devastation and disappointment is performed in public by athletes such as Alicia Sacramone, who fell twice during a gymnastics routine. Expressions of exhaustion and dismay crossed the faces of the American women's soccer team when they lost to Norway. These athletes know the cameras are upon them, and that what they do and say enters the theater of world television.

The Olympics fan will find performances outside of the actual athletic events as well. Often these are our own performances: we have friends over and cheer wildly for our favorite athletes. We go into work and speak knowledgeably about last night's competition. "Go for the Gold!" I am urged by a flier from Time Warner Cable television in my mailbox, asking me to become part of the games by subscribing. The advertisement features a picture of a swimmer bursting from out of the television into my living room. These performances strengthen our senses of identity and group belonging.

We observe the performances of others as well, both the famous and the infamous. These performances by athletes, politicians, coaches, and hangers-on begin to suggest some of the rhetorical, political impact of the games. The flag bearer for the United States team was Lopez Lomong, a "Lost Boy" originally from the Sudan. His proud and smiling figure at the head of the American squad was a performance of America's diversity and international allure, despite recent diplomatic blunders. There is a rhetoric at work in popular culture in this example, as audiences experiencing entertainment may be influenced toward specific political and social attitudes.

Some performances around sports and games are explicitly connected to rhetorical effects in politics. Russian prime minister Vladimir Putin and American president George Bush both attended opening ceremonies, putting on performances in press conferences and interviews, until Putin had to rush home to manage his country's invasion of the Republic of Georgia. President Bush remained to project a performance of calm leadership on the world stage in a time of crisis. Swedish wrestler Ara Abrahamian threw his bronze medal to the ground in disgust, as his coach complained that his being denied the gold was nothing but "politics." Photographs were widely circulated of the Spanish basketball team mocking the Chinese national team by making Asian "slant-eyes," an ethnic slur that caused outraged reactions around the world. These are performances within the games, and counter-performances by observers around the world, with important political and social impact. In the Spanish-Chinese incident, racial politics are played out on a stage created by sport.

The Olympics have often been a site of performances with rhetorical impact as a focal point for nations and groups to send persuasive messages to the world. President Carter directed that the United States boycott the 1980 Olympics to protest the Soviet invasion of Afghanistan. There was some discussion of boycotting the 2008 Olympics to protest alleged Chinese human rights violations, especially in Tibet. Evening news broadcasts often reported on the activities of protestors who used the publicity offered by the Olympics to broadcast their messages to the world. For many years, apartheid South Africa was barred from participation in the Olympics, and in many other international sporting events.

The Olympics are not by any means the only site where sports, games, rhetoric, politics, and social issues are manifest in public performances. Sports and games are highly performative. Most sports are spectator sports, even if the spectators are the neighborhood kids hanging around a local basketball court. Players know they enter onto a stage when they enter into the game, and many a neighborhood star makes the most of her celebrity through showy displays on the court or field. From the Olympics to pickup basketball to street stickball to chess in the park, sports and games are a place where people perform so that others may see them. These performances are rhetorical in that they influence how people think about social and political issues. In creating these influences, sports and games have tremendous effect in popular culture. These are the issues examined in the chapters of this book.

This book is a collection of scholarly essays that study the rhetorical, performative dimensions of sports and games, exploring the ways in which social and political work is accomplished through performance in popular culture—specifically, the popular culture that is sports and games. Chapters include studies of sporting events, of actual games played, of performance surrounding games and sporting events, of "fake" sports that are almost all performative and hardly sports at all, and of widespread cultural performative activities that use sports as a repertoire of signs. We explore such questions as the following: How are sports and games performative, and to what social and political end? What does it mean to say that sports and games, or activities connected to sports and games, are performative? What is it about sports and games in their various forms and places in our culture that specifically calls for performative analysis? How are major social and political struggles carried out in part or in whole through games or sports-related performance?

The book is organized in three parts: Part One introduces the subject of the book and discusses general dimensions of performance in sports and games. The Rachel Kraft and Barry Brummett chapter comes first and is the broadest of the three, introducing basic concepts, defining key terms, and setting the agenda for the rest of the book. Roger Gatchet's chapter looks at the theme of "making monsters" across sports to argue that the performative dimensions of sports and games are used widely to rhetorical effect throughout the culture. Gatchet's study shows how, in general, performance in sports and games plays a wider role in rhetorical struggles. Sunshine Webster's chapter agues that stylized images found in the performance of female athleticism give us a repertoire of ways to think about an important instrument of rhetoric in culture.

Part Two looks "inward" toward texts of performance in sports and games, while Part Three looks "outward" toward the use in the wider culture that is made of performances found in sports and games. Both assess the effects of these performances as rhetorics of popular culture. Part Two looks within actual sports and games, or more precisely within the texts of their public appearances and presentations. This section of the book examines the ways in which performances are part of how the sports and games are played. The rhetorical effects of such performances are considered in each case. Carlnita Greene studies the highly performative events of Silver League Base Ball, showing the rhetorical work of creating collective memory that is carried out in the games. Greene's study examines the restructuring of the past, with rhetorical effect, in the performances of these games. Luke Winslow shows how masculinity is performed within the sport of bull riding, and the rhetorical effects created by such performances. Jaime Wright studies the performative standard of perfection coached in the texts of the Japanese television show Ninja Warriors and considers its rhetorical effect in culture. Alexis Carreiro's chapter studies the Roller Girls phenomenon to examine the performance of female identity within those events. Jay Childers finds political, rhetorical impact in the performance of poker in tournaments carried on television. Laura Barberena identifies the rhetorical effect of the performance of class struggle within the highly performative sport of Mexican Lucha Libre.

Part Three keeps one eye on sports while examining the ways in which images, actions, objects, and signs are mined from sports and games and used performatively in the broader culture beyond sports and games. Part Three thus considers performances in sports and games as a kind of symbolic repertoire used by people in performances throughout the culture beyond those sports and games. Jeanine Congalton's chapter studies the ways in which eating contests are taken up into the broader culture as integral parts of wider events such as state fairs and so forth. Kevin Johnson's chapter looks at the dialectic between the signs and performance of hip hop as a broad cultural system and sports and games as a parallel system, noting the ways in which signs and performances are borrowed back and forth. His study considers both directions of cultural borrowing found in our other chapters, for he shows how NBA and street basketball incorporate performative signs from the hip hop system and ways in which hip hop uses signs taken from the NBA. Tim Steffensmeier sees collegiate football tailgating as the performance of "sacred" rituals of weekend life for many observers. Fans who gather in stadium parking lots around the nation conduct their own performances with one another, with rhetorical effect. Finally, Meredith Bagley's chapter studies the Don Imus and Rutgers women's basketball controversy, focusing on the ways in which images and stereotypes connected to sports performance are taken up into broader social struggles that chain out in the culture.

■ Part One

General Dimensions
of the Rhetoric
of Performance
in Sport and Games

■ Introduction

Part One contains three chapters. The first chapter, by Rachel Kraft and Barry Brummett, introduces major terms and concepts that will be important through the rest of the book. Pay particular attention to the key terms of rhetoric, sport and games, performance, and popular culture. Note where these terms converge and how attention to one idea necessarily leads you to another idea. The second chapter, by Roger Gatchet, discusses how "monsters" are made out of the material provided by prominent sports figures who go astray in the public eye. Think about why Gatchet uses the term "monster." What do monsters do for the public, generally? Also, think of other public examples of making monsters. The third chapter, by Sunshine Webster, argues that traditional, stereotypical expectations of femininity are difficult to avoid. Even sports figures who do not want to feminize sports in traditional ways may be pushed by the public in ways beyond their control. Ask yourself if this sort of constraint also operates for race, class, sexual orientation, and so forth.

1

■ Why Sport and Games Matter

Performative Rhetorics in Popular Culture

❏ Rachel Kraft and Barry Brummett

Are there any cultural activities around the world that engage people more than sport and games? Europeans, Asians, Africans, and Central and South Americans cheer passionately for their favorite soccer (or football, in their usage) teams. The sight of nattily attired young men playing cricket practically screams "British Empire." American young people have made video games a billion-dollar industry. Baseball has been called our "national pastime," while Friday, Saturday, and Sunday are reserved for high school, college, and professional football. Yet it has not always been so. In the United States at least, this high passion for sport and games is of fairly recent historical vintage, having begun its upward climb only in the late nineteenth century.

Since sport and games became components of the American social landscape, we have played and watched them with a kind of mania. The evidence abounds: Amateur and professional athletes alike will train diligently for competition, sometimes foregoing all other occupations in the hunt for perfect performance. The spectator audience for sport is huge and committed. Some Red Sox fans paid upward of $600 a seat to watch the baseball team from

Boston during the 2007 Major League Baseball playoffs. The record-sized television audience following the 2004 Olympics in Athens could watch real-time competitions at two and three in the morning if they could not stand to wait for delayed airings later in the day.

Not too many decades ago, people would watch a handful of major sports on television or listen to them on the radio: baseball, football, hockey, and the like. Today, spectator sport has become a major source of pleasure to fans across many media (Brummett and Duncan; Duncan and Brummett, "Mediation"). One can see people playing poker, table tennis, or skateboarding mediated on cable television, and people go online to participate in endless games of simulation such as Second Life; mediated spectator sports are everywhere (McAllister; Rowe). The increasing popularity and availability of alternative sport and competitions caused CBS to cover 2007 Guitar Hero and World of Warcraft video and computer game competitions on television, becoming the first major broadcast channel to cover these games as if they were sporting events. Now individuals who enjoy playing the air guitar can compete against others in twenty-four cities around the United States and non-traditional sport and games have become a multibillion dollar industry.

What do we mean by sport and games, and why do we put them together in the same category? Both terms are so familiar to us that, paradoxically, precise definitions may be neither possible nor desirable. Common to both is a sense of play (Huizinga). Although participants may be in great earnest about sport and games, they are essentially playing, engaging in activities outside the usual humdrum context of work and obligation. People engage in sport and games because they want to—those who do so under obligation are going to work or fulfilling a gym class assignment but are neither sporting nor playing. Competition is usually a component of sport and games, although not always—someone is trying to win, to outscore, perhaps to improve one's own best performance. One may engage in sport and games either as a player (go out onto the soccer field, sit down to a game of poker) or as a spectator (sit in the stands, watch poker on television).

Sport and games denote some level, great or small, of physical exertion, at least for the players. Nearly everything we call a "sport" is physically challenging. So are many games, however—chess, for instance, is notoriously taxing physically. Try sitting at a board for hours on end thinking furiously if you doubt this. Sport and games also denote some level, great or small, of mental exertion, at least for the players. Never mind the stereotype of the dumb athlete. There are many ways to be smart or dumb, and on the court or field the athlete must be mentally skilled in the context of that sport, or she won't be an athlete for long. And games, of course, require mental exertion in the context of preparation for the game and the game itself. To return to the example of chess, a great deal of mental exertion, even genius, is required. But the sad example of American chess genius Bobby Fischer, whose personal life was a maelstrom of paranoia and instability, shows that the mental intensity of chess players before the board can be just as great, and just as limited, as the mental intensity of a great baseball hitter judging an incoming fastball.

In this chapter, we argue that sport and games, whether those we watch as spectators or those we engage in directly, have tremendous social and political consequences. Sport and games are increasingly important components of popular culture around the world (Birrell and McDonald; Farrell). But although these are games, they are not merely games. There is a rhetoric in sport and games: they are persuasive communications, texts that, intentionally or unintentionally, influence the social and political attitudes held by the public. As Bob Krizek observes, "the intersection of Sport and Communication is a complex terrain supporting a wide-range of interesting and culturally important topics" (103). Sport and games rhetorically influence how we think about some major social issues. We argue also that sport and games are highly performative, that is, taking on a role by exhibiting behaviors, stances, costumes, and so forth that will be widely understood as having social and political meaning. The athlete entering an arena is much like the teacher entering a classroom: one must take on a role, put on a mask, to become that athlete or teacher in the theatrical space of that activity. Sport and game participants enact socially defined roles, they play to audiences; participants know they are being observed and they tailor their behaviors in these performances to audience presence. In fact, we argue, it is largely through their performative dimension that sport and games have their rhetorical effects in popular culture.

To develop our argument we first argue that sport and games are major ways in which people form personal and social identity these days. We see ourselves as chess players or Cubs fans, we are golfers at our core, we cheer on the Olympic athletes from our own countries or countries we like with a sense of national pride—in short, we create ourselves individually and as social groups in large part through the sport and games of popular culture. We will argue, second, that through sport and games we construct difference, saying who we are not, saying who is normal and who is not. If we cheer for our own nation's Olympic athletes, we hope for the downfall of athletes from countries of which we disapprove. We follow the latest steroid or doping scandal to reassure ourselves that at least "we" are not like "them." Third, in this chapter we return to the idea of performance to identify it as a main mechanism by which, through sport and games, we create who we are and who we are not. It is in these social and personal performances that sport and games have such rhetorical effect, shaping attitudes and motives. Let us turn now to the ways in which sport and games create personal and social identity.

■ Sport and Games: Personal and Social Identity

Participants and fans often define themselves by what they play or which teams they support. This is what Michael Butterworth calls "sport's power to shape who we are as a people" ("Purifying" 146). It is on the playing fields and the courts, on our home computers, through print media, sport television, and the Internet that sport and games have become a central part of individual and social character. This happens largely because sport and games are sources of meaning and shared symbols in our society. Everybody will understand that a reference to Michael Jordan underscores athletic brilliance and mastery, and the meanings he facilitates as a symbol have been central to the ways in which many a youngster has defined himself. Whether participating or watching, sport and games have become "site[s] for the production of meanings" (Oates 76). They not only hold our attention but also have become critical tools used for identity and social development. As Richard Gruneau contends, sports are creations of "human agency" (31). How we participate in or watch sport and games operates within historical and cultural contexts. Fans buy the jerseys of players whose on- or off-field style they can relate to, and fans get together with friends to watch events with great diligence and devotion. Neal Gabler argues that moviegoers model their lives around film; the same may be said for sports fans and their games.

Though many view sport and games as harmless pastimes, our obsession with them has social, political, and economic meaning; how we think about and react toward sport, games, and players symbolizes social and political ideology surrounding race, gender, and citizenship, revealing which cultural and individual values are important to society. How sport and games interacts with other discourses also has meaning (Meân 792). As Butterworth argues, "it is impossible to separate sport from the field of politics" even if "fans and media alike continue to insist that sport remains divorced from the political and social terrain" ("Purifying" 147). Butterworth shows, for instance, how the Iraqi national soccer team became an agency of national identity ("Politics"). Younghan Cho studies the politics of another soccer encounter. Sport is not outside our system of values, beliefs, and identities.

It is useful to think about sport and games as messages, as ways to communicate about important social and political issues. As Kurt Lindemann and

James L. Cherney observed in their study of wheelchair rugby, "participating in wheelchair rugby is itself a communicative act that sends a complex message to both the community of sport and our broader social collectives that counters ableist assumptions about what persons with quadriplegia can accomplish" (108). The same is true for all sport and games: participating in synchronized swimming sends different messages—about gender, sexuality, masculinity, femininity, national allegiance and origins, and so forth—than does participating in Thai kickboxing.

Sport is not only an outlet for exhibiting unspent energy or congregating with friends, it is a "socializing agent" (Fuller 4). People form communities around sport and games, and the shared symbols of those activities ground the community (Aden). In the right places, cries of "Hook 'em Horns!" or "Woo, Pig! Sooie!" or "Gig 'em!" will draw together friends or foes. Similar senses of identity form at the national level; Butterworth observes that "sport is a common site for the production and communication of national identities" ("Purifying" 145). The actions of both players and fans makes rhetorical use of a set of shared codes about how athletes are supposed to behave in and out of the sporting or gaming arena (Fuller 4).

Several scholars have explored the social and historical evolution of physical activity and sport (Baker; Whannel; Zeigler). This history has been connected to our attitudes toward identity regarding gender. Lindemann and Cherney observe that "involvement in the community of sport is restricted by certain social characteristics and such involvement draws upon traditional notions of gender and ability" (108). This has proved true since industrialization and immigration took root in the United States, causing sport to take on significant cultural importance. Men and boys began engaging in sport and games in large numbers in the late nineteenth century and the early twentieth century as a way to improve strength and fitness and ready them for battle against impending threats from abroad. As Lindsay Meân writes, "the sports field is frequently represented as a battle field in which male athletes are powerful and aggressive, with bodies characterized as weapons or tools" (790). Even Teddy Roosevelt believed that sports could build strength and character that would produce men who could make the United States into a formidable presence on the world stage (Zirin 18). Women, by and large, participated for vastly different reasons—to instill camaraderie and friendship but not in aggressive or vigorous ways. Hardin and Shain highlight this distinction between male and female participation, noting that "male superiority and female inferiority" have held constant through the evolution of sport (323).

We form identity individually and in groups by defining the cultural groups to which we belong and through declaring our class status and aspirations. Sport and games have long been a way to express the commonly held values of our class and, perhaps more importantly, to provide ways for people to improve their class status. Some have viewed athletic participation as an equalizer, an element of society in which individuals were able to start from nothing and achieve great fame and renown by embodying social values such as diligence, perseverance, hard work, and determination. It was an arena in which athletes from all backgrounds could come together and show their dedication to American values and ideals of physical fitness. Baseball, among other sports, came to epitomize sport as the social and economic equalizer. It symbolized a forum in which heroes could be made and ordinary people could attain success (Trujillo 3). These views of sport as a means to personal and social improvement continue today, of course. Basketball and boxing have long been regarded as a "way out" of dead end inner city living. Football in small town Texas provides the same dream, if not reality, for young men. All sorts of athletics are assumed to build character in young people. With the rise of new media, interactive multiplayer computer games allow players to create their own identities, talk online with others, and build teams. Computer and video games have become as social as kickball or watching one's college football team with a group of like-minded friends (Humphreys 38).

Our personal and cultural identities are formed through defining our gender and what it means to be male or female, masculine or feminine. While men and boys readily participated in sport and games, early participation for women and for people of color operated under a certain set of spoken and unspoken rules and largely operated outside the realm of "traditional" sport until the passage of major Civil Rights legislation in the 1960s and Title IX in 1972. These laws required programs receiving federal money to allot equal amounts to male and females sport. Scholars who have detailed the historical participation and understanding of women and people of color in sport explore not only ceiling-breaking athletes but also what their participation has meant for the social and political fabric (Cahn; Festle; Smith; Bloom and Willard). As they explain, women were supposed to dress in feminine ways, so as not to attract any suspicion that they might be overly mannish or lesbians. In the early days of sport and games, many were barred altogether since sport were believed to cultivate aggression, determination, and physical strength—traits that were regarded as male characteristics and as qualities that would incite hysteria, inhibiting women's ability to have children and rear a family. Whether females have participated in or been excluded from sport and games, both have served as means of defining identity in society.

We also form our various identities and allegiances through declaring our ethnicities and races (Butterworth, "Race"; Delgado). Athletes of color who displayed impressive athletic ability were viewed as hyper-human and sexually deviant, dismissed as abnormal and abhorrent. They were left out of popular sport and competitions, save for a few exceptional athletes such as boxer Jack Johnson, sprinter Jesse Owens, and baseball player Jackie Robinson, whose athletic prowess came not without significant public criticism. It was not until the twenty-first century that athletes such as Tiger Woods and the Williams sisters (Venus and Serena) largely contended with color lines drawn around the boundaries of sport and games traditionally played by whites such as golf and tennis.[1] This is one reason why, when major league baseball was segregated by race, the old Negro Leagues were such a source of pride for African Americans. It is also a reason why there was so much at stake socially when Jackie Robinson integrated major league baseball by playing for the Brooklyn Dodgers in 1947.

■ Sport and Games: Constructing Difference

Both societies and individuals need to say who they are and often use sport for that purpose, as we saw in the first section. But to say who you are also entails saying who you are not. To construct ourselves as salt of the earth, we need to have an idea of who is elitist and distant. If we are honest and hardworking, we need images of who is lazy and a cheater. Sport and games are also central to the ways in which individuals and societies construct difference. Descriptions that position athletes as heroes or villains, exemplary sportsmen or bad boys, or other portrayals that locate behavior or appearance in one "good" category or its perceived "bad" opposite create binary categories in sport and games that communicate palatable forms of experiencing identity. Lindsey J. Meân and Jeffrey W. Kassing, for instance, argue that for many women "performing female athletic identity involved marking difference" (137).

We construct difference within sport: we have heroes and villains on the court. We know which wrestlers are the good guys and which are not. But we also construct differences between ordinary mortals and prominent athletes. Highly stratified designations in sport and games work to communicate particular ways of acting and being within athletic and gaming communities. Within conventional and well-established social, political, and economic historical contexts for sport, stereotype and stigma surrounding social identity groups have become part of an American system of normativity. In it, ideals of model citizenship are produced and communicated to the sport and game-consuming public from multiple areas of our culture. Through collaboration with other institutions that are part of society, such as family, education, government, media, science, and law, sport has become a central institution through which individuals come to understand themselves and differentiate others, and to participate in the continuous making and remaking of social norms by conforming to or lashing out against them. Sport methodically casts individuals who are not "normal" into a constricted and confining end of a binary mold that places limits on difference and agency. For instance, LaFrance and Rail studied public sentiment toward Dennis Rodman while he played for the Chicago Bulls basketball team. Rodman, who often dressed in women's clothing and rejected the traditional images of masculinity in men's basketball, became a phenomenon because he broke from the binary mold of how male athletes are supposed to act. Though he was a professional athlete who helped the Bulls win several national championships, his appearance off the court did not align with the type of image that successful basketball players are viewed as typically having.[2] It was clear that Rodman received the attention that he did because he helped the public define difference.

On the other hand, Nick Trujillo's analysis of legendary Major League Baseball pitcher Nolan Ryan shows how Ryan was constructed as a hero, in contrast to some other athletes, who embodied widely held values. Difference was employed in this case to build up a hero, by comparison. Trujillo suggests that in spectatorship, the meanings that are gathered from watching sport are applied to lived experiences of individuals and "reflect underlying attitudes, values, and beliefs" of that viewing public (3). Nolan Ryan was a great pitcher not only because of his low earned runs average, his complete games, or his career that lasted into his forties. Ryan was considered a heroic player also because he personified the values of fans and fit their image. To viewers, Ryan was the epitome of success. He was a pitcher with exceptional ability and prowess who was a rancher in the off season and appreciated simplistic living. The media liked to characterize Ryan as "almost perfect," a man who was "legendary" and shared an ethic of how men are supposed to pursue their passions and show strength (3). Through depictions of Ryan, viewers could experience a shared sense of reality surrounding a white male athlete in a sport that is systematically described as the American pastime that exemplifies bodies that are aesthetically pleasing and physically fit (Trujillo 117).

Judith Butler describes how constructing difference between normal and deviant individuals perpetuates a system of social ideals that is arbitrary and serves to uphold systems of power ("Athletic"). She identifies specifically the power structure of racism and heterosexual patriarchy. Dichotomous (black-white, male-female) categorizations are created in order to "fix" identity—to classify, name, and recognize how individuals fit into the national framework. As part of binary groupings, "normal" bodies usually go unrecognized. Nothing about them is perceived as irregular to call attention. Conversely, impressions of deviance label non-normative individuals as either godlike or as pariahs.

They serve as hyper-visible examples counter to traditional concepts of appropriate and palatable identity. Race and gender are part of a "system of binary oppositions" (Butterworth, "Pitchers" 140). Society regards race as black or white, gender as man or woman, and individuals as normal or abnormal and as insiders or outsiders.

Two important examples of the dichotomous construction of difference are gender and sexuality. Meân and Kassing argue that "due to its cultural prominence the community of sport provides a powerful site for the re/production of hegemonic forms of knowledge about gender and gendered practices" (127). Gender is conflated with sexuality to imply a straight or gay identity. This binary construction of race and gender, amongst other categories, positions groups within each dichotomy as strict opposites. Michael Butterworth explains: "interpretations of gender and sexuality within popular culture tend to essentialize men and women as clearly marked opposites based on biological sex differences" (Butterworth, "Pitchers" 140). Men and women alike participate in these constructions, but categories of "normal" would not exist without distinct categories or the "other." Duncan and Brummett, however, show how spectator sport may also contain sources of female empowerment through refusal of masculine hegemony ("Liberal").

Sport has always been a site for the construction of normative masculinity through difference, often in contrast to femininity as well as to gay masculinities (Butterworth, "Pitchers"). Lindemann and Cherney observe that "communication in a team sport can create and sustain an organizational culture that emphasizes and encourages particular meanings and enactments of masculinity" (110). For example, in 2007, CBS Sports and other television channels repeatedly showed Tony Joiner, a football player for the University of Florida Gators, kissing teammate and quarterback Tim Tebow on the cheek after Tebow completed a touchdown pass to another player. Clearly, the behavior and the athletes involved were regarded as different from the norm because it involved public display of emotion and affection in a sport dominated by images of brute strength and aggression. Repeated media attention showed how behavior in sport that is widely considered abnormal, in this case a male athlete kissing another male athlete, is highlighted as a sort of public spectacle.

■ Sport and Games: Performance

One particular dimension of our discussion so far that we now bring to the foreground is that of performance. "Performance" is a term widely used in social and humanistic studies today to emphasize the social and rhetorical construction of identity and experience (Bial; Butler, *Bodies, Gender,* "Performative"; Pacanowsky and O'Donnell-Trujillo; Schechner). Sports often involve showing oneself and others how to be masculine, how to possess cultural values such as loyalty or aggressiveness, in short, they involve "communicative performances of enculturation" (Lindemann and Cherney 120). Many fans of basketball have taken on the look and culture of hip-hop while young girls don the jerseys of their favorite soccer players. Increased media attention toward sport, games, and athletes and ever-pervasive advertisements for sporting goods, products, and the athletes themselves have made performances of race, gender, sexuality, and nationality in sport and games into a critical component of popular culture. For example, Susan Burris contends that sports industries such as the National Basketball Association made professional sport a key component of popular culture at the end of the twentieth century (85). According to Boyle and Haynes, "the media are important, in the sense that they help foster a wider feeling of collective identification among members in the social group" (13). Whether it is news or sport, the media has the ability to determine what viewers see as important by determining how often they show particular sporting acts, what time slots and channels on which they show sports, and how many resources are devoted to promoting an event. Thomas Oates describes sport as a series of moments where identities are played out, transformed, and situated within a particular narrative or context, a context often created by television channels and commentators (76). No forum other than attending or participating in a game facilitates this sense of purpose more than mediated television. Television and other media have their eye on sport precisely because sport and games are so highly performative, especially in the current state of affairs, where high-definition viewing rules the day and twenty-four hour cable sports channels rake in the money. The expression "spectator sport" itself insists on seeing that which is viewed as a performance. And every weekend athlete, every girl on an after-school soccer field, is aware of how she presents herself to her public whether large or small. Paul D. Turman, for example, studies the effects of coaches' performance of "immediacy behaviors" as motivating factors for teams (162).

When Olympic volleyball star Misty May-Treanor wipes off her sand-clad feet and puts on dancing shoes in *Dancing with the Stars* or when Dennis Rodman wears women's clothing and makeup, each athlete is putting on a performance: enacting a role in public that has social and political implications. Gender identity is fruitfully understood as performative in many studies (Butler, Bodies, Gender; Lockford; Walker). Because the public has used Rodman as a way to construct difference, it may seem as if only the strange and different perform. This is not at all the case. Every football player who spikes the ball in the end zone after a touchdown—every basketball player who hangs on the rim after a slam dunk—every Texas Hold 'Em poker player who dons shades and pulls a wide brimmed hat down over her eyes so that her expression cannot be seen—all of them are performing. One cannot merely be a player or an athlete. You must perform that identity; you must show it to others. Athletes, gamers, and fans participate in this performance, "the idea of actively and intimately 'doing,' 'sensing,' and 'living'" (Hargreaves and Vertinsky 5).

Meân and Kassing study ways in which women specifically "do or perform [female] athleticism" (127). Female athletes must cope with the perceived mutual exclusivity of aggressiveness and femininity too—often through carefully managed performances. In the July 1997 edition of *Sport* magazine, female professional basketball player Lisa Leslie exposed the image women in sport and games are expected to perform when she said, "When I'm playing, I'll sweat and talk trash. However, off the court, I'm lipstick, heels and short skirts. I'm very feminine, mild-mannered and sensitive" (Festle 45). In the 1990s, world renowned track star Marion Jones personified palatable experiences of race and gender within sport because she performed the role of the elegant black athlete who could don spike shoes and outpace all competition in the 100-meter sprint and then pose for the cover of *Vogue* magazine in a stylish evening gown (Heywood and Dworkin xvii, 81). Before her recent admission of steroid use, resulting in her being stripped of all Olympic medals that she had won, Jones was a palatable sporting figure because she did not disrupt ideals of race or gender and instead performed them. She became more like an object of sexual desire, a position that black track athletes have occupied since black women began to excel on the track in the 1920s and the 1930s. As a woman who wore dresses and posed for fashion magazines, she did not blur the lines of femininity or destabilize traditional paradigms surrounding black female athleticism.

Butterworth discusses how the locker room has arguably become the most important space for performances and embodiments of gender and sexuality ("Pitchers"). In his analysis of the rhetoric surrounding Major League Baseball pitcher Mike Piazza and the speculation that he may be gay, Butterworth discusses the performances that Piazza undertook to reinforce his heterosexuality and deny validity to gay identity in sport. He did so by managing difference, by showing himself as ostentatiously not gay in performance. As Butterworth describes, Piazza, aware of the gay rumors about him, was routinely seen with women on either side of him after games or at clubs where he might be seen by the media. At a press conference, Piazza recognized the rumors surrounding him and vehemently denied homosexuality ("'I'm Not Gay'"). "I'm not gay," he said, "I'm heterosexual." By embodying traditional ideals of masculinity and by showing a preference for women and coming out as straight, his performances reinforced heterosexuality as the norm and homosexuality, along with its associations of passivity and sexual deviancy, as an abnormal identity that has no place in either sport or society. In Piazza's case, heterosexuality was being re-performed again and again to reinforce cultural norms and to make him seem hyper-heterosexual.

Lindemann and Cherney note that in wheelchair rugby, athletes are drawn to "living the ruby 'lifestyle'" which perpetuates a "masculinist culture" through ostentatiously performing "the daredevil attitude that characterizes talk about the sport" (117). These performances involve a great deal of "macho posturing," they note (118). They point to the violent actions of wheelchair rugby as a highly performative way to assert strength and masculinity, for "the on-court displays may seem reckless in terms of the potential for injury" (113). In countless sports where athletes are required to profess palatable forms of their gender, not doing so could cost a player respect from teammates and fans alike.

One reason why performance in sport conveys social and political attitudes so well is that performance is fueled by commodification. In an age where star athletes have to do well both on and off the court, field, or arena to succeed, performance sells. We want to see over-the-top performances in professional wrestling, we hope to see anger and violence performed in hockey games. Team owners and advertisers know this, and so they encourage performance. That means, at the same time, encouraging the demonstration of social and political attitudes. The rise of sport media on television, in newspapers and magazines, and on the Internet has contributed to the reinforcing of norms and cultural identity.

As they have become increasingly popular not only to play but also to watch, athletes have become commodities—figures that can be bought and sold by consumers and team owners for profit. In an age of consumerism, where each person consumes about three thousand advertisements a day, the athlete has become entertainment, a good and a brand that can be manufactured in a certain way to attain maximum attention and yield. Being a fan is about consuming a brand of figure, athleticism, or ideals with which a fan identifies. Famous basketball players can now have their own shoe lines so that fans can do more than just support their favorite athlete or team—they can wear what their favorite athlete or team wears and inherit the image of that athlete or team. Athletes sell not only sport drinks and athletic equipment but also a whole host of other goods not related to sports at all, ranging from deodorant to cars. Sport franchises, the Olympics, and college sport have all become business interests in addition to forums where athletes can display their physical ability. With the pervasive availability of sport and games on air in our homes, "televised sport not only provides our main connection to sport itself, but also our ideas about nationality, class, race, gender, age, and disability" (Boyle and Haynes 11).

The commodification of sport and games has extended its range beyond traditional activities. With the advent of technology that has allowed for fantasy sport leagues and online computer game competitions and with the increasing popularity of alternative sport and games, many of the sociopolitical dynamics of traditional sport and games have transformed new outlets and new media, reaching participants and fans who are not interested in soccer, football, basketball, baseball, and other traditionally popular sport. Mary McDonald notes:

> In contemporary mediated capitalist culture, gendered racial politics are firmly immersed in an economy of signs, texts, images, and commodified bodies seemingly, but not actually, detached from the continuing imperatives seeking dominance, privileges, and presumed superiority for white bodies. Perhaps nowhere is this sensibility more vividly articulated than in the realm of mediated sport, where mythological images of meritocracy and transcendence are incessantly promoted. (248)

Since sport and games became increasingly mediated in new forms, spectatorship and fandom have become a considerably important part of sport culture, national identity, and performance.

Performance is not only on the field or screen. As we sit with friends in front of the television we show our passion physically and vocally, for the benefit of others. By becoming fans, spectators engage in certain kinds of "pleasures," fulfilling their own desires through fetishism, voyeurism, and narcissism (Duncan and Brummett, "Types and Sources"). "Televised sport creates fetishes by commodifying athletes and their actions, that is, by relating the material of sport goods to be closely examined, appraised, and assessed" (Duncan and Brummett, "Types and Sources" 199). Through looking and viewing, spectators attach themselves to a particular image or brand. This kind of performance also conveys a rhetoric with social and political implications. Fans as well as athletes often perform gender roles. Bryan Curtis, for example, studied "the way men really talk sport," concluding, "For most of us, the act of arguing about sport is akin to trench warfare" (4). Masculinity is constructed and reinscribed in the performances we offer as fans discussing sport.

Being a fan is a kind of performance. Notice the performative behavior of fans at televised football games as they shed clothing, paint themselves team colors, and put on funny hats in hopes that the camera will find them. As Elana Shefrin also explains, "Participatory fandom is marked by a sustained emotional and physical engagement with a particular narrative universe" (273). Watching sport and games is enjoyable for spectators because people attain pleasure from imagining themselves in the sporting scene—"satisfying" themselves by fetishizing the players on the court, field, or arena—or from looking without being invited to do so (Duncan and Brummett, "Types and Sources" 198).

Zagacki and Grano discuss fandom in their essay on the Louisiana State University football team and the radio programming surrounding the team. They note, "Talk radio gives Tiger fans opportunities to share creative interpretations of events. This helps them cope with moments of perceived crisis when the team loses, solidifies their community identity and shapes fans' understandings of the productions of institutionalized athletics" (276). In the sporting fan world, teams and players are vilified or lauded. Radio sport talk and the spectating community "reaffirm identity through mediated interactions in which heroes, martyrs, villains, and the role of the fans are recalled and renewed in common appreciation" (Zagacki and Grano 46). Through a community of spectatorship, the supporters have a common sense of identity and purpose. Much of this identity is related to "regional pride," felt being part of a Louisiana state school. But a community identity and mythic connotations surrounding the team also consist of a brand of masculinity and race that solidify character and self. In all these cases, the performative dimensions of fans and spectators are important.

■ Conclusion

In the introduction to this book, these questions were raised: How are sport and games performative, and to what social and political end? What does it mean to say that sport and games, or activities connected to sport and games, are performative? What is it about sport and games in their various forms and places in our culture that specifically calls for performative analysis? How are major social and political struggles carried out in part or in whole through games or sports-related performance?

In this first chapter we have made but a start at suggesting some directions to take in answering those questions. To really address them, scholars must examine particular sport and games, from the point of view of both participants and spectators. That is what the chapters in the rest of this volume do. We want to close by emphasizing one main theme here, and that is that sport and games—which are central components of popular culture in the United States and around the world—are highly rhetorical, with social and political importance. The next time you strap on the cleats or pull up a chair before the television to enter the world of sport and games, remember that you are not doing so neutrally. Sport and games are so connected with who we are as individuals and as groups that we are constantly performing those identities as we engage sport and games. This subject matter is not mere entertainment, it is important.

Works Cited

Aden, Roger C. *Popular Stories and Promised Lands: Fan Cultures and Symbolic Pilgrimages.* Tuscaloosa: U of Alabama P, 2007.

Baker, William J. *Sports in the Western World.* Urbana: U of Illinois P, 1988.

Bial, Henry, ed. *The Performance Studies Reader.* New York: Routledge, 2004.

Birrell, Susan, and Mary G. McDonald. Introduction. *Reading Sport: Critical Essays on Power and Representation.* Ed. Susan Birrell and Mary G. McDonald. Boston: Northeastern UP, 2003. 3–13.

Bloom, John, and Michael N. Willard, ed. *Sports Matters: Race, Recreation, and Culture.* New York: New York UP, 2002.

Boyle, Raymond, and Richard Haynes. *Power Play: Sport, the Media and Popular Culture.* New York: Pearson, 2000.

Brummett, Barry, and Margaret Carlisle Duncan. "Theorizing Without Totalizing: Specularity and Televised Sport." *Quarterly Journal of Speech* 76.3 (1990): 227–46.

Burris, Susan. "She Got Game, but She Don't Got Fame." *Sport, Rhetoric, and Gender: Historical Perspectives and Media Representations.* Ed. Linda K. Fuller. New York: Palgrave, 2006. 85–96.

Butler, Judith. "Athletic Genders: Hyperbolic Instance and/or the Overcoming of Sexual Binarism." *Stanford Humanities Review* 6.2 (1998): n. pag. *Google Scholar.* Web. 12 Nov. 2008.

———. *Bodies That Matter: On the Discursive Limits of "Sex."* New York: Routledge, 1993.

———. *Gender Trouble: Feminism and the Subversion of Identity.* New York: Routledge, 1999.

———. "Performative Acts and Gender Constitution: An Essay in Phenomenology." *Performing Feminisms.* Ed. Sue-Ellen Case. Baltimore: Johns Hopkins UP, 1990: 270–82.

Butterworth, Michael L. "Pitchers and Catchers: Mike Piazza and the Discourse of Gay Identity in the National Pastime." *Journal of Sport and Social Issues* 30.2 (2006): 138–57.

———. "The Politics of the Pitch: Claiming and Contesting Democracy Through the Iraqi National Soccer Team." *Communication and Critical/Cultural Studies* 4.2 (2007): 184–203.

———. "Purifying the Body Politic: Steroids, Rafael Palmeiro, and the Rhetorical Cleansing of Major League Baseball." *Western Journal of Communication* 72.2 (2008): 145–61.

———. "Race in 'The Race': Mark McGwire, Sammy Sosa, and Heroic Constructions of Whiteness." *Critical Studies in Media Communication* 24.3 (2007): 228–44.

Cahn, Susan. *Coming On Strong: Gender and Sexuality in Twentieth-Century Women's Sport.* Cambridge: Harvard UP, 1994.

Cho, Younghan. "Rituals in Sport: Theorizing a Spectacle of the Left During 2002 Korea-Japan World Cup." Annual Meeting of the International Communication Association. New York. 25–30 May 2005. Conference paper.

Curtis, Bryan. "Talking Sport the Way Men Really Talk Sport." *New York Times* 24 Aug. 2008: 5.

Delgado, Fernando P. "Golden but Not Brown: Oscar De La Hoya and the Complications of Culture, Manhood, and Boxing." *International Journal of the History of Sport* 22.2 (2005): 196–211.

Duncan, Margaret Carlisle, and Barry Brummett. "Liberal and Radical Sources of Female Empowerment in Sport Media." *Sociology of Sport Journal* 10.1 (1993): 57–72.

———. "The Mediation of Spectator Sport." *Research Quarterly for Exercise and Sport* 58.2 (1987): 168–77.

———. "Types and Sources of Spectating Pleasure in Televised Sport." *Sociology of Sport Journal* 6.3 (1989): 195–211.

Farrell, Thomas B. "Media Rhetoric as Social Drama: The Winter Olympics of 1984." *Critical Studies in Mass Communication* 6.2 (1989): 158–82.

Festle, Mary Jo. *Playing Nice: Politics and Apologies in Women's Sport.* New York: Columbia UP, 1996.

Fuller, Linda K. *Sport, Rhetoric, and Gender: Historical Perspectives and Media Representations.* New York: Palgrave, 2006.

Gabler, Neal. *Life the Movie: How Entertainment Conquered Reality.* New York: Knopf, 1998.

Gruneau, Richard S. *Class and Social Development.* New York: Human Kinetics, 1999.

Hardin, Marie, and Stacie Shain. "'Feeling Much Smaller than You Know You Are': The Fragmented Professional Identity of Female Sport Journalists." *Critical Studies in Media Communication* 23.4 (2006): 322–38.

Hargreaves, Jennifer, and Patricia Vertinsky, ed. *Physical Culture, Power, and the Body.* New York: Routledge, 2007.

Heywood, Leslie, and Shari Dworkin. *Built to Win: The Female Athlete as Cultural Icon.* Minneapolis: U of Minnesota P, 2003.

Huizinga, Johan. *Homo Ludens.* Boston: Beacon, 1950.

Humphreys, Sal. "Productive Players: Online Computer Games' Challenge to Conventional Media Forms." *Communication and Critical/Cultural Studies* 2.1 (2005): 37–51.

"'I'm Not Gay': Piazza Sets Record Straight about Sexual Orientation." *CNNSI.com.* CNN/Sports Illustrated, 21 May 2002. Web. 6 Jan. 2009. <http://sportsillustrated. cnn.com/baseball/news/2002/05/21/mets_piazza_ap/>.

Krizek, Bob. "Introduction: Communication and the Community of Sport." *Western Journal of Communication* 72.2 (2008): 103–06.

LaFrance, Melisse, and Genevieve Rail. "As Bad as He Says He Is?" *Reading Sport: Critical Essays on Power and Representation.* Ed. Susan Birrell and Mary G. McDonald. Boston: Northeastern UP, 2003. 74–107.

Lindemann, Kurt, and James L. Cherney. "Communicating in and through 'Murderball': Masculinity and Disability in Wheelchair Rugby." *Western Journal of Communication* 72.2 (2008): 107–25.

Lockford, Lesa. *Performing Femininity: Rewriting Gender Identity.* AltaMira, 2004.

McAllister, Ken S. *Game Work: Language, Power, and Computer Game Culture.* Tuscaloosa: U of Alabama P, 2004.

McDonald, Mary G. "Mapping Whiteness and Sport: An Introduction." *Sociology of Sport Journal* 22.3 (2005): 245–55.

Meân, Lindsey J. "Identity and Discursive Practice: Doing Gender on the Football Pitch." *Discourse and Society* 12.6 (2001): 789–815.

Meân, Lindsey J., and Jeffrey W. Kassing. "'I Would Just Like to be Known as an Athlete': Managing Hegemony, Femininity, and Heterosexuality in Female Sport." *Western Journal of Communication* 72.2 (2008): 126–44.

Oates, Thomas P. "The Erotic Gaze in the NFL Draft." *Communication and Critical/Cultural Studies* 4.1 (2007): 74–90.

Pacanowsky, Michael E., and Nick O'Donnell-Trujillo. "Organizational Communication as Cultural Performance." *Communication Monographs* 50.2 (1983): 126–47.

Rowe, David. *Sport, Culture, and the Media: The Unruly Trinity.* Maidenhead: Open UP, 2004.

Schechner, Richard. *Performance Studies: An Introduction.* New York: Routledge, 2002.

Shefrin, Elana. "Lord of the Rings, Star Wars, and Participatory Fandom: Mapping New Congruencies between the Internet and Media Entertainment Culture." *Critical Studies in Mass Communication* 2.3 (2004): 261–81.

Smith, Earl. *Race, Sport and the American Dream.* Durham: Carolina AP, 2007.

Trujillo, Nick. *The Meaning of Nolan Ryan.* College Station: Texas A&M UP, 1994.

Turman, Paul D. "Coaches' Immediacy Behaviors as Predictors of Athletes' Perceptions of Satisfaction and Team Cohesion." *Western Journal of Communication* 72.2 (2008): 162–79.

Walker, Lisa. *Looking Like What You Are: Sexual Style, Race, and Lesbian Identity.* New York: New York UP, 2001.

Whannel, Garry. "Sport Stars, Narrativization and Masculinities." *Leisure Studies* 18.1 (1999): 249–55.

Zagacki, Kenneth S., and Dan Grano. "Radio Sport Talk and the Fantasies of Sport." *Critical Studies in Media Communication* 22.1 (2005): 45–63.

Zeigler, Earle. *History of Physical Education and Sport.* Champaign: Stipes, 1988.

Zirin, Dave. *What's My Name Fool? Sports and Resistance in the United States.* Chicago: Haymarket, 2005.

Notes

1. Although the Williams sisters are largely regarded as being the first black female tennis players to break the image of tennis as a sport played by whites, Althea Gibson broke many of the same designations in the 1950s.

2. While LaFrance and Rail discuss Rodman's non-traditional appearance and behavior, they argue that Rodman's performance of race and gender ultimately reinforced binary categories instead of breaking them down.

2

■ The Rhetoric of Monstrosity in Professional Sports Controversy

□ Roger Gatchet

> The monstrous body is pure culture.... Like a letter on the page, the monster signifies something other than itself: it is always a displacement, always inhabits the gap between the time of upheaval that created it and the moment into which it is received, to be born again.
>
> —Jeffrey Jerome Cohen (4)

On March 14, 2004, veteran professional wrestler Chris Benoit won the World Wrestling Entertainment (WWE) World Heavyweight Championship belt in a "triple threat" match against famed wrestler Shawn "The Heartbreak Kid" Michaels and then-reigning champion Hunter Hearst Helmsley, better known to fans by his moniker Triple H. In the match's final, suspense-filled moments, Benoit reversed a hold by Triple H, pulling his bloodied opponent to the canvas into his signature finishing maneuver, the "Crippler Crossface." The celebration that took place in the squared circle after Triple H tapped out to the submission move was an emotional display, further embellishing the spectacle of performed violence and bloodshed that had entertained the cheering 20,000-plus in attendance at the sold-out Madison Square Garden in New York City.

Three years later, the nation was shocked to discover that the man who would later be described by his wrestling colleagues as "calm and relaxed," a "model employee," and a "caring, heart filled guy" had murdered both his wife and son before hanging himself using the wires from a weight-lifting machine ("Wrestler Kills Wife"). Three days after the bodies were found, WWE chairman Vince McMahon made a much-anticipated appearance on the *Today* show to discuss the double murder-suicide. When co-host Meredith Vieira pushed McMahon to explain why the WWE had rejected the possibility that steroid abuse may have contributed to Benoit's violent actions, the head of the company stated, "There was no indication whatsoever that this man could possibly turn into this monster and do what he did." As the interview came to a close, McMahon once again calmly reiterated that "there was no way of telling this man was a monster, no way of knowing that whatsoever. He was a mild-mannered individual."

The notable term McMahon used twice to describe Chris Benoit, "monster," has been frequently applied also to another polemical in-ring competitor, former world heavyweight boxing champion "Iron" Mike Tyson. While Tyson has been at the center of numerous controversies throughout his troubled career, the boxer once known as the "baddest man on the planet" made headlines in the summer of 1991 after being arrested for raping Desiree Washington, then the reigning Miss Black Rhode Island. His conviction the following year led to more media attention, which included an op-ed piece published in the *New York Times* describing Tyson as "a brutal and monster-like public figure" (Wu 10). Benoit and Tyson are not the only sports figures to be called monsters, however. More recently, ex-Atlanta Falcons quarterback Michael Vick was the subject of public outrage when he was accused (and later convicted) for operating the Bad Newz Kennel, an illegal dogfighting operation located on his Virginia estate. Consistent with the views of many who voiced their disgust toward the allegations was one anonymous individual whose thoughts were broadcast on CNN's *Paula Zahn Now* program in the summer of 2007: "Put this monster in the cage where he belongs, not on a football field" ("Michael Vick Pleads Not Guilty to Dogfighting").

This chapter is about monsters. Not the other-worldly beasts and ghostly apparitions of Stephen King novels and Hollywood horror films, but rather *human* monsters of our own creation. The rhetoric of monstrosity is a mode of performative, constitutive name-calling that frequently occurs in the diverse texts that circulate throughout popular culture. As Barry Brummett notes in the opening pages of *Rhetorical Dimensions of Popular Culture,* popular culture is "inherently rhetorical," the "cutting edge of culture's instruments that shape people into what they are" (xxi). As such, the realm of popular culture is a dynamic site of struggle over meaning and power as social actors seek to understand themselves in relation to others, often by constituting those others through difference—by attempting to understand *them* as radically different from the rest of *us.* This has important consequences for how we come to understand ourselves in relation to others, because understanding this process as a performance reveals the ways in which language constitutes our reality and makes us better equipped to examine how complex discourses of difference go beyond name-calling or scapegoating. The stakes are especially high with monster-talk, because, as MIT professor and cultural critic Henry Jenkins III explains, "the monster can have no legitimate point of view. The monster has no culture, generates no meaning, and respects no values. The monster exists simply to negate the moral order" (301).

This chapter explores the ways in which competitive and performative sports become a source of images and signs for the purposes of monster-making. More to the point, it argues that a performative rhetoric of monstrosity is a central feature of public responses to controversial sports figures such as Chris Benoit, Michael Vick, and Mike Tyson. Monster-talk is frequently employed to describe athletes like these who cross legal, moral, or ethical lines, but the effects of such talk *as* performance go beyond mere description. What are the social, cultural, and political consequences of monster-making? How is the discursive category of monstrosity mobilized to not only describe but also constitute difference? How does the "monster" label function as both "the ultimate incorporation of our anxieties," as Jeffrey Jerome Cohen argues, and as a rhetorical means of disguising those anxieties (xii)?

To address these questions, the chapter first discusses the relationship between speech act theory, performance, and the construction of alterity in the rhetoric of popular culture. The word *alterity* refers to the assignment of difference or "otherness" by one individual or group onto another, as is the case when someone is labeled a "monster" on a popular daytime news program such as the *Today* show, or in a leading national newspaper such as the *New York Times.* This section provides a theoretical foundation for understanding the performative nature of discourse—or as J. L. Austin puts it, how we "do things with words"—by examining the rhetoric of monstrosity and its creation of alterity as a type of performative speech act, a way of creating a reality *through* language.

Next, the chapter takes a closer look at this dynamic through a series of three interrelated case studies. Each case examines the relationship between controversy and alterity in popular culture through the lens of performative public and media responses to three controversial athletes: NFL quarterback Michael Vick, former heavyweight champion boxer Mike Tyson, and professional wrestler Chris Benoit. The emergent discourses of difference circulating around these controversial sports figures are sites where multiple alterities converge into what professor Edward J. Ingebretsen calls a discourse of *monstrosity*. Once labeled as monsters, the athletes become "occasions of dense exchange" that are simultaneously admired and reviled (Ingebretsen 1–2). After examining each athlete and the relationships between their representations in the media, the chapter concludes by arguing that one of the consequences of the performative rhetoric of monstrosity in sports is that it dehumanizes and exceptionalizes the athletes involved, allowing the rest of us to avoid confronting how the athletes-made-monsters may be symptomatic of larger social structures that transcend the individual sports in which they participate.

■ The Performance of Difference in the Rhetoric of Popular Culture

"We live in a time of monsters," Jeffrey Jerome Cohen observed in 1996 (vii). The same can be said for us today. Indeed, Americans seem to be obsessed with monsters, and there is no shortage of examples in the performances found throughout popular culture that highlights this. In 2008, *The Dark Knight,* director Christopher Nolan's highly anticipated second entry in the Batman film franchise, became one of the highest grossing films that year, largely based on audiences' fascination with the haunting performance of Heath Ledger as Batman's arch nemesis, the Joker. Ledger's Joker, who is all the more disquieting given the actor's death from an accidental drug overdose before the film was released, was described by many film critics in terms of monstrous descriptors such as "tongue-flickingly reptilian" (Mondello) and "a god of chaos" (Turan). Yet behind the smeared makeup and maniacal grin of the Joker, however terrifying, is the face not of a monster, reptile, or god, but of a human (granted, a psychopathic human). It is this intentional transformation of human into monster that is one of the key features of monster-making, an explicitly violent form of othering that Ingebretsen describes as being pervasively "soul-deep" in US culture today (200).

Monster-making is distinct from other forms of name-calling due to the ways in which it dehumanizes those who are targeted by such rhetoric, thus shaping them into evil, and despised by others, thus isolating them from the rest of society. The term "other" is used throughout this chapter in a way that you may not be accustomed to seeing it—as a verb and a noun that relates to both the construction and embodiment of difference. As rhetorical critic Lisa Glebatis Perks explains, "Othering refers to cultural representations that depict groups of people as backward, primitive, degenerate, or otherwise inferior" to another group of people (72). These representations can also be understood as a way of constructing individual and collective identities through discourse, a way of establishing a sense of who we *are* in terms of what we *are not*. As performance studies scholar D. Soyini Madison explains, this fundamental process of identity formation calls for the moral imperative to interrogate "how our subjectivity *in relation to the Other* informs and is informed by our engagement and representation of the Other" (9, original emphasis; see also 96–99). Speech act theory offers a framework for doing just that.

In 1955, philosophy professor J. L. Austin delivered a lecture series at Harvard University that was later published from his notes under the title *How to Do Things with Words.* The lectures and the subsequent book are famous for initiating what became known as speech act theory, the study of (as the book's title suggests) how people use words to get things done. Austin abandons traditional philosophical concerns over truth and falsehood and instead examines the subtleties of a category of performative utterances "in which to *say* something is to *do* something" (12, original emphasis). The kinds of utterances Austin has in mind are the standard stuff of everyday discourse—promises, apologies, bets, judgments passed down in judicial courts, marriage pronouncements, and so on. If, to borrow one of Austin's examples, someone warns you "to cross the track by the bridge only," the statement has performed the warning and has, as a result, shaped your reality (Austin 57). The warning was not just described or explained but also created, and hence performed, through language. Another category of speech acts identified by Austin contains those that produce effects at some future date after the utterance is spoken and involve acts "such as convincing, persuading, deterring, and… surprising or misleading" (109).

Austin's lectures led to later work on speech acts by his student John R. Searle (*Speech Acts*), Jacques Derrida (the collection *Limited INC*), and Judith Butler (*Excitable Speech*), among others. Although a survey of these works is beyond the scope of this chapter, it will be helpful to focus briefly on Butler's extension of Austin's framework. Butler, who is widely known both inside and outside the academy for her influential work on gender as a rhetorical, performative construct, has a lot to say about the complex relationship between language, performance, and lived experience. In *Excitable Speech,* she examines injurious speech acts that go beyond marriage pronouncements and poker bets. From hate speech to pornography to homophobic military policy, Butler shows how injurious speech affects and is resisted by those who are subject to such discourses. If one is subject to a racial slur, for example, the resulting "linguistic injury appears to be the effect not only of the words by which one is addressed but the mode of address itself, a mode…that interpellates and constitutes a subject" (2). Injurious speech is thus a double-edged sword, because it carries the latent potential to both constitute one's identity *and* influence or shape one's world long after the words are spoken. This is especially evident in the courtroom, Butler argues, where judicial decisions that restrict or define injurious speech actually extend discourses of racism, sexism, and hate, because the injury does not exist in the eyes of the court until the court says it is so (96–97).

Although Butler does not discuss monstrosity as such, I would argue that monster-talk parallels hate speech and the other hurtful rhetorics she analyzes. Just like racial slurs and other vituperative insults, rhetorics of monstrosity flex their performative muscles to constitute others as evil and subhuman. As monsters, their presence poses a serious threat to the collective, and their punishment or expulsion (or even death) is justified in the name of that collective. Groups forge their collective identity on top of the body of the vanquished monster, making this hated other one of the defining characteristics of American identity throughout the history of the United States. "The cultivation of hate is practically synonymous with civility," Ingebretsen explains, and "monster-talk is an integral feature of the arsenal of fear which underlies the practice of those modern, liberal states who nonetheless come to self-definition by making 'perfect enemies'" (10).

The performative power of these utterances is further amplified by their repeatability. As Della Pollock points out, "At its most basic level, performance is a repetition. It is a *doing again of what was once done,* repeating past action in the time of acting" (11, original emphasis). Through the repetition of monster-talk in popular culture, any violence that may have been caused by the original utterance is reperformed, and wounds are reopened. For example, Vince McMahon's move to distance himself and the WWE from Chris Benoit by calling him a monster constitutes Benoit as a monster in that moment, while it also affects the way others come to understand him in the future. As McMahon's words tour throughout popular culture, replaying in television interviews, newspaper articles, and on YouTube, their injurious potential expands accordingly. Transformed into monsters, athletes like Chris Benoit, Michael Vick, and Mike Tyson become "metaphors of our anxiety"; they represent an impoverished attempt to signify the traumatic encounters with our own alterity, that is, with the possibility that we may be more similar to our monsters than different (Kearney 117).

This possibility of similarity between the individuals in a society and their monsters, in spite of the rhetorical efforts made to prove otherwise, leads to an interesting paradox in the rhetoric of monstrosity. Although social actors may go to great lengths to express their disgust and to deny their own resemblance to the vilified monsters they create (or that are created for them), Ingebretsen argues that "monsters are obliquely sources of admiration…and amazement. Merely identifying the monster as terrible, as awful and perverse, is only one of the fearful ceremonies designed around them. Displaying the monster as desirable is of equal (though hidden) value" (2–3). They are publicly loathed, yet privately loved. Continuing, Ingebretsen observes how "the monster-face is a mask placed on someone whose offense is obliquely desirable to us, however much we disguise that knowing from ourselves or call it something else…. They get away with murder and that fascinates us. Monsters are supposed to do just what they desire, and that frightens us" (3–4). Similarly, Cohen argues that "we distrust and loathe the monster at the same time we envy its freedom, and perhaps its sublime despair" (17).

Examples of this are not hard to come by in the world of sport and games. Just think of the media blitz and the public fascination and disgust surrounding O. J. Simpson's 1995 double-murder trial, which emerged again in 2008 when he was tried and convicted for robbery and kidnapping. Former champion figure skater Tonya Harding, best known for her involvement in the attack on fellow skater Nancy Kerrigan, also returned to the spotlight in 2002 on Fox's short-lived *Celebrity Boxing* program (to fight Paula Jones, no less) despite being thoroughly vilified in the media years earlier. This love-hate dialectic mirrors the discourses of good and evil that lie at the center of all monster stories (both fictional and true) and helps explain why Nolan resurrected the Joker character after he was previously killed in Tim Burton's *Batman,* or why masked murderer Jason, just when he appears to have finally been vanquished for good, returns in yet another *Friday the 13th* sequel. In sports, it also explains how a despised Mike Tyson could avoid permanent banishment from professional boxing after biting a chunk out of Evander Holyfield's ear in their infamous 1997 rematch for the heavyweight championship, or why baseball fans packed stadiums in 2007 to watch Barry Bonds, the player who "used a wealth of forbidden chemicals to make a monster of himself," narrow the gap on Hank Aaron's career homerun record ("A Baseball Tragedy").

■ Case Studies

In the three case studies that follow, I examine the monster-making rhetoric of each controversial athlete as reflected in print and televised media outlets. Using the *Lexis-Nexis* and *ProQuest* databases, I searched major print news sources such as the *New York Times, Washington Post, Boston Globe, USA Today,* and *Los Angeles Times.* I also searched the transcripts of programs aired on major broadcast networks and cable channels such as ABC, NBC, and CNN. In some examples, such as the case of Chris Benoit, I supplement this data with information from Internet websites and documentary footage. All three athletes—Vick, Tyson, and Benoit—were at one time considered to be one of the best practitioners of their respective sport. Chris Benoit, a veteran grappler of the two largest professional wrestling promotions in the United States, was hailed as one of the best technical wrestlers in sports entertainment; comparisons were drawn between Mike Tyson and Muhammad Ali early in his career; and Michael Vick, who broke a number of NFL records before his conviction for illegal dogfighting, garnered MVP buzz while still a second-year rookie for the Atlanta Falcons.

Although the individual controversies in which each was involved were markedly different, Vick, Tyson, and Benoit were all constituted as monstrous through a series of mediated performative utterances and as such were part of a rhetorical process that defined the subjectivity of the athletes' accusers in terms of what those accusers were *not.* This "not" is precisely the locus of alterity for each athlete. In the case of Michael Vick, his alterity was constructed through a racialized monstrosity that also served as a platform for critiquing contemporary race relations in the United States; in the case of Mike Tyson, depictions of this controversial public figure take a theological turn when he is represented as the locus of a monstrous evil, and as a villainous figure in a series of ongoing morality plays that pitted good against evil; in the case of Chris Benoit, whose profession perhaps best exemplifies the category of performative sport, a monstrosity of the real emerges as the WWE struggles to control its image and contain the public dialogue that seeks to understand the underlying motive behind Benoit's violent actions.

Michael Vick and Racialized Monstrosity

> The immortal Dante tells us that Divine Justice reserves special places in hell for certain categories of sinners. I am confident that the hottest places in hell are reserved for the souls of sick and brutal people who hold God's creatures in such brutal and cruel contempt.
> —*Senator Robert Byrd on the US Senate Floor, 19 July 2007*

In July 2007, West Virginia senator Robert Byrd delivered an impassioned speech on the floor of the US Senate decrying the abuse of dogs in illegal dogfighting operations across the country. Although the senator denied that his comments were directed at Michael Vick specifically, the timing and specificity of his speech left little doubt that he was speaking about the recent federal charges brought against Vick and his co-conspirators. The draft of the speech released by Byrd's press office uses damning terms such as "sadistic," "barbaric," and "depravity," setting the tone for further remarks addressing what he considers to be an epidemic of dogfighting in the United States. In his public performance of the speech, Byrd also advocates capital punishment as an appropriate measure for dogfighters: "I have seen one individual in my lifetime electrocuted in the electric chair—in my time. It is not a beautiful spectacle. So I can say I could witness another one if it involves this cruel, sadistic, cannibalistic business of training innocent and vulnerable creatures to kill" (*Cong. Rec.* 9569). The following month, a "Summary of the Facts" filed in US District Court by federal attorney Chuck Rosenberg offers a detailed list of the actions taken by Michael Vick and others that would eventually lead to Vick's sentencing in December of that year to twenty-three months in prison. The Atlanta Falcons' star quarterback admitted to financing an illegal gambling operation from his Smithfield, Virginia property that sponsored fights between pit bulls, many of which were trained and housed on the property, and ran a business he and his partners called the Bad Newz Kennel. Of the many federal charges brought against Vick, one that perhaps drew the worst of the public's ire was his approval of the torture and killing of several pit bulls by methods such as drowning and hanging ("Summary" 5, 9). While Vick maintained his innocence when the accusations first arose, he eventually pleaded guilty and signed a plea agreement on August 23, 2007.

Much like the remarks made by Senator Byrd, public and media responses around the time that Vick pleaded guilty framed the troubled athlete as a monstrous force. Although Vick claimed to have found God and promised to "redeem" himself and make himself "a better person" ("Virginia Grand Jury"), Chris DeRose, the president of the nonprofit animal rights organization Last Chance for Animals, made an appearance on CNN's *Nancy Grace* program where he argued that pit bulls are not inherently vicious, locating their violent aggressiveness instead in "the monsters...behind the dogs" ("Virginia Grand Jury"). Jim Goodwin, another well-known animal rights advocate from the Humane Society of the United States, when interviewed by CNN anchor Soledad O'Brien on *Anderson Cooper 360 Degrees,* called dogfighters like Vick "sick" and "sadistic" ("Alberto Gonzalez"). O'Brien opened the interview with an equally provocative statement asking Goodwin, "is the pit bull inherently a vicious, evil dog, or is it the owners who are vicious, evil people who train their dogs to do bad things?" O'Brien's question indirectly describes Vick as a vicious and evil individual, an interesting if not unexpected portrayal given that "Westerners have a limited repertoire of language for characterizing" those actions that they organize under the banner of "evil," such as the torture and abuse of animals for monetary gain (Gunn, "The Rhetoric" 3). Elsewhere, ESPN columnist Chris Mortensen was quoted describing Vick as "simply ignorant or evil" ("Guilty Plea"), and former district attorney Jeanine Pirro categorized Vick's actions as "all about evil" ("Michael Vick Pleads Not Guilty"). As Butler argues in regard to hate speech, all this monster-talk similarly "*constitutes* its addressee at the moment of its utterance; it does not describe an injury or produce one as a consequence; it is, in the very speaking of such speech, the performance of the injury itself, where the injury is understood as social subordination" (18, original emphasis).

Monster-talk always says more than it appears to say on the surface. Sportswriter Michael Wilbon of the *Washington Post,* for example, observed that Vick "can be the devil incarnate or the persecuted victim of a racially motivated attack that has ignored the basic tenet of due process." Indeed, one way to understand these descriptions of monstrous evil is to recognize the way in which they perform certain kinds of alterity, which is one of the primary functions of the rhetoric of monstrosity. The production of alterity in Vick's case can be seen in the way racial identities and stereotypes are mapped onto signifiers such as "monster," "evil," or "barbaric," suggesting that Vick was constituted as other not solely for his participation in an illegal dogfighting operation. As Ingebretsen observes, "Firewalling racial difference in the terms of monstrosity is an American commonplace," and monstrosity can serve as a convenient discursive category for channeling collective anxieties over contemporary race relations, especially in the context of the US criminal justice system (276n60).

R. L. White, the president of the Atlanta chapter of the NAACP, recognized the alterity of race hidden behind monstrous depictions when he asserted that Vick was being persecuted in the media, his treatment akin to a "lynching" of his personality ("NAACP Official"). White's use of the trope of lynching here is significant, as it recasts a term identified with the long history of racially motivated violence against Blacks, particularly in the southern United States (Vick himself was born in Virginia, the state in which the capital of the Confederacy was located), to describe the symbolic violence done by references to Vick's monstrosity. Others described portrayals of Vick as "racial profiling" and "a witch hunt targeting a successful black man" ("Michael Vick Dog Fighting Case"). Boyce Watkins, a professor at Syracuse University, noted the "racial undertone in terms like…monster and thugs" used to describe Vick in the media ("Race in the Court"). Pointing out the similarities in media portrayals between Vick and other popular African American sports stars such as Terrell Owens, O. J. Simpson, and Barry Bonds, Watkins used the Vick case as an opportunity to address the relationship between monstrosity and racism (especially toward African Americans) in popular culture. "Typically," the professor states, "you only see black men on television when they are playing the sport or committing a crime." Whoopi Goldberg also pointed to the racial and cultural implications of the accusations against Vick when she argued on *The View* that "instead of just saying [Vick is] a beast and he's a monster, this is a kid who comes from a culture where this is not questioned" (de Moraes).

The speech acts that constitute Vick as an evil monster perform a symbolic, discursive violence against him as both an explanation and a form of redress for the real violence he enacted on the pit bulls at his Virginia estate. The above comments also suggest that Vick, however evil and monstrous his portrayal as the ringleader of Bad Newz Kennel may be, was never the subject of unanimous condemnation. Butler notes that "not all utterances that have the form of the performative…actually work," opening up the possibility for more humane, more responsible representations of those whose actions fall outside societal norms and standards for behavior (16). Dogfighting is indeed a terrible crime, and given Vick's guilty plea there is little doubt that he committed the crimes he was accused of. That said, Vick was also constituted as a rhetorical symbol of evil, just as dogfighting was routinely reviled as an evil, monstrous activity—perhaps to alleviate a collective guilt for our inability to control the growing practice of dogfighting in the United States ("Dogfighting a Booming Business"), or as part of a disguised racial (or racist) commentary on the relationship between dogfighting and the African American community. Once Vick was made into a monster, efforts to explore the deeper causal factors behind his behavior were consistently eschewed in favor of a more dominant portrayal of him as a soulless, monstrous criminal.

Mike Tyson Fighting in a Holy Field: The Monstrosity of Evil

> Boxing, of all sports, is the most perfectly suited to be the morality play: strong versus weak, good versus evil, black versus white.
> —*New York Times columnist William C. Rhoden*

As is true with all monsters, boxing fans and non-fans alike have followed the career and personal life of Mike Tyson with both fascination and disgust over the past three decades. Described alternately as both "'evil incarnate'" and a "'folk hero,'" the former heavyweight champion from Brooklyn has been the subject of much criticism and vilification in the press, a perhaps unsurprising statement considering both the criminal activity and the downright bizarre behavior he has engaged in, both inside and outside the ring (qtd. in Gildea, "The Dark"). As sportswriter William Gildea comments, Tyson "wanted to 'eat' his opponent's children. He wanted to make some other fighter his 'girlfriend.' Rage is his arsenal. Unpredictable, sometimes violent, Tyson has shown us—plainly—the reality of boxing. Still, we have never been able to stop ourselves from watching. Monsters attract us, too" ("A Sport").

One might argue that to some extent, Tyson's monstrosity is self-inflicted. He did, after all, employ a centuries-old monster archetype with his expressed desire to eat, Saturn-like, the children of his opponent Lennox Lewis, in addition to causing the actual leg bite he inflicted on Lewis in 2002 during a melee at a press conference to hype their upcoming championship bout and biting off Evander Holyfield's ear during their 1997 match. Clearly, in terms of his self-performance Tyson has not done himself any favors.

It is not surprising, then, that Tyson is often read by the media as a performative figure, which further adds to the complexity of the monster-talk that has circulated around him depending on the controversy that was making headlines at the time. Shortly after Tyson's conviction for rape in early 1992, *New York Times* writer Robert Lipsyte reflected how multiple, nested alterities are organized under the rubric of a performative monstrosity when he observed that "for the next few days, Mike Tyson will be a symbolic character in various morality plays, a villain-victim of the Gender War, the Race War, the Class War and the Backlash against Celebrity Excess." Although Lipsyte could not have known it at the time, Tyson would continue to maintain symbolic status as an actor in "morality plays" for years to come. Indeed, one of the dominant themes that is consistently evoked in media coverage throughout Tyson's professional career is the notion of "good versus evil," where Tyson's otherness is channeled through the complex alterity marker "evil."

As I mentioned in the previous section on Michael Vick, the term "evil" is often employed in injurious performative utterances because we have few linguistic resources for signifying so-called evil acts. In the West, evil is commonly associated with religious rhetorics of darkness and the demonic, especially the figure of Satan. Various communities, philosophical movements, and popular culture texts in general have all characterized Satan and evil in different and at times even contradictory ways, but Jeffrey Burton Russell argues that the common thread running through these diverse interpretive logics is that Satan has remained "a long-lived and immensely influential concept aimed at the truth about evil" (22). The evil that the Devil represents, Russell points out, is usually of human origin (23). In this sense, Satan and evil can be understood as sites for the collective projection of the most unpleasant, terrifying

> aspects of humanity itself, and as a therapeutic symbol that allows communities to avoid confronting those dark aspects of human nature. In The Death of Satan, Andrew Delbanco similarly argues that evil is "the blamable other," someone who "can always be counted on to spare us the exigencies of examining ourselves" (234).

One can see how this dynamic plays out in representations that constituted Tyson as a figure who performed multiple identities or personalities, which helped further reinforce the view of those who depicted him as an evil force at battle with the good, even God-like opponents he faced before retiring from professional boxing in 2005. In the press coverage of his 1992 rape trial, for example, Tyson's behavior was characterized as an inner struggle similar to that between Dr. Jekyll and Mr. Hyde (Shaw,), and he has been described as having a "disordered personality" (Gildea, "The Dark"), and "a psychological smorgasbord" with "bipolar appeal" that "can prompt sympathy and horror simultaneously" (Sandomir). Lipsyte saw Tyson as a "sullen villain" whom he calls "Irony Mike," a cartoon character "who might have sprung from the Saturday morning boys' TV ghetto."

Tyson's alterity as a performative, multiple personality-schizophrenic serves to prop up references to the struggle between good and evil that surfaced primarily in the rhetoric surrounding Tyson's two bouts with Evander Holyfield in the 1990s. When Desiree Washington first accused Tyson of raping her in 1991, Holyfield was scheduled to defend his heavyweight championship against Tyson in a fight later that year. Musing on what impact the rape allegations would have on the future bout, one columnist said, "The fight was going to be a good vs. evil [sic]. Now it's good vs. more evil" (Hiestand). Elsewhere, Holyfield was described as "God's Warrior," while Tyson played the part of the "Devil's Disciple" (Borges, "It's Now"); Tyson, a "thug of a champ" and "the prince of darkness," was contrasted with Holyfield, the "good American" who is "honest, clean-cut" and whose "only flaw is a bad heart that was checked and cleared" (Rhoden).

Given Evander's unique surname in this context—Holy-field—perhaps it was overdetermined that media coverage of the fight would take a theological turn. But what are the social consequences of such rhetorical depictions? As John M. Sloop argues in a 1997 essay on the rhetoric of Tyson's rape trial, dominant representations such as these encourage audiences to see Tyson as "the 'black thug'"—a sexually promiscuous, evil, African American monster whose guilt was assumed in advance (114). More importantly, an additional consequence of this rhetoric is that it works to close up possibilities for further consideration of the motivations behind Tyson's behavior. As disgusted *Boston Globe* columnist Ron Borges asserted after the 1997 Holyfield bout, "Nobody wants to hear any more about Mike Tyson's tortured background" ("Same Old"). Another sportswriter who admits that "we helped create this boxing Frankenstein" nonetheless vividly describes Tyson's "inner core" as "soulless" and "so contaminated from childhood that it's likely beyond purification" (Saraceno). The monstrous, evil Tyson, as Ingebretsen puts it, is a cipher of anxiety and serves a therapeutic function by calling attention away from the similarities between himself and his persecutors (171). Yet running just under the surface of these performances is the notion that, although the other "may be coded as foreign," he or she is perhaps more like us than we would care to admit—hence the monster's continual re-formation and re-presentation in popular discourse, a staving-off of the threat they pose to reveal our own monstrosity (Ingebretsen 203).

Chris Benoit and the Monstrosity of the Real

> In the ring, and even in the depths of their voluntary ignominy, wrestlers remain gods because they are, for a few moments, the key which opens Nature, the pure gesture which separates Good from Evil, and unveils the form of a Justice which is at last intelligible.
> —*Roland Barthes, "The World of Wrestling" (25)*

In the 2004 documentary *Hard Knocks: The Chris Benoit Story*, professional wrestler Chris Benoit describes his appearance in the main event at the twentieth annual Wrestlemania, the largest pay-per-view organized by the WWE each year, as the crowning achievement of his career: "If I had to pick one match that would define everything I've ever dreamed of, everything I've ever aspired to be, everything I've ever wanted with this industry, it would have to be Wrestlemania XX." After working for nearly twenty years in the business, Benoit's underdog victory on the "grandest stage of them all" smacked of a fairy-tale ending, the "pure gesture" Barthes identifies as carrying the symbolic weight of a good wrestling match.[1] In the celebration that followed, huge clouds of colored confetti rained down into the arena, and Benoit, cradling the championship gold in his hands, openly wept as his father, wife, and son embraced him in the ring. The "justice which is at last intelligible" was unveiled.

Benoit's championship victory in the main event at Wrestlemania XX is considered by many wrestling fans to be one of the highlights of his professional career with the WWE, an opportunity awarded to a select few performer-athletes whom the company considers able to carry the responsibilities that come with being in the top tier of its competing roster. Three years later, Benoit appeared poised to earn yet another championship at the *Vengeance: Night of Champions* pay-per-view event but missed the show after placing a telephone call in which he claimed his wife and son were suffering from a serious case of food poisoning. The following day, June 25, 2007, Benoit, his wife Nancy, and their seven-year-old son Daniel were discovered dead at their Georgia home. This shocking turn of events led to a frenzy of media coverage in the ensuing months, with current and past members of the wrestling industry, doctors, legal analysts, and others all struggling to make sense of what happened. Public speculation immediately turned to the subject of steroids and whether or not "roid rage" was a cause of Benoit's violent actions, despite the WWE's claim, released just one day after the bodies were found, that "it is entirely wrong for speculators to suggest that steroids had anything to do with these senseless acts" ("WWE Shocked").

The shocking nature of the double murder-suicide was amplified by virtue of its having occurred within the boundaries of the professional wrestling industry, a form of "sports entertainment" where matches are often choreographed and outcomes are scripted by promoters in advance. Laurence de Garis, a professor of sports management who has wrestled professionally for two decades under the names Larry Brisco and "The Professor," argues that professional wrestling is a highly performative sport where the success of each match turns on its believability, logical coherence, and narrative appeal (200–09). Although "'Drama' has become the dominant metaphor for writing about professional wrestling" (de Garis 193), de Garis contends that

> the credibility of professional wrestling as "fake" sport is important to fan enjoyment of the performances. The reason that credibility is important is so that fans can experience a pro-wrestling match as they would a sports event. The best matches in wrestling are those that mimic the oohs and ahs of a sports contest. The best matches have reproduced the formula that makes those "miracle moments" in sports so miraculous: the home run in the bottom of the ninth to win the game, the last-second field goal, the final-round knockout while you are behind on the judges' scorecard. (201)

De Garis is explaining how this performative sport appeals to an audience's desire for real, albeit scripted, entertainment. Sharon Mazer describes this dynamic as the "phantom of the real" that lies "at the heart of professional wrestling's appeal" (82).

This tension between "real" and "fake" that is maintained in the interactions between promoters, wrestlers, and fans and "generates much of the heat in wrestling" was shattered with the news of Benoit's double murder-suicide (Mazer 68). Suddenly, terribly, the "fake" that "binds fans to wrestlers, and to each other, creating a performance of denial and complicity that in its ambivalence and ambiguities eludes moral and academic authority" had given way to the very real deaths of three individuals at the hands of one of the WWE's top performers (Mazer 68). Traumatic moments such as this one are ripe for rhetorics of monstrosity. As Cohen observes, the monster is a "harbinger of category crisis" and as such "notoriously appears at times of crisis as a kind of third term that problematizes the clash of extremes" (6).

In this case, the violent clash of extremes between the fake and the real produced the conditions for monster-talk, which was most evident in Vince McMahon's portrayal of Benoit as a monster on the *Today* show. By constituting Benoit as a monster, McMahon was attempting to address the growing concerns about the murder-suicide as well as close the tragedy off to further speculation. Benoit was a monster, end of discussion. McMahon would appear a few months later in the CNN documentary *Death Grip: Inside Pro Wrestling*, reinforcing his earlier statements by again calling Benoit a monster and defending the actions of his company: "Nothing from the WWE, under any set of circumstances, had anything at all to do with Chris Benoit murdering his family. How would we know that Chris Benoit would turn into a monster?" ("Death Grip"). As the national conversation about Benoit continued, commentators such as Jeanine Pirro (who also offered thoughts on Michael Vick) echoed McMahon's assessment of Benoit when she criticized attempts to look "for an excuse for someone to murder his wife and his child. I don't think that we need an excuse. It's just about good and evil.... He killed his wife and child, but if you want to blame it on drugs, do that" ("Toxicology Results"). And in a comment that reinforced the alterity of Benoit and his wife, professional wrestling icon Hulk Hogan linked Benoit's actions to "devil-worship stuff," which he claimed Benoit's wife participated in both inside and outside her own professional wrestling career ("Hulk Hogan").

The WWE further distanced itself from Benoit by pulling merchandise related to him from store shelves and stopping production on the *Hard Knocks* documentary (which is no longer available for purchase through the company's website). References to the wrestler also began disappearing from the WWE's official website. On the page dedicated to covering the history of its popular *Royal Rumble* pay-per-view event, for example, visitors will notice an entry missing for 2004, the year Chris Benoit won the competition ("Royal Rumble"). The company's hurried disassociation with Benoit, although not atypical behavior when a major corporation is faced with a crisis that has the potential to damage its reputation, is nonetheless interesting considering the centrality of violence in the performative economy of professional wrestling. The performance of pain and violence, what Barthes described as a "rhetorical amplification," is the bread and butter of WWE programming, played out each week in nationally televised matches and signified on/through the bodies of the wrestlers themselves (23). Yet it was for this very reason that Benoit was constituted as a monstrous figure, his alterity defined by his violation of the performative boundaries of his sport. Inside the ring, he was known as the "Canadian Crippler" and praised as a performer "with deadly focus" who was also "cold-hearted" and "absolutely ruthless" (*Hard Knocks*); outside the ring, his actions spilled over into the excessive and the profane by disrupting the illusion of reality the public has come to expect from professional wrestling performances.

Butler argues that performative speech "is always in some ways out of our control" (15). Although this increases its potential for causing injury (in the case of hate speech or monster-talk, for example), it also suggests that such speech can signify something that was not intended by its original source. A question she poses regarding the consequences of hate speech and the possibility of resisting it can likewise be applied to the rhetorics of monstrosity discussed in this chapter: "Is there a repetition that might disjoin the speech act from its supporting conventions such that its repetition confounds rather than consolidates its injurious efficacy?" (20). During McMahon's *Today* show interview, Vieira inverted his monster comment by asking the company chairman what role the wrestling industry played in Benoit's double murder-suicide. "And in any way does pro-wrestling contribute to the creation of monsters?" she asked. "Absolutely not," Vince asserted, "Everyone that's in this organization, to my knowledge, is well-adjusted, family people. They go to work like everybody else, except their definition of what their job is, is to put a smile on somebody's face. They're performers, and they do their jobs very, very well." McMahon's response affirms Benoit's monstrosity while it simultaneously denies the chairman's participation in the monstrous rhetoric he uses to describe the wrestler. By "displacing our fearful fascination onto spectacular stories of horror, monstrosity and violence," McMahon's rhetoric insists that the WWE played no role in the creation of Benoit the monster, and that there are no further explanations for Benoit's actions (Kearney 8). McMahon effectively naturalizes Benoit's status as a monster, disguising the motivations behind his violent actions, whatever they may have been, in a veil of otherness.

■ Conclusion

This chapter has shown how sports can become a source of images and signs for making monsters out of controversial athletes, and how popular culture is a site of struggle where the rhetoric of monstrosity is both created and contested. Using the coverage of controversies surrounding Michael Vick, Mike Tyson, and Chris Benoit as representative examples, it has argued that monstrosity is a complex signifier of alterity that is constituted through performative utterances and functions as a powerful symbol that both disguises and channels a variety of ideological motivations. The chapter also suggests that one of the motivating factors behind monstrous discourses is the construction of identity through negative identification, that is, by defining oneself against the evil actions of the sports-figure-turned-monster.

At this point, you may be wondering what actions a collective can take to avoid the symbolic and material violence that is often the end result of monster-making, whether in a sports context or in other social, political, and cultural settings. Posing this question need not be taken as a denial or defense of the often terrible acts of violence perpetrated by those who are labeled as monsters. Rather, posing it is to express a concern for the ethics of representation in the texts of popular culture, and how a collective can go about understanding its "monsters" without describing them as such, and without dehumanizing them in the process. In his book *Strangers, Gods and Monsters,* Richard Kearney argues that societies can better understand monsters and scapegoats through an ethics of tolerance and self-reflexivity. The goal is not to abandon monsters completely, "For how are we to address otherness at all if it becomes totally *unrecognizable* to us?" Kearney asks (10, original emphasis). He locates the source of monster-talk in "the refusal to acknowledge oneself-as-another," a refusal to consider the ways in which we may be more like our monsters than we are different from them (11). When faced with the other, Gunn recommends "humility and openness" and "a degree of hospitality in order to avoid fashioning others into gods and monsters" ("Review Essay" 98). As sports controversies continue to surface with each coming season, the rhetorical constructions of athletes at the center of those controversies will be affected by the ability of consumers of popular culture to look inward before speaking out.

Works Cited

"Alberto Gonzalez Announces Resignation; Michael Vick Pleads Guilty." *CNN.com*. Cable News Network, 27 Aug. 2008. Accessed on 30 July 2008. <http://transcripts.cnn.com/TRANSCRIPTS/0708/27/acd.01.html>.

Austin, J. L. *How to Do Things with Words.* 2nd ed. Ed. J. O. Urmson and Marina Sbisà. Cambridge: Harvard UP, 1962.

Barthes, Roland. "The World of Wrestling." 1957. *Mythologies.* Trans. Annette Lavers. New York: Hill, 1972. 15–25.

"A Baseball Tragedy." *New York Times* 9 Mar. 2006, late ed., sec. A: 22. *LexisNexis.* Accessed on

23 July 2008.

Borges, Ron. "It's Now a Holy Field. Boxing is the Lord's Work for This Champion." *Boston Globe* 20 April 1994, city ed.: 77. *LexisNexis.* Accessed on 23 July 2008.

———. "Same Old Trick; On Boxing." *Boston Globe* 1 July 1997, city ed.: C1. *LexisNexis.*

Accessed on 23 July 2008.

Brummett, Barry. *Rhetorical Dimensions of Popular Culture.* Tuscaloosa: U of Alabama P, 1991.

Butler, Judith. *Excitable Speech: A Politics of the Performative.* New York: Routledge, 1997.

Byrd, Robert C. "Byrd Condemns Dogfighting." *U.S. Senator Robert C. Byrd.* N.p., 19 July 2007. Accessed on 31 July 2008. <http://byrd.senate.gov/2007_07_19_Byrd_Condemns_Dogfighting.pdf>.

Cohen, Jeffrey Jerome, ed. *Monster Theory: Reading Culture.* Minneapolis: U of Minnesota P, 1996.

Cong. Rec. 19 July 2007: 9534–9574. *LexisNexis.* Accessed on 31 July 2008.

de Garis, Laurence. "The 'Logic' of Professional Wrestling." *Steel Chair to the Head: The Pleasure and Pain of Professional Wrestling.* Ed. Nicolas Sammond. Durham: Duke UP, 2005. 192–212.

de Moraes, Lisa. "Whoopie on 'The View,' Day Two: She Doesn't Condone Michael Vick's Dogfighting." *Washington Post* 6 Sept. 2007, Met 2 ed.: C07. *LexisNexis.* Accessed on 20

July 2008.

"Death Grip: Inside Pro Wrestling." *CNN.com.* Cable News Network, 7 Nov. 2007. Accessed on 31 July 2008. <http://transcripts.cnn.com/TRANSCRIPTS/0711/07/siu.01.html>.

Delbanco, Andrew. *The Death of Satan: How Americans Have Lost the Sense of Evil.* New York: Farrar, 1995.

Derrida, Jacques. *Limited INC.* Evanston: Northwestern UP, 1988.

"Dogfighting a Booming Business, Experts Say." *CNN.com.* Cable News Network, 19 July 2007. Accessed on 31 July 2008. <http://www.cnn.com/2007/US/07/18/dog.fighting/>.

Gildea, William. "The Dark Fascination with Tyson: Public Is Still Riveted by Troubled Former Heavyweight Champion." *Washington Post* 5 June 2005, final ed.: E01. *LexisNexis.* Accessed on 23 July 2008.

———. "A Sport Embodying Both Beauty and the Beast." *Washington Post* 24 Feb. 2002, final ed.: D03. *LexisNexis.* Accessed on 23 July 2008.

Glebatis Perks, Lisa. "The Evil Albino: Cinematic Othering and Scapegoating of Extreme Whites." *Uncovering Hidden Rhetorics: Social Issues in Disguise.* Ed. Barry Brummett. Thousand Oaks: Sage, 2008. 71–84.

"Guilty Plea for Vick; Jail Time?" *World News with Charles Gibson.* ABC. 20 Aug. 2007. *LexisNexis.*

Accessed on 20 July 2008.

Gunn, Joshua. "Review Essay: Mourning Humanism, or, the Idiom of Haunting." *Quarterly Journal of Speech* 92.1 (2006): 77–102.

———. "The Rhetoric of Exorcism: George W. Bush and the Return of Political Demonology." *Western Journal of Communication* 68.1 (2004): 1–23.

Hard Knocks: The Chris Benoit Story. WWE Home Video, 2004. DVD.

Hiestand, Michael. "Cameras Won't Leave Field, Despite Walter Incident." *USA Today* 11 Sept. 1991, final ed.: 3C. *LexisNexis.* Accessed on 20 July 2008.

"Hulk Hogan Talks to *US* about the Killer Wrestler." *Usmagazine.com.* US Weekly, 3 July 2007. Accessed on 28 Nov. 2008. <http://www.usmagazine.com/

hulk_hogan_talks_to_i_us_i_about_the_killer_wrestler>.

Ingebretsen, Edward J. *At Stake: Monsters and the Rhetoric of Fear in Public Culture.* Chicago: U of Chicago P, 2001.

Jenkins, Henry III. "Afterword, Part I: Wrestling with Theory, Grappling with Politics." *Steel Chair to the Head: The Pleasure and Pain of Professional Wrestling.* Ed. Nicolas Sammond. Durham: Duke UP, 2005. 295–316.

Kearney, Richard. *Strangers, Gods and Monsters.* London: Routledge, 2003.

Lipsyte, Robert. "The Tyson Verdict: From Spark to Flame to a Roaring Blaze." *New York Times* 12 Feb. 1992, late ed., sec. B: 13. *LexisNexis.* Accessed on 23 July 2008.

Madison, Soyini D. *Critical Ethnography: Method, Ethics, and Performance.* Thousand Oaks: Sage, 2005.

Mazer, Sharon. "'Real' Wrestling/'Real' Life." *Steel Chair to the Head: The Pleasure and Pain of Professional Wrestling.* Ed. Nicolas Sammond. Durham: Duke UP, 2005. 67–87.

"Michael Vick Dog Fighting Case Opens Racial Divide." *ESPN.com.* Walt Disney Internet Group, 3 Aug. 2007. Accessed on 27 Nov. 2008. <http://sports.espn.go.com/espn/ wire?section=nfl&id=2960337>.

"Michael Vick Pleads Not Guilty." *Hannity and Colmes.* FOX. 27 July 2007. *LexisNexis.* Accessed on 30 July 2008.

"Michael Vick Pleads Not Guilty to Dogfighting Charges; How Widespread Is Dogfighting in America?" *Paula Zahn Now. CNN.com.* Cable News Network, 26 July 2007. Accessed on 27 July 2008. <http://transcripts.cnn.com/TRANSCRIPTS/0707/26/ pzn.01.html>.

Mondello, Bob. "In Gotham, a Long Look into the Heart of Darkness." Rev. of *The Dark Knight,* dir. Christopher Nolan. *NPR.org.* National Public Radio, 18 July 2008. Accessed on 28 July 2008. <http://www.npr.org/templates/story/story.php?storyId= 92534168>.

"NAACP Official: Vick Shouldn't Be Banned from NFL." *CNN.com.* Cable News Network, 23 Aug. 2007. Accessed on 27 Nov. 2008. <http://www.cnn.com/2007/US/law/08/22/ vick/index.html#cnnSTCVideo>.

Pollock, Della. "Introduction: Remembering." *Remembering: Oral History Performance*. Ed. Della Pollock. New York: Palgrave, 2005. 1–17.

"Race in the Court of Public Opinion." *News and Notes*. National Public Radio. 6 Aug. 2007. *LexisNexis*. Accessed on 20 July 2008.

Rhoden, William C. "Sports of the Times: A Modern Morality Play, in 12 Rounds." *New York Times* 9 Nov. 1996, late ed., sec. 1: 31. *LexisNexis*. Accessed on 23 July 2008.

"Royal Rumble." *WWE.com*. World Wrestling Entertainment, Inc., n.d. Accessed on 27 Jan. 2008. <http://www.wwe.com/shows/royalrumble/3973952/>.

Russell, Jeffrey Burton. *Mephistopheles: The Devil in the Modern World*. Ithaca: Cornell UP, 1986.

Sandomir, Richard. "TV Sports: Good and Bad Tyson on Display." *New York Times* 14 July 2003, late ed., sec. D: 4. *LexisNexis*. Accessed on 23 July 2008.

Saraceno, Jon. "Tyson's Outlook Won't Set Him Free." *USA Today* 8 Feb. 1999, final ed.: 3C. *LexisNexis*. Accessed on 23 July 2008.

Searle, John R. *Speech Acts: An Essay in the Philosophy of Language*. Cambridge: Cambridge UP, 1969.

Shaw, Mark. "Prosecution Plays on Intellect." *USA Today* 31 Jan. 1992, final ed.: 7C. *LexisNexis*. Accessed on 20 July 2008.

Sloop, John M. "Mike Tyson and the Perils of Discursive Constraints: Boxing, Race, and the Assumption of Guilt." *Out of Bounds: Sports, Media, and the Politics of Identity*. Ed. Aaron Baker and Todd Boyd. Bloomington: Indiana UP, 1997. 102–22.

"Summary of the Facts." *USAToday.com*. Gannett Co., Inc., 24 Aug. 2007. Accessed on 30 July 2008. <http://www.usatoday.com/sports/columnist/hiestand-tv/2007-08 -26-MNF-Vick_N.htm>.

Today. NBC. 28 June 2007.

"Toxicology Results Released in Chris Benoit Case." *Hannity and Colmes*. FOX. 17 July 2007. *LexisNexis*. Accessed on 23 July 2008.

Turan, Kenneth. "'The Dark Knight': Through Shadows and Hype." Rev. of *The Dark Knight*, dir. Christopher Nolan. *NPR.org*. National Public Radio, 18 July 2008. Accessed on 28 July 2008. <http://www.npr.org/templates/story/story.php?storyId =92534170>.

"Virginia Grand Jury Indicts Michael Vick on Dog Charges/Polygamist Leader Jeffs Found Guilty." *Nancy Grace*. *CNN.com*. Cable News Network, 25 Sept. 2007. Accessed on 30 July 2008. <http://transcripts.cnn.com/TRANSCRIPTS/0709/25/ng.01.html>.

Wilbon, Michael. "The Tug-of-War over Vick." *Washington Post* 8 Aug. 2007, Met 2 ed.: E07. *LexisNexis*. Accessed on 20 July 2008.

"Wrestler Kills Wife, Son and Him." *Larry King Live*. *CNN.com*. Cable News Network, 9 July 2007. Accessed on 27 July 2008. <http://transcripts.cnn.com/TRANSCRIPTS/ 0707/09/lkl.01.html>.

Wu, Amy. Letter. *New York Times* 8 Aug. 1993, late ed., sec. 9: 10. *LexisNexis*. Accessed on 23 July 2008.

"WWE Shocked at Latest Developments in Benoit Tragedy, Concerned by Sensationalistic Reporting." *WWE.com*. World Wrestling Entertainment, Inc., 26 June 2007. Accessed on 31 July 2008. <http://corporate.wwe.com/news/2007/2007_06_26.jsp>.

Note

1. For an excellent analysis of what makes for a good wrestling match, see "The 'Logic' of Professional Wrestling" by pro wrestler-cum-academic Laurence de Garis.

3

■ It Is a Girl Thing

Uncovering the Stylistic Performance
of Female Athleticism

□ Sunshine P. Webster

"I am an athlete," world champion tennis player Serena Williams shouts into a giant megaphone along with other famous female athletes as part of Nike's new advertising campaign aimed at giving voice to female athletes. Armed with tag lines such as "It's not a girl thing," the campaign encourages viewers to focus less on femaleness and more on the athleticism of female athletes. Nike as well as other sports marketing companies have produced similar ads over the past fifteen years, but despite overt foregrounding of skills and athleticism over femininity and femaleness, these and other similar sports marketing campaigns inextricably link gender and athleticism. Stylistic images of female athletes shape our understanding of the performance of sports. For female athletes, it is a girl thing. Gender becomes more important than athleticism.

Stylistic images of professional athletes position the body as the locus of athletic style. Style refers to the coalescing of signs on the physical body. These signs encompass artifacts adorned on the body such as clothing, hairstyles, and tattoos as well as gender, race, and socioeconomic class. The body represents the site of meaning and the performative site of style. Professional

athletes wear, act, and perform their sport stylistically. Popular media emphasize style over athleticism and in doing so construct and define notions of
femininity, masculinity, race, and class. By reading the athletic body, we begin
to uncover meanings, contradictions, intent, and lack thereof. Likewise, we
also discover the ways these stylistic images are gendered, raced, and
classed.

Media outlets delight in portraying stylistic images of athletes. The July/
August 2007 issue of Men's Health magazine features professional quarterback
Brady Quinn wearing a tight-fitting athletic shirt with text reading, "The Male
Body" (Quill). In addition, January 2007, *ESPN the Magazine* features two
Denver Nugget basketball players clad in headbands highlighting the display
of tattoos across both players' wrists, forearms, biceps, and necklines. The
January 28, 2008 issue features snowboarder Gretchen Bleiler sporting tight
clothing and exposing a bit of her midriff. Similarly, immediately following
the 2004 Olympic Games, FHM men's magazine and Playboy Magazine
featured "sexy" Olympic female athletes emphasizing the femininity of their
bodies and enhancing their sex appeal. These examples reinforce the link
between style and sports.

This chapter explores the ways stylistic images and messages provide an
avenue for understanding the performance of sports. A focus on style becomes
a focus on the performance of sports and brings to light the gendered, raced,
and classed nature of sports. Specifically, this chapter offers a case in point
by examining mass-mediated messages of female athletes to illustrate how
style becomes the performance of sports. The female bodies portrayed in
mediated messages demonstrate how the body becomes the performative
site of style, style becomes gendered, and style shapes our ideological views
about athleticism, female athletes, and femininity. Emphasizing style over
athleticism leads to significant rhetorical implications regarding identity formation and ideology. Moreover, a media emphasis on style over athleticism
positions sports as a site of social struggle.

■ Style as a Rhetorical Construct

Goods, commodities, and artifacts exist within a social network and work
together to construct meaning. Together, these goods and signs create style.
The physical body is key to understanding style because the body provides
the surface upon which signs coalesce. Students of popular culture quickly
discover that style is not accidental. On the contrary, Stuart Ewen contends,
"style has emerged as the predominant expression of meaning" (241). Mary
Douglas and Baron Isherwood argue that goods exist within a system of signs

and function to attribute meaning (15). Understood as signifiers indicating certain conditions, goods may be interpreted for significance. This implies that goods and their uses compare with semantic, syntactic, and pragmatic uses of language. Much like words making up a sentence, signs must adhere and conform to understood definitions, rules, and practices in order to communicate. Within a variety of texts, authors position the physical body as the locus upon which signs coalesce. For these authors, the body, with its adornment of goods, represents the site of meaning and the performative site of style. "The study of fashion in popular culture is often preoccupied with how clothing, hairstyles, make-up, and accessories are brought into a system of meanings generated through use and reappropriation" (Guins and Cruz 148). In a society saturated with messages and signs (Debord 110), popular media exists as a commodity for consumption. As Fredric Jameson suggests, we live "in a world in which everything, including labor power, has become a commodity" (117). Everything has its price, but that does not imply that popular media encompasses everything for sale. For John Fiske, "Popular culture is made by the various formations of the people at the interface between the products of capitalism and everyday life" (216). Further, Stuart Hall connects popular culture to the mass commercialization of cultural forms such as music, books, films, jerseys, uniforms, sporting events, and other consumable products (66).

Viewing popular culture as a commodity is undeniably important; however, these cultural forms and artifacts do not exist in a vacuum. Rather, they exist in a dynamic relationship between objects, signifiers, and social actors. For instance, a Mia Hamm jersey represents a commodity for sale and consumption, but the messages and signs surrounding the jersey may construct a reality that transcends the $50 purchase price. The historical and current notoriety of the player influences the meaning of the jersey. In addition, the timing or current framing of the jersey to contemporary exigencies such as a winning or a retiring season could produce greater interest and desire. Likewise, a celebrity endorsement from a famous personality such as Oprah Winfrey would undoubtedly create a mass appeal and increase demand for the jersey. Such a scenario is quite common and expected. "What it brings to light, and the significance of which cannot be overstated, is the complicated energies that corporations employ to produce meaning through popular culture" (Guins and Cruz 147). Producers of popular media know very well the potential economic and social impact of commercialization. When we consume popular mediated messages, we construct meaning within a web of historical, cultural, ideological, and material relationships. "Viewers, listeners and readers do their own symbolic work on a text and create their own relationships to technical means of reproduction and transfer" (Willis 243).

Because the commodity, the modern unit of exchange, is the site where value and meaning cohere and are contested, it bears upon how we understand the objects that surround us and through which we negotiate our relationship to the culture that surrounds us (Guins and Cruz 83). We symbolically construct meaning of our lives through our act of consumption. "For symbolic work and creativity mediate, and are simultaneously expanded and developed by, the uses, meanings and 'effects' of cultural commodities. Cultural commodities are catalysts, not product; a stage in, not the destination of, cultural affairs" (Willis 242). Commodities exist within the dynamic interchange between consumers, producers, industries, histories, and institutions. For athletes, their bodies become commodities and style defines the performance of their bodies. The performance of sports unfolds through fashion, goods, and signs upon the physical, athletic body.

In addition to fashions, language use, gestures, and mannerism operate together to produce style. "The expression and understanding of style as a cultural and social force marks a complex relationship between time and place that is significant because of the immanent relationality of culture that it exemplifies" (Guins and Cruz 349). With its adornment of goods and signs, the body becomes the performative site of style and the site of meaning. Thus, the body becomes an important site with which to read.

■ The Body as the Site of Style

In his work *Sport, Culture, and the Media,* David Rowe explores the (re)production and interpretation of media sports "texts" (11). Within these texts, Rowe discovers how the media images of female athletes emphasize style (125). That is, the media images of female athletes focus on dress, appearance, and looks rather than athletic ability. Adorned with skimpy clothing and exposed skin, female bodies become the site for constructing and reading female athletic style.

Recent images of female athletes illustrate how style overshadows athleticism for professional and non-professional female athletes alike. On the *Her Sports + Fitness* web site, editors claim to offer a "real magazine for real women who want to lead a healthier and active life." Within the pages, the magazine delivers images, editorials, training plans, and nutritional tips on female athleticism. Readers learn what "real" female athletes look like and wear. Examining four years of magazine covers, spanning from 2004 to 2007, reveals a very interesting take on "real women." Over this course of time, only five covers did not show bare abdominals. In addition, all but one cover positioned the model(s) as jogging or posed, facing the camera. All covers featured attractive, white women appearing between the ages of twenty-two and thirty-five. The stylistic images of the magazine covers appear consistent throughout the four-year time frame. Clearly, the bodies on the magazine covers emphasize style over athleticism despite contrary claims. Moreover, images of athleticism are taken for "real" rather than actual athletic ability. To be a female athlete she must wear a particular style upon her body and look the part. Nike's "If You Let Me Play" campaign also emphasizes style and the body over athleticism.

Within the "If You Let Me Play" campaign, Nike emphasizes style to push for the inclusion of girls in sports. Most of the young girls featured in the advertisement are dressed similar to the older, female athletes featured in *Her Sports + Fitness*. For instance, many of the girls are shown wearing sports bras or bikini tops and shorts. Most of the young girls have bare abdomens and shoulder. Camera angles move in closer to the bare shoulders and bellies giving the appearance of more skin. One girls is featured in a dress, and two additional girls are shown wearing athletic t-shirts. Only one girl is shown wearing pants. Of the twenty-two children in the ad, six are non-white. The lack of diverse representation within the Nike ad mimics the same lack of diversity portrayed within the pages of *Her Sports + Fitness*. Both the Nike campaign and *Her Sports + Fitness* depict female athleticism for non-professional women in similar ways. Both highlight the stylistic adornment of skin-revealing clothing on the body and offer little to no focus on non-white female representation. Women and girls perform sports by dressing and looking a certain way. Moreover, this emphasis of style over athleticism has serious rhetorical effects. For non-professional female athletes, little room exists outside the narrow stylistic depictions. These messages not only marginalize women of color and bodies of size but also deny women real athleticism. Emphasizing style over athleticism leads to rhetorical implications. Women who do not fit within this narrow cultural construction experience social struggle as a result. Media images of professional female athletes depict a similar portrait as well.

Analyses of images within *ESPN the Magazine*, *Sports Illustrated (SI)*, and *Sports Illustrated for Women* magazines reveal that media portray male and female professional athletes differently. For instance, Laurie Gordy's exploration into fifty *SI* and *SI for Women* magazines uncovers a stark contrast in media images of female athletes (7). *SI* emphasizes appearance and attractiveness of women in magazine more so than *SI for Women*; however, both magazines still emphasize style over athleticism. For *SI*, style refers more narrowly to outwardly "wearing" sports rather than playing sports. That is, the *SI* images showed women posing in athletic gear/uniforms rather than playing sports.

In contract, *SI for Women* included both. Similar to *SI*, *ESPN the Magazine* emphasizes "wearing" of sports more than playing. Covers of the bimonthly magazine over the three-year period 2006–2008 featured women on three covers. Of the three, professional athletes appear on two: Venus and Serena Williams on one and Gretchen Bleiler on another. All three women appear in white clothing from head to toe, and both covers emphasize style over athleticism. Venus and Serena wear white formal gowns revealing their muscular arms and toned abdominal areas. Likewise, Gretchen wears snug-fitting white t-shirt, white pants, and reveals her abdomen as well. Both of these covers portray female athletes as sexy, wholesome, and with moderately toned muscles. However, their femininity is highlighted to a much greater degree than their athleticism. In fact, none of the three women is shown playing her sport, nor are any of these women shown in their sports uniform. Rather, each woman performs professional athleticism stylistically. Moreover, their bodies become the site of this feminine portrayal. The performance of sports becomes a performance of gender.

■ Gendered Bodies

Michel Foucault teaches that bodies are not only socially produced but also discursively defined (45, 49). The body is not a "natural, trans-historical object" (Malson 49). Rather, the body itself is a production of culture. Susan Bordo furthers this notion by suggesting, "The body that we experience and conceptualize is always mediated by constructs, associations, images of a cultural nature" (35). Following Foucault, Bryan Turner explains that "the body has been subject to a long, historical process of rationalization and standardization" (218). Culture creates standards and boundaries by which bodies should conform. Moreover,

> with the decline of formal religious frameworks in the West which constructed and sustained existential and ontological certainties residing outside the individual, and massive rise of the body in consumer culture as a bearer of symbolic value, there is a tendency for people on high modernity to place even more importance on the body as constitutive of the self. (Shilling 2, original emphasis)

Mediated images of athletes construct notions of masculinity and femininity. Relying heavily on the work of Michel Foucault, Lisa Walker positions the body as a text through which to read meaning and style. Citing Foucault, she writes,

> The body manifests the stigmata of past experiences and also gives rise to desires, failings, and errors. The elements may join in the body where they achieve sud-

den expression, but as often, their encounter is an engagement in which they efface each other, where the body becomes the insurmountable conflict. The body is the inscribed surface of events. (168)

For Walker, reading the body enables one to uncover meaning, contradictions, intent, and lack thereof. She questions aspects of bodily style and mannerisms that communicate and perform sexual orientation, gender, race, and class. Candace West and Don Zimmerman as well as West and Sarah Fenstermaker argue that gender is performed through social interactions and constructions. "The 'doing' of gender is undertaken by women and men whose competence as members of society is hostage to its production. Doing gender involves a complex of socially guided perceptual, interactional, and micropolitical activities that cast particular pursuits as expressions of masculine and feminine 'natures'" (West and Zimmerman 131–32). In addition, "doing gender" leads to "doing difference" (West and Fenstermaker 55). Gender, class, race, and sexual orientation become markers of difference. In reference to sexual orientation, Walker notes that there is nothing in a person's face to suggest that they are homosexual; rather, "signs of gayness, a repertoire of gestures, expressions, stances, clothing, and even environment that bespeak gayness" exist to signify homosexual style (9). Again, the body, adorned with signs and goods, becomes the surface with which to communicate and read style. The body is the performative site that induces rhetorical implications.

Citing Judith Butler, Lesa Lockford urges one to read "gender...as a corporeal style, an 'act,' as it were, which is both intentional and performative" (3, original emphasis). Much like Walker, Lockford emphasizes the intentionality of performing a certain style. For Lockford, people choose to enact the style of femininity. She claims that "gender is a compulsory performance mandated by cultural and social dictates" (6). As such, culture imposes femininity upon women and the female body decides whether to embody and perform. Lockford then relates the intentionality of feminine performative style with feminist embodiments. She states, "Although becoming a feminist may occur in many ways and may result in various ways of being, it is surely evident that becoming a feminist influences the way a woman enacts her self-performance" (33). In other words, the body becomes the site of performing gender. For Walker and Lockford, performing gender involves some elements of intentionality and effort.

For female athletes Vikki Krane, Precillia Y. L. Choi, Shannon M. Baird, Christine M. Aimar, and Kerrie J. Kauer claim that women exist at a difficult juxtaposition between conflicting cultures. That is, they argue, women in sports experience a clash between the masculinity of sport culture and the femininity of "women culture" (315). Images of female athletes such as the *ESPN the Magazine* cover of Venus and Serena Williams illustrate the women's toned, muscular bodies and their femininity simultaneously. Wearing sleeveless dresses, these Wimbledon champions show impressive bicep muscles as well as grace and beauty. Such a juxtaposition of masculinity and femininity may not be as easy for other female athletes. The clash may appear more visible. In addition to studying sexual orientation, Walker examines how individuals perform and "wear" gender as well as race in order to explore aspects of style that are not so easily modified. Referencing a character within the fictional work *Loving Her*, Walker states, "She also has the capacity to 'wear [her] gender according to a particular class style' that gives her access to the privilege of whiteness" (128). Within this statement, we see the body as adorned with both gender and race. Moreover, this statement implies that one has complete control over self-representation and style. However, such may not be the case especially with mediated messages. We are not viewed as having objects and experiences, but as appearing as objects and experiences. With media focus on style over athleticism, style defines female athletes. Such a focus on style and appearance marks a distinction between reality/ self and the social representation of reality and self. The symbolic representation of the commodity dominates our understanding of the social reality such that style becomes a medium of reflecting, creating, and tainting reality and identity.

Social practices define standard or good bodies as well as deviant and Other bodies. Mediated images frame the female athlete as good or Other. Walker articulates clearly notions of Other that are based upon her own experiences. As a femme lesbian, her voice is often silenced within the lesbian community because she does not wear the "correct" lesbian style. For female athletes, the signs of their gender, class, sexual orientation, and/or race may contradict with expectations of femininity or the standards of style for the sport they play. Media portrayals of female athletes support stereotypical, traditional views of femininity that supersede athletic ability (Fink and Kensicki 315) and privilege heterosexuality (Meân and Kassing 128). In their study of female athleticism and identity, Lindsey Meân and Jeffrey Kassing discovered that female athletes construct their identities in multiple ways (126). For instance, many of the female athletes interviewed align with Mike Featherstone's notion that consumption constructs identity. Many of these women experience tension between being a woman and being an athlete. One athlete insisted, "Being a woman or being feminine and having muscles; there's nothing wrong with that" (Meân and Kassing 136). A coherent system of signs meeting expectations might perpetuate hegemonic ideologies and preference one style, or set of commodities, over others (Daniels, Spiker, and Papa).

Many scholars suggest that media constructions of female athletes perpetuate hegemonic discourse (Fink and Kensicki 315) and limit feminine possibilities (Meân and Kassing 128), rendering female athletes disempowered. Marking themselves as Other and different from non-athletic women, these athletes in Meân and Kassing's study consume in order to create a less problematic identity. Still, others in the study suggest they perform a more "true" identity conforming to societal standards. Female athletes who conform to media constructions and ideals feel empowered by their athleticism despite the perpetuation of hegemonic ideals (Kitchens 1). In contrast, women who do not conform to expected ideals attempt to render gender invisible to make sense of their lack of conformity (Meân and Kassing 131). Walker echoes this sentiment by noting, "Witness the unease that some femme lesbians will evidence when they sit with their legs thrown apart, in proper butch stance, and the inability of some butches to look 'natural' in a dress" (10). For some, style is less intentional. Not all female athletes are able to conform to societal standards of athletic beauty.

Relating back to Douglas and Isherwood (15), styles serve as a system much like language: all the pieces must fit together in order to provide a coherent meaning. For instance, a woman of size on the cover of *Her Sports + Fitness* magazine would appear grammatically incorrect. The body, as an inscribed surface, would signify an "error" in style when commodities and signs do not "fit" together. WNBA star Lisa Leslie points to the inherent contradictions with the title of her new autobiography *Don't Let the Lipstick Fool You*. Shown on the cover of her book wearing a short, sleek, sleeveless, and low-cut black dress, Lisa Leslie epitomizes sexiness representing a sport rarely associated with such a description. With this title and picture, Leslie draws attention to not only the stylistic nature of sports but also the potential contradictions. Here, lipstick represents a commodity used to construct the stylistic portrayal of a professional basketball player. That is, readers assume she wears lipstick as part of her performance as a basketball player. Moreover, the lipstick represents her desire to appear feminine while she plays. At the same time, the lipstick also illuminates a stark contrast to what people would assume a female athlete participating in a stereotypical masculine sport to look like. With her statement "Don't let the lipstick fool you," Leslie points to ideological questions concerning the relationship between femininity and athletic performance. She can look beautiful and play well simultaneously. Interesting ideological questions arise: Can serious female athletes appear sexy while they play? Can the public take female athletes seriously when they appear sexy while they play? These and other questions bring to light rhetorical implications of the stylistic performance of sports.

Emphasizing style over athleticism denies female athletes the merits of their skills, strength, and accomplishments. More attention becomes placed on whether they perform correctly. That is, female athletes are measured by the degree to which they perform sports according to stylistic standards of beauty and body size. Moreover, non-conforming bodies become marginalized, silenced, and blocked from view, leaving little room for difference and change.

Thus far, much of the discussion has centered on media images of femininity, and Lisa Leslie's book offers a great case in point. The book provides an in-depth account of her career from childhood through college to the WNBA. Her title, framing, and marketing emphasize her stylistic performance as a female athlete. "Gendered forms of athleticism re/presented in the media become inextricably linked with the performance of actual athletic identities" (Meân and Kassing 128). Lisa Leslie's challenge to basketball spectators suggests she "wears" a different uniform. Throughout her work, Walker questions the relationship between style and identity. For instance, relating to issues of visibility, Walker claims, "Visibility and identity are linked by showing that the construction of identity relies on the repudiation of differences that have been marked as Other within the economies of the visible" (137). Likewise, citing Mouffe's argument from appearance, Walker writes, "Everything presenting itself as different can be reduced to identity. This may take two forms: either appearance is mere artifice of concealment, or it is a necessary form of manifestation of an essence- in other words, appearance either conceals or manifests the 'essence' of its subject" (188).

Based on two perspectives offered by Mouffe's quote above, Walker posits identity as a differencing agent. That is, identity becomes evident through the designation of Other. The visibility of otherness points to the essence of the marked individual. However, Walker critiques this perspective claiming that some, for instance, the femme lesbian, may "pass," which positions the passer's identity and essence within dominant hierarchies. Meân and Kassing's interviews with female athletes illustrate Walker's concern. As female athletes attempt to reconcile differences between societal expectations of their physique and/or their sexual orientation, they turn to dominant discourse hoping to render the differences invisible and pass (Meân and Kassing 126). Walker urges society to question cultural assumptions of femininity as well as sexual style in order to allow for differences in representation. She further notes,

> If the primary mode of identity politics is an insistence on the self, and the primary mode of visibility politics is a public self-fashioning, in claiming the "label" femme, I manipulate both modes, quietly believing that there is something inherent about

my identity, and putting that identity on display in a way that I hope demands a rethinking of what a lesbian looks like. (213)

Although questioning cultural assumptions concerning the performance of femininity and sexual style allow for different modes of representing one's essence, such questioning may undermine how style functions as a coherent system of signs. If the performance of a lesbian encompasses a variety of visual representations, how then does one attribute meaning? Likewise, how does "essence" become manifested through multiple visual representations? These questions hint at contradictions embedded within the representational model. Walker supports multiple interpretations of signs, which is much like the aesthetic model mentioned above, but suggests an essence exists despite the variations of meaning. Such contradictions may account for Walker's reluctance to move beyond questions in search of answers. Nonetheless, Walker's questions of identity and representation grow out of her experiences feeling silenced as a femme lesbian who could not wear her desired style. Maneuvering within societal boundaries becomes difficult when personal choices, desires, and physical makeup exist outside the approved boundaries. Within the boundaries, signs make sense and communicate consistently. More importantly, ideologies make sense within the boundaries. Bodies out of bounds raise questions.

■ Style as Ideology and the Controversy of the Running Skirt

While most of the researchers thus far focus their analyses on the ways the body performs gender, class, racial, and sexual orientation styles, Lesa Lockford examines how style relates to ideology (2). More specifically, she hopes to "illuminate how ideology is inscribed upon the performing body" (3). Further, she cites a number of feminist scholars such as Judith Butler, Paula Bartley, and Simone de Beauvoir indicating their acceptance of the performative nature of femininity and its ideological meaning. For Lockford, this perspective derives "from a presumption that a surface inscription of corporeal style is an outward expression of core identity" (53). Such an approach assumes that a material, "extra-discursive" reality exists apart from the contingent knowledge of the "real" (Malson 39). The contingency of knowledge presupposes that knowledge is ideological because not all views can be represented.

Viewing the body as the performative site of personal and ideological style highlights the inherent social nature of style. Cecilia Hartley contends, "The construction of the body is undoubtedly a social act" (63). Performances of style hinder the satisfaction of both performer and audience. That is, the body engages in a performative act and in doing so communicates meaning to both herself as well as to an audience. As the body is read, both performer and audience assess the conglomeration of goods, commodities, and signs in order to attribute meaning. However, as seen, contradictions between performer and audience lend themselves to (mis)interpretations. Disruptions and inconsistencies within the system of signs may render the body illegible. Voice becomes enabled or constrained in the construction of meaning. Significance and emphasis is placed on the coherency of the appearance and image of style. "The ultimate form of commodity reification in contemporary consumer society is precisely the image itself" (Jameson 117). A recent debate within a particular athletic community highlights this tension between commodities, style, femininity, and ideology.

Style often informs ideology. Over the past three years, runners have engaged in a somewhat heated discussion regarding the running skirt. In 2005, *Runner's World* ran a series of features discussing this new fashion trend, and more recently in 2008 *Runner's World* again devoted an entire issue to the debate. The August 2008 issue contains an editorial exposé written by Kristen Armstrong (a small article expressing a dissenting view) and a three-page spread product review. As readers peruse the pages of the product review, they may learn which skirt is designed to fit their body type, details of fabric, and suggested retail price. Even though this issue looks more informative than controversial, the great running skirt debate is hotly contested within running circles. Some women—such as Armstrong, who challenges women to "bring it on like a man but not look like one" (26)—find the skirts fun and feminine. Others find running skirts distracting from the athleticism of the sport. For instance, one female runner comments, "I prefer to forget my outward appearance as much as possible so I can give myself over to something much more important: what's going on inside" (27). Because of this debate, blogging sites have emerged as a site for women to continue this discussion. The *St. Petersburg Times* posted a blog entitled, "The Running Skirt: Sexy or Stupid" on July 30, 2008, to which a number of women commented. Both sides of the argument cite feminism as ground for support. Jill Barker, a contributor to the *Calgary Herald*, writes in reference to the running skirt, "I'm too emotionally invested in ensuring women can be athletic without worrying about looking good at the same time." Such a comment prompted a number of replies, including the following comment posted on August 29, 2008:

> Wow, I didn't realize we were still in the early feminist era when women felt they had to choose between looking good and being athletic. Hate to break it to Jill, but being athletic has the side benefit of making a woman look good. Perhaps

she should quit working out and wear baggy clothing lest she draw the objectifying male gaze as she trots by, slim and beautiful, in her running shorts. Shorts,
skorts, I run in both, because I'm grateful that my sisters fought for my right to
choose. I ignore those misguided "feminists" who think feminism is about making women feel bad for choosing to honour their bodies and to show them off
in the way that best pleases them. (canada.com)

On both sides of this debate, style and perceptions of style shape ideological beliefs about female runners and female athleticism. As they debate the
propriety of the running skirt, these women construct notions of female athletic style. Clearly, this debate constructs a false dilemma suggesting that
female athleticism involves choosing between femininity and athleticism.
Accordingly, women may choose to conform to more traditional, masculine
athletic styles and be athletic, or they may choose to look feminine while
they exercise. Both sides suggest style communicates some truth about women,
femininity, and female athleticism and both suggest significant implications
for athletes.

■ Implications: Why Care about the Controversial Skirt

The heated running skirt debate helps illustrate the multiple implications of
emphasizing style over athleticism. This emphasis does not only deny actual
athleticism (as discussed earlier) but also limits construction of identity and
notions of self. An athlete's identity is determined by this discourse and by
discourses that depict, describe, and define that individual. Identity may be
known only within those social and discursive practices. For instance, the
female athletes within Meân and Kassing's study frame their identity according to stereotypical, hegemonic notions of femininity despite their contradictory feelings and physique. Discursive practices deny the true experience of
the athletes by denying them the ability to create their own discursive formation in order to express their experiences. Experiences can be articulated only
within the current space. Moreover, the current space constructs a monolithic
reality in which other possibilities are shut off or silenced to the world. The
athlete becomes dominated by the social order that labels, constructs, and
stigmatizes experiences according to a specific set of discursive practices
aimed at locating deviations from normality. Current discourses illustrate a
reality that discourages the possibility of knowing outside the discourse.
Dominant cultural ideals concerning normal, attractive bodies become constituted through discursive practices of the members of the dominant class.
For male, female, black, white, slender, and rubenesque bodies, identity can-

not exist apart from the discourse. This discourse constructs a reality for athletes offering room for some while excluding others.

In addition, this exploration into the stylistic performance of sports brings to light the role sports play in a larger system. Analyzing these advertisements, campaigns, and magazines illustrates how sports and style play a key role in our culture and commodification. Athletes as well as spectators and consumers exist within this highly performative weave of fabric. More interestingly, because of the interconnectedness between style, culture, and commodification, sports become sites of social struggle. Identity emerges from the performance; yet, social pressures and standards set boundaries for performances. Performing bodies outside the lines struggle to be seen and struggle to be. "The commodity thus exercises considerable influence over the establishment of hegemony, a concept that is central to numerous considerations of the exercise of style and identity through popular practice" (Guins and Cruz 84).

Addressing the marginalizing implications mentioned above, many scholars call for a re-reading of the body to allow for multiple identities. For instance, Lockford calls for a decentering of preconceived notions of gender. She states, "Destabilizing and denouncing the original meaning makes the construction of alternative conceptions of femininity possible and opens the way for more performative choices" (53). She further calls for multiple readings of gendered style in order to recognize the substance of individuals performing such style. In doing so, she aligns her argument with Postrel in the hope of accounting for multiple and varied interpretations of identity. Although Lockford does not fully align with the aesthetics of identity presented by Postrel, she does not fully support the representational model of Walker either. Rather, she views style as an opportunity to present substance and calls for the allowance of multiple readings and interpretations to do so. As such, mediated images of athletes would allow for multiple perspectives and multiple bodies.

Allowing for multiple readings of athleticism would create space for difference and grant voice to those who have been silenced by current portrayals of athleticism. Works of both Walker and Lockford illustrate constraining forces limiting their assertions of particular identities. Athletes who do not conform to notions of femininity, masculinity, race, or class also become marginalized and silenced (Meân and Kassing 130). Analyzing and evaluating mediated messages allows researchers to "articulate identity, to give voice to its existence and transformations" (Guins and Cruz 279). Although it may always be a guy, black, or girl thing when reading athleticism, with multiple bodies we may broaden our definition of what that means.

Works Cited

Armstrong, Kristen. "The Rise of Skirt Culture." *Runner's World* Aug. 2008: 25–28.

Barker, Jill. "Hemming and Hawing over Running Skirts." *Calgary Herald* 28 Aug. 2008. Google Search. Accessed on 1 Dec. 2008.

Bordo, Susan. *Unbearable Weight: Feminism, Western Culture, and the Body.* Berkeley: U of California P, 1993.

Canada.com. Canwest Publishing Inc., 29 Aug. 2008. Accessed on 18 Sept. 2008. <http://www.canada.com/topics/lifestyle/style/story.html?id=cc556e2e-f827–40e6–8522–576b309bbee4&p=2>.

Collean, Deal Diva. "Running Skirt: Sexy or Stupid?" *tampabay.com. St. Petersburg Times,* 30 July 2008. Accessed on 1 Dec. 2008. <http://blogs.tampabay.com/deals/2008/07/running-skirt-s.html>.

Daniels, Tom D., Barry K. Spiker, and Michael J. Papa. *Perspectives on Organizational Communication.* 4th ed. New York: McGraw, 1997.

Debord, Guy. "The Commodity as Spectacle." *Popular Culture: A Reader.* Ed. Raiford Guins and Omayra Zaragoza Cruz. London: Sage, 2005. 109–14.

Douglas, Mary, and Baron Isherwoord. *The World of Goods: Toward an Anthropology of Consumption.* London: Routledge, 1979.

Ewen, Stuart. *All Consuming Images: The Politics of Style in Contemporary Culture.* New York: Basic, 1999.

Featherstone, Mike. *Consumer Culture and Postmodernism.* London: Sage, 1991.

Fink, Janet S., and Linda J. Kensicki. "An Imperceptible Difference: Visual and Textual Construction of Femininity in *Sports Illustrated* and *Sports Illustrated for Women.*" *Mass Communication and Society* 5.3 (2002): 317–39. *Google Scholar.* Accessed on 28 Sept. 2008.

Fiske, John. "Popular Discrimination." *Popular Culture: A Reader.* Ed. Raiford Guins and Omayra Zaragoza Cruz. London: Sage, 2005. 215–22.

Foucault, Michel. *The Archeology of Knowledge and the Discourse of Language.* Trans. A. M. Sheridan Smith. New York: Pantheon, 1972.

Gordy, Laurie. "The Gendered World of Sports: An Analysis of *Sports Illustrated for Women* and *Sports Illustrated.*" Annual Meeting of the American Sociological Association. Atlanta. 2003. Conference paper. *Google Scholar.* Accessed on 28 Sept. 2008.

Guins, Raiford, and Omayra Zaragoza Cruz, ed. *Popular Culture: A Reader.* London: Sage, 2005.

Hall, Stuart. "Notes on Deconstructing 'The Popular.'" *Popular Culture: A Reader.* Ed. Raiford Guins and Omayra Zaragoza Cruz. London: Sage, 2005. 64–71.

Hartley, Cecilia. "Letting Ourselves Go: Making Room For the Fat Body in Feminist Scholarship." *Bodies Out of Bounds: Fatness and Transgression.* Ed. Jana Evans Barziel and Kathleen LeBesco. Berkeley: U of California P, 2001. 60–73.

Home page. *Her Sports + Fitness.* N.p., n.d. Accessed on 27 July 2008. <http://hersports.com>.

"If You Let Me Play." Dir. Samuel Bayer. Wieden+Kennedy, 1995. Accessed on 13 Feb. 2009. <http://www.wk.com/?#/works/258/>.

Jameson, Fredric. "Reification and Utopia in Mass Culture." *Popular Culture: A Reader*. Ed. Raiford Guins and Omayra Zaragoza Cruz. London: Sage, 2005. 115–28.

Kitchens, Erica N. "The Negotiation of Gender and Athleticism by Female Athletes." MA Thesis. Georgia State U, 2006. *Google Scholar*. Accessed on 28 Sept. 2008.

Krane, Vikki, Precilla Y. L. Choi, Shannon M. Baird, Christine M. Aimar, and Kerrie J. Kauer. "Living the Paradox: Female Athletes Negotiate Femininity and Masculinity." *Sex Roles* 50.5–6 (2004): 315–29.

Lockford, Lesa. *Performing Femininity: Rewriting Gender Identity*. Walnut Creek: AltaMira, 2004.

Malson, Helen. *The Thin Woman: Feminism, Post-Structuralism, and the Social Psychology of Anorexia Nervosa*. London: Routledge, 1997.

Meân, Lindsey J., and Jeffrey W. Kassing. "'I Would Just Like to be Known as an Athlete': Managing Hegemony, Femininity, and Heterosexuality in Female Sports." *Western Journal of Communication* 72.2 (2008): 126–44. *Google Scholar*. Accessed on 5 Aug. 2008.

Postrel, Virginia. *The Substance of Style: How the Rise of Aesthetic Value Is Remaking Commerce, Culture, and Consciousness*. New York: Harper, 2003.

Quill, Scott. "The Brady Quinn Workout: Our Cover Guy Shows You How to Sculpt an All-American Body." *Men's Health*. Rodale Inc., n.d. Accessed on 2 Feb. 2009. <http://www.menshealth.com>.

Rowe, David. *Sport, Culture, and the Media: The Unruly Trinity*. Philadelphia: Open UP, 2000. *Amazon Book Search*. Accessed on 10 Sept. 2008.

Shilling, Chris. *The Body and Social Theory*. London: Sage, 2003. *Amazon Book Search*. Accessed on 10 Sept. 2008.

Turner, Bryan. *Medical Power and Social Knowledge*. London: Sage, 1987.

Walker, Lisa. *Looking Like What You Are: Sexual Style, Race, and Lesbian Identity*. New York: New York UP, 2001.

West, Candace, and Don H. Zimmerman. "Doing Difference." *Doing Gender, Doing Difference: Inequality, Power, and Institutional Change*. Ed. Candace West and Sarah Fenstermaker. London: Routledge, 2002. 55–80. *Google Scholar*. Accessed on 25 Sept. 2008.

West, Candace, and Sarah Fenstermaker, ed. *Doing Gender, Doing Difference: Inequality, Power, and Institutional Change*. London: Routledge, 2002. *Google Scholar*. Accessed on 25 Sept. 2008.

Willis, Paul. "Symbolic Creativity." *Popular Culture: A Reader*. Ed. Raiford Guins and Omayra Zaragoza Cruz. London: Sage, 2005. 241–48.

■ Part Two

Performance Within Texts of Sports and Games

■ Introduction

When we play sports and games, we put on a performance. This is true whether we are professionals or amateurs. Part Two examines the performances within sports and games themselves, to learn ways in which those performances do social and political work. This is the largest unit of the book, with six chapters. Carlnita Greene begins with a study of the nostalgic performance of Silver League Base Ball. Today's athletes who perform this early form of baseball from the late nineteenth century are enacting nostalgia for an era in which they never lived. Spectators often join the performance, arriving in period costume. Pay close attention to the rhetoric of these performances, and to the social and political effects achieved. Luke Winslow's chapter focuses on a rhetoric of masculinity in the performance of televised bull riding. Note the ways that different characters enact different types of masculinities. Consider the effects of these performances on audiences. Jaime Wright's study of televised Ninja Warriors is keyed to the idea of perfection, grounded in the theoretical works of Kenneth Burke. Note the rhetorical effects explained by

Wright, and think about where else perfection is an element of performance in sports and games.

Feminine identities are created in performances of televised Rollergirl derbies. Alexis Carreiro studies these performances in her chapter. Compare her findings to those of Webster in Part One and Bagley in Part Three for a range of rhetorics of women's identity. Jay Childers studies performances in televised Texas Hold 'Em poker. He argues that issues of globalization are worked out rhetorically for the audience in these performances. Note the ways that wide-ranging issues can be addressed in sports and games that may seem to be only entertainment. Another form of entertainment is the phenomenon of *Lucha Libre*. Laura Barberena studies this highly popular form of entertainment in Mexican culture and explains the ways in which class struggles may take place within the ring. Note her comparisons of *Lucha Libre* to sports in the United States, including professional wrestling.

4

■ Towards a Rhetoric of Nostalgia and Cultural Memory

Silver League Base Ball
and the Performance of the Past

□ **Carlnita P. Greene**

Proposing that we live in a postmodern age, many scholars claim that contemporary society has no connection to the past. Instead, it is characterized by fluidity, hybridity, and bricolage (P. Smith 214–15; Harvey 39–65; Jameson 3). However, inside significant segments of our society, the past is ever present through performance. From television shows such as VH1's *I Love the 90s* to consumer products such as the PT Cruiser and sports memorabilia, we are a society that not only is obsessed with the past but also continually wants to reexperience these bygone moments. That is to say, as a cultural phenomenon nostalgia is both ubiquitous and pervasive. It is for this very reason that we need to further consider how nostalgia functions within contemporary, postmodern society. However, I claim that, unlike how it was in the past, our experiences with nostalgia are increasingly both vicarious *and* performance-based or what I label *vicarious nostalgic performances*.

I contend that these experiences are prevalent especially within the realm of sports because sports rely upon the past for performances within the present. Moreover, I propose that vicarious nostalgic performances also contribute to the popularity of sports because they draw audiences deeper into the experiences due to their interactivity. Therefore, I argue that vicarious nostalgic performances are more suasory than other forms of nostalgia because they involve embodiment, enactment, and/or performativity. As such, these performances contribute to and create a rhetoric of nostalgia steeped in an idealized past that acts as a counter to the present and functions as a "site of struggle" in discourse.

Utilizing "Silver League Base Ball," a text that is both a game and a reenactment, I will address in this chapter how and why vicarious nostalgic performances are a hallmark of amateur sports. Asserting that performance is a key dimension of nostalgia today, I will outline the characteristics of nostalgic performances and suggest why these performances are especially prevalent within sports. Then to further demonstrate vicarious nostalgic performances at work, I turn to an analysis of "Silver League Base Ball." Finally, I suggest future implications for the relationship between nostalgia and performance as well as how scholars could utilize this approach for considering the rhetoric of nostalgia within other areas of popular culture. Therefore, I begin by defining nostalgia and outlining how it functions within contemporary, postmodern society.

■ As Time Goes By: Defining Nostalgia

According to Fred Davis in *Yearning for Yesterday: A Sociology of Nostalgia,* the term "nostalgia" originated with the work of the seventeenth-century Swiss physician Johannes Hofer (1). Nostalgia, as defined by Hofer, was a medical condition of "extreme homesickness" that was felt by Swiss soldiers abroad (Davis 1). It included symptoms such as "despondency, melancholia…profound bouts of weeping…and, not infrequently, attempts at suicide" (1–2). Hofer's work on nostalgia was developed and extended by other physicians such that historically it was considered a "disease" (Davis 2–3). However, as the word's usage spread, Davis suggests that it became "demilitarized and demedicalized," which reflects our understanding of the notion today (4).

In its current usage, nostalgia refers to a general homesickness and/or longing for a past that was considered "better, simpler, or full of hope" and is most often associated with positive feelings (Davis 8; Meyers 6). Yet, as Malcolm Chase and Christopher Shaw explain in "The Dimensions of Nostalgia": "Our present usage of the word is therefore distinctly modern and metaphorical. The home we miss is no longer a geographically defined place, but rather a state of mind" (1). That is to say, people are nostalgic for former times in their lives, or reconstructions of these times, that are seemingly different than their present state of affairs.

In 1979, Fred Davis undertook perhaps the most comprehensive study on nostalgia to date. He claims that nostalgia is not just a longing for the past but a "dialogue" between the past and the present in which the past is always favored (16). People who are nostalgic compare their current situations with their pasts, which are always viewed as comparatively better (16). He notes that there are different levels of nostalgia that range from *first order,* or simple nostalgia, in which people unreflectively believe that the past is better, to *third order* nostalgia in which people are reflective, reflecting not only on the reality of the past but also on why they are having these nostalgic feelings in the first place (17–24).

He also deems that people cannot be nostalgic for periods in which they did not live and/or of which they have no experience either firsthand or secondhand through someone else's experiences (8). However, I contend that since Davis's initial study, the phenomenon of nostalgia has greatly expanded to include times in which people have not lived and/or periods that they only have secondhand knowledge of through popular culture and media. Furthermore, while Davis insists that nostalgia was a feature of modernity, I argue that within contemporary society, the very nature of nostalgia has changed significantly from what it was in the past.

■ "You Must Remember This...": Nostalgia in Contemporary Society

Although nostalgia certainly was an element of modernity, today it is more prevalent than in the past because the influence of postmodernity has significantly altered the ways that we view society and ourselves (Bauman 18–26). First, within postmodernity there is a collapse of the stable social categories and grand narratives of the past such that people often are drawn to past times that seem more stable, easily explicable, and/or significant in contrast to an otherwise chaotic present (Lyotard 60). For example, many Americans believe that the 1950s were a "simpler time" because there was a postwar economic boom, families seemed closer, and life was supposedly much more predictable. In other words, many people long for the 1950s of the "Leave it to Beaver" mythology in which Mom, Dad, Wally, and the "Beaver" lived just around the corner.

Secondly, due to mediated experiences our conceptions of time and space also have altered such that our society is more fast-paced and societal changes seem to occur more rapidly. In this sense, some would reason that because of our fast-paced, hyper-mediated society, people are continually looking towards the future and progress. Yet, I argue that the opposite trend is occurring within society. Instead of focusing on the present or future, people are repeatedly drawn to the past because it provides them with an idealized world in which life was seemingly better than it is today. Yet, employing the past is reassuring also because it has already happened and, therefore, lacks the uncertainly of the future.

For example, as Stephanie Coontz argues in *The Way We Never Were: American Families and the Nostalgia Trap:* "Despite ever mounting evidence that families of the past were not as idyllic and families of the present are not as dysfunctional as they are often portrayed…the myths themselves remain remarkably resistant to change" (xi). Similarly, in "Memories for Sale: Nostalgia and the Construction of Identity in Old Pasadena," Greg Dickinson explains that in the launching of "Old Pasadena" in Los Angeles, the historic Pasadena was replaced by a nostalgic one such that the space becomes a sanitized version of the past stating: "since what is now Old Pasadena was once the very sort of old town most feared…[The new version of] Old Pasadena must cover over not only the histories of other old urban sites, but its own past" (10). In other words, the nostalgic past is often mythologized and people find comfort in the myths.

For this reason, nostalgia is especially employed by "the culture industry" for our popular culture, consumption, and entertainment experiences. As such, nostalgia is everywhere we turn, from *Transformers* to other movie remakes. Because it is so appealing, Oren Meyers explains, "nostalgic themes are, indeed abundant in current consumer society" (8). Therefore, reiterating the ubiquity of nostalgia, Diane Lamude claims, "It is difficult to find a person who has not experienced nostalgia from some media experiences" (37).

Finally, these two aspects combined with a decreased involvement in community-based organizations and civic engagement offers evidence that, as Robert Putnam suggests, we are "bowling alone" (15–31, 48–65). In other words, many of the past social and community organizations no longer hold the appeal that they once had nor do they hold the same function within society, such that some maintain there is a lack of community. Thus, many scholars assert that today people feel more fragmented, dislocated, isolated, and disempowered while simultaneously seeking out their own individualized means of entertainment and consumption (Giddens 5; Jameson 3). As a result of these feelings, people turn to the past as a coping mechanism such that buying a doll might remind a person of his or her youth and a happier time, or watching the movie *Mrs. Brown* (1997) might lead one to imagine that life was indeed better for the Victorians than it is for us.

Our nostalgic experiences today not only are more prevalent but also operate at a much faster rate over a shorter period of time. That is to say, we are nostalgic not only for a past that was ten, twenty, or even thirty years ago. We are nostalgic for last year, last week, and even yesterday. For example, a popular show on VH1 is *The Best Week Ever* where numerous hosts recount the previous week's popular culture and celebrity news. Furthermore, because of mediated experiences and technology, we can not only record our every moment as it passes but also continually relive these moments anytime that we want to and/or share them with others via YouTube. Thus, the process of nostalgia operates at a more accelerated pace than in the past.

Nostalgia has not only accelerated and multiplied, its very nature is more complex than it was in the past. As Christina Goulding argues in "Romancing the Past: Heritage Visiting and the Nostalgic Consumer," we should not assume that nostalgia is a simple notion because "nostalgia is more than just memory; it is a complex emotion with different causes and different manifestations" (568). That is to say, nostalgia as a cultural phenomenon is fluid and ever-changing. It is also "a particular way of ordering and interpreting the various ideas, feelings, and associations we experience when thinking of the past" (K. Smith 509).

Because it is a way that we make sense of the world and because it is rife with meanings that vary from individual to individual, I propose that nostalgia also should be considered as a form of rhetoric that involves political and social struggle. While nostalgia can be used for political ends as scholars Shawn J. and Trevor Parry-Giles suggest, it is also a "site of struggle" in discourse (420). In other words, people can and do struggle over meanings associated with nostalgia and nostalgic experiences. For example, while some people view the Kennedy presidency as "Camelot" and believe that this period in history was a better time in our nation, others do not agree that this time was ideal nor that he was a successful president nor simply accept this version of the past as the "good old days." People often compare nostalgia with their own lived experiences or other forms of nostalgia such that meanings are constantly being questioned and struggled over. Furthermore, what one is nostalgic about also can be struggled over.

In this way, the rhetoric of nostalgia is a form of discourse that is in conflict with other discourses. As Bruce Gronbeck avows in "The Rhetorics of the Past: History, Argument, and Collective Memory": "The past can be endlessly argued over and argued with. It can itself be a battleground or it can be raided, rebuilt, and perverted for any number of human purposes" (49). As such nostalgia and nostalgic experiences may conflict with other meanings within culture and society such that it has significant rhetorical, social, and political implications. Yet, increasingly the way that nostalgia functions today also is significantly different than it did in the past because these experiences are primarily vicarious and at the same time involve performances as key components.

■ The Past Experienced through Other Lenses: Vicarious Nostalgia

Arguing against Davis, I propose that the past can be experienced both first-hand and as Goulding, in "Romancing the Past: Heritage Visiting and the Nostalgic Consumer," suggests *vicariously* (585). Because representations of the past are more readily available in various forms of history, consumer products, popular culture, and media, our ability to draw upon it for our own use is commonplace. In this way, individuals or groups can be nostalgic for times and places in which they have never lived or experienced. As Oren Meyers argues in "Advertising, Nostalgia and the Construction of Commodities as Realms of Memory": "While nostalgia is supposed to connect a person to his own past, studies show that nostalgic recollections tend to blend the private with the public. Furthermore, people can feel nostalgic not only about historical events in which they personally did not take part, but also about times in which they did not live" (7). In other words, sometimes we are nostalgic for times that are completely removed from our realms of experience.

Therefore, as Goulding asserts today people often experience "secondary or vicarious nostalgia" in which "nostalgia…[is] rooted in secondary sources, as none of the informants [in her study] had any first-hand experience of the movements they related to" (585). Following Meyers and Goulding respectively, I argue that within contemporary society, people are able to connect with pasts that may be even several generations before their times or that they have knowledge of only through mediated experiences (Meyers 7; Goulding 585). However, aside from including the idea of experiencing the rhetoric of nostalgia vicariously, I argue that a key way we experience nostalgia today is through performance such that *nostalgic performances* are a hallmark of contemporary society.

■ The Past Imbues the Present: Characteristics of Nostalgic Performances

Within recent years, *performance* has taken on considerable importance as it is studied throughout a wide variety of academic disciplines ranging from theater to cultural studies. Because it is a significant yet multifaceted phenomenon, Marvin Carlson asserts that "as its popularity and usage have grown so has a complex body of writing about performance, attempting to analyze and understand just what sort of human activity it is" (1). In "Performance Studies: The Broad Spectrum Approach," Richard Schechner proposes that performance needs to be considered in broader terms, claiming it "is a broad spectrum of activities including at the very least, the performing arts, rituals, healing, sports, popular entertainments, and performance in everyday life" (7).

If performance needs to be considered within a wider context and if it is a key aspect of our daily lives, then it seems likely that our experiences with the rhetoric of nostalgia also would involve performance because as Ray Birdwhistell suggests: "Performance is an inherent constituent of all communication" (qtd. in Bial 44). Therefore, I begin by outlining a definition for performance that will be used throughout this chapter and then suggest how it can provide us with a more in-depth view of how we experience nostalgia today.

Perhaps one of the earliest studies on performance comes from the work of scholar Erving Goffman. Pointing to the theatricality of everyday life, he advocates that we are like actors on a stage in which we enact various behaviors and mannerisms according to our social situations and the roles that we play within society (18–20). Goffman asserts that, rather than being isolated from particular groups, we all are "performing selves" because our social behaviors are both constrained by and vary according to both contexts and audience expectations (Goffman 106–07). Therefore, Goffman discloses that any situation will be defined by the roles that participants play, how consistent these are to pre-established roles, and how well participants interact in these performances (17–76, 106–40). In this sense, we can view our performances in everyday life as actions, behaviors, and/or enactments that are socially based and constrained yet allow for fluidity and play.

In *Performance Studies: An Introduction,* Richard Schechner points to the multiple uses of performance within society asserting, "Performances mark identities, bend time, reshape and adorn the body, and tell stories. Performances—of art, rituals or ordinary life—are 'restored behaviors,' 'twice-behaved behaviors,' performed actions that people train for and rehearse...."

Any and all of the activities of human life can be studied 'as' performance"
(28–29). Paralleling my earlier point, if Schechner's assessment of performance
is correct and if the rhetoric of nostalgia is a key feature of contemporary,
postmodern society, then it seems likely that our nostalgic experiences would
involve performance as a hallmark. Therefore, I claim that within society
there are specific kinds of performances that are steeped in nostalgia or what
I label *nostalgic performances.*

Following Alison Blunt's definition of "productive nostalgia" or, as she
explains it, the idea that nostalgia can be *"embodied and enacted in practice* rather
than solely in narrative or imagination," I argue that, within contemporary,
postmodern society, people engage in nostalgic performances (722, emphasis
added). These performances are imbued with elements of the past in meaningful ways such that an idealized or imagined past is a hallmark of the performances. In other words, nostalgic performances involve someone's attempt
to re-present, re-create, or simulate a nostalgic past through enactment and
embodiment. These nostalgic performances not only draw upon the past but
can also be a reappropriation of the past for use in the present.

However, as Barbara Kirshenblatt-Gimblett, argues in "Performance
Studies," performances are linked not only to people. They can involve places
and objects as well because "if the body is one site of performance analysis,
objects are another…object performance provides a particularly rich arena for
the relationship between people and things" (50). Therefore, I propose that
often our performances in everyday life are dependent not just on our own
embodiments but also on where these performances occur and which objects
we use in the employment of said performances. Similarly, a place or an
object—such as a stadium, shopping mall, or, as Kirshenblatt-Gimblett suggests, a museum (50)—can possess performativity in its own right.

In this way, nostalgic performances can involve also objects and places
that may hold special significance for someone, such as an old car, or historical
relevance, for example, objects in a museum or an old house. Again, because
"the culture industry" often relies on the selling of nostalgic items, these too
may be linked to nostalgic performances or can be employed in the creation
of them. As Veronica Della Dora suggests in "The Rhetoric of Nostalgia:
Postcolonial Alexandria between Uncanny Memories and Global Geographies,"
"nostalgia draws by handfuls from the vast repertoire of symbols and signs
which constitutes territory…. These perceptible fragments or memorative
signs act as synecdoche for a whole complex of images and experiences" (211).
In other words, people use objects to evoke nostalgic pasts in their performances. These performances also are situated within various spaces or places
such that, as Dickinson argues, some places such as simulations or museums
can "evoke a whole range of emotion laden-memories while providing the

possibility for *bodily participation* in the evocation of the memory" (4, emphasis added).

If we combine the idea that our experiences with the rhetoric of nostalgia today are mainly vicarious and that they involve performance, then one would assume that we would find experiences where both of these elements play significant roles. Therefore, I use the term *vicarious nostalgic performances* to label those experiences that are secondhand and at the same time involve performative dimensions. I also maintain that these vicarious nostalgic performances have stronger suasory potential than other forms of nostalgia because they involve embodiment, enactment, and/or performance. In this way, I believe that people enact these kinds of performances when there is an attempt to rely upon the rhetoric of nostalgia to perform, such as when people create identities to participate in reenactments and/or to engage in sports.

■ Reliving the Glory Days: Sports and Vicarious Nostalgic Performances

Although some would argue that sports occur only within the *present* moment, I assert that sports are often imbued with vicarious nostalgic performances. As Karl Raitz argues in *The Theater of Sport*: "The sporting experiences may even include the past environments retained in nostalgic memory, upon which expectations for future experiences are built" (ix). Within sports there often is a level of nostalgia that pervades the actual play, talk of games won and lost, historic rivalries, and reminiscence about great players from days gone by.

Furthermore, because sports is a form of entertainment, its main objects, memorabilia, also have become a primary means for fans to maintain the past within the present. For example, some fans collect old baseball cards or football jerseys of retired players. This rhetoric of nostalgia operates also on a wider scale within the professional sports industry with museums such as the Pro Football Hall of Fame or the National Baseball Hall of Fame and Museum. Finally, sports documentaries, films, and TV channels such as ESPN Classic often focus on the "golden years" of particular teams or replay old games such as past Superbowls or World Series games.

One could even suggest that vicarious nostalgic performances are a key reason for the popularity of sports today because participating in them may give people a chance to relive the "glory days" of their youths or to participate vicariously in the successes and failures of others. Yet, perhaps the sport in which nostalgia is most often appropriated is baseball because, as Dawidoff says, "America is so swamped in baseball nostalgia that the game threatens to be obscured by a cloud of kitsch" (qtd. in Aden 20). Therefore, to further demonstrate how these kinds of performances operate within sports, I turn to an analysis of Silver League Base Ball as a text.

■ Performing the Past: Silver League Base Ball as a Text

Part game, part reenactment, Silver League Base Ball is a sport in which amateurs dressed in period-style uniforms play in an old-fashioned ball park according to the game's 1866 rules. Founded in 2001, Silver League Base Ball occurs annually at the Genesee Country Village and Museum, which recreates nineteenth-century living and is located twenty minutes outside of Rochester, New York. According to the museum's website, "Silver League" attempts to portray "base ball" (as spelled and known during that time) by creating "a comprehensive 19th century base ball program including the first replica 19th century base ball park in America" where "visitors will hear, see, touch, and taste base ball on its rise to national pastime status" ("19th Century Base Ball Field"). Because "Silver League," as a text, relies on both the vicarious nature of nostalgia *and* performance, I propose that it provides ideal examples of vicarious nostalgic performances. Now, I will explain how the game operates as such for players and audiences as well as outline its rhetorical, social, and political implications.

The Vicarious Nature of the Experience

Although the game's action is experienced firsthand by the players, the kind of nostalgia that is experienced by both players and audiences is vicarious. In other words, it is highly unlikely that players or audience members lived during the nineteenth century, although some may have a distant relative who lived during this time. Nevertheless, this kind of experience means that players' performances and audiences' observations are rooted primarily in a rhetoric of nostalgia that is activated by the social and political frameworks of history, media, books, popular culture, and, one could argue, even the museum itself. That is to say, as a living history museum, the Genesee Country Village and Museum creates a representation or version of the past that players and spectators may use to inform their ideas about nostalgia and/or their nostalgic performances.

Within Silver League Base Ball, not only is the game played according to the 1866 rules, the park itself includes bleachers; an outfield fence sporting period-style advertising; a manual scoreboard operated by two young lads on scaffolding; a press box; a tower for the tallykeeper and announcer; special seating for unattended young ladies; and a refreshment tent serving peanuts, birch beer and other period-appropriate food. ("19th Century Base Ball Field")

In this way, the replication of a "base ball" stadium and the ability to purchase foods from the nineteenth century contribute to the nostalgic performances that occur at the museum because, as stated earlier, places and objects can be used to evoke nostalgic feelings. Moreover, the vicarious nature of the experience is heightened because participants, who have no firsthand knowledge of the period, can imagine what it was like to be either a player or a spectator at a stadium during the nineteenth century. This vicarious nature of the experience works in conjunction with the multiple levels of performance both within and outside of the game.

Levels of Performance

Because the game is located within a living history museum, its performativity also is heightened—for both players and audiences. The minute that players or audiences set foot in the Genesee Country Village and Museum they are transported back to the nineteenth century. Wandering around the village, they can view what life was like during that time, by looking into houses or gardens, viewing animals, visiting the general store, and/or talking to the blacksmith about his trade. Therefore, by the time audiences or players reach Silver Park, the "base ball" stadium, they are already immersed in nineteenth-century life such that their nostalgic performances are reinforced and intensified. These aspects set the stage for performances within the game and contribute to the rhetoric of nostalgia as whole.

Although the degree of performativity varies according to the role one plays, Silver League Base Ball operates as vicarious nostalgic performance for both players and spectators alike. Since it is both a game and a reenactment, it is a unique kind of nostalgic performance that blends both the present and the past. Players are performing in a given moment according to the rules of the game and spectators are watching in the present. However, these rules of the game are from the nineteenth century and the style of play also follows this historic timeframe, which is very different from today's game. For example, as Priscilla Astifan notes in "Baseball in the 19th Century": "The ball could be caught either in fair or foul territory and on the first bound as well as on the fly. No balls were called on the pitcher, but strikes on refused balls would eventually be called on a batter if he appeared to be prolonging the game by refusing good pitches" (8). Similarly, in the nineteenth century, the players wore no protective equipment (Astifan, "Baseball in the 19th Century" 11).

Therefore, the players are able to experience and perform what it was like to play "base ball" during the nineteenth century. Their performances rely upon their dress, use of equipment, rules of the game, and their own embodiments of said performances. However, their nostalgic performances are complicated by the fact that the players do not pretend to be another person someone (real or fictional) that who played "base ball" during the nineteenth century. Instead, the players retain their own identities and simply participate in a nineteenth nineteenth-century game. Yet, this complication also certainly could contribute to their immersion in the vicarious nostalgic performances as a whole because they are in a unique position to image how it *might* have been to live during this time. In this sense, these performances are a means of connecting the players not only to history, but also to their own pasts.

Because the sport is an amateur's game, it allows players to tap into past times when they played baseball as children simply for fun because, as Patrick Bietsy argues in "If It's Fun, Is it Play?: A Median Analysis," "amateur baseball is a game set aside from everyday activity and engaged in for fun and winning" (qtd. in Mergen 65). And although players in "Silver League" certainly play to win, the game is played mostly for fun, as none of the players is a professional athlete. Therefore, perhaps these performances help them to recapture their own youths, as the men and women who play are mostly between the ages of forty and sixty. As such, the nostalgia of youth also underlies and pervades the actual performances of the past.

Although the nostalgic performances operate individually for players, they also operate collectively for teams as a whole. Players have specific positions as members of a team, such as the pitcher or batter, and have to work together to "pull off" these performances to win games. This collectively is reinforced through historic team names such as "The Knickerbockers" (Rochester's first "base ball" club during the nineteenth century) and "The Live Oaks," "the city's first official champions" (Astifan, "Baseball in the 19th Century" 4, 7). In this sense, the rhetoric of nostalgia operates not only to join the teams but also to connect them with the region's past.

Finally, the Genesee Country Village and Museum website notes the interactivity of the game, not just for the players, but also for audiences because "visitors will also meet and interact with the players as well as members of the press, the umpire, the hawker selling his snacks, the unattended young ladies there to keep the game respectable and the rest of the fans" ("19th Century Base Ball Field"). Paralleling the players' experiences, the vicarious nostalgic performances operate both individually and collectively for spectators although more indirectly. For example, an audience member observes the nostalgic performances, not just of the players, but also of other actors in the ballpark—such as the scorekeepers, refreshment stand operators, and the announcer. She can grab a bottle of sarsaparilla or some popcorn and sit in the bleachers to watch the game while rooting for her favorite team.

However, an audience member could become more immersed in the vicarious nostalgic performances by dressing up in the period costume and performing "as if" she were living in the nineteenth century and just happened to be attending the day's game. Nevertheless, most spectators do not dress up and instead happily remain garbed in their twenty-first-century attire. Therefore, spectators, unlike the players, are somewhat removed from a full immersion in the nineteenth century because they are simply watching others play the game. Further, the audience's experiences could be labeled as doubly vicarious or *hyper-vicarious* because they have no firsthand knowledge of the nineteenth century and are not directly experiencing the action of the game.

Yet, as many of the spectators are friends and/or family members of the players, group and community identities are reinforced because audiences can root for a historically regional team while simultaneously having a specific person to support. Because it is an amateur game, the sport is also a way for audiences to tap into their own nostalgias of youth. Further, as none of the players is a professional, there often are the kinds of mistakes that make the games more lively, fun, and interesting. Therefore, spectators are encouraged to remember their own performances and/or observations of past amateur games. Each of these aspects of performance and the vicarious nature of the game contribute to the text's rhetoric of nostalgia as a whole as well as its social and political implications.

Competing Social and Political Implications

Overall, Silver League Base Ball creates a rhetoric of nostalgia, steeped in an idealized past, with competing social and political implications. It is a means of both situating baseball within Rochester's history and re-appropriating the past for the present. Yet, although many of the meanings the text creates seem beneficial and/or positive for inhabitants of the region, these meanings are often contradictory and can best be viewed as "sites of struggle" within conflicting discourses about the origins of "base ball" and the region's past.

On the one hand, the text creates a shared form of cultural memory and collective, community-based nostalgia for inhabitants of the region. Since the players and spectators get a chance to participate in and/or observe how a game would have been played during the nineteenth century, this connection to the past taps into regional community lore about "base ball," because "the game's roots here can be traced all the way back to the early 19th century when baseball was played on a meadow not far from the banks of the Genesee River" (Altobelli xiii). This rhetoric of nostalgia suggests the prominence of baseball in the region as a whole because some people speculate that the game started, not in Cooperstown, NY, but in Rochester somewhere around the Genesee Valley region that is the same area where the "Silver League" game is played today (Mandelaro and Pitoniak 1–3).

Similarly, the rhetoric of nostalgia that operates within Silver League Base Ball harkens back to the sport's popularity as the region's favorite neighborhood pastime. During the nineteenth century, "base ball' was played by a number of Rochesterians regardless of race, class, gender, and/or occupation. There were not only women's teams, but also several teams that were racially mixed; as Priscilla Astifan explains, "Before the Civil War, in Rochester and many other American communities, black players shared club membership with white players" ("Part Two" 7). It was also a highly popular game during that time; as Astifan notes, "One newspaper in 1858 gave an exaggerated figure of at least a thousand clubs that had formed in the Rochester area" ("Baseball in the 19th Century" 7). She also states that "the baseball craze in Rochester and apparently all of western New York continued…As an editorial in a Buffalo newspaper declared, 'Almost everyone is affected with the ball club fever this season. Almost everything pertaining to the game of the hour is of necessary interest'" ("Baseball in the 19th Century" 7–8). Therefore, while the "Silver League" game recaptures some of the cultural memory about the sport's origins in the area, it also connects Rochesterians to the region's history as a whole.

In this sense, the rhetoric of nostalgia that is created about the region's history serves as a counter-narrative to the present. During the nineteenth century, Rochester as a city was in an economic boom as the headquarters for Eastman Kodak Company and one of the first to have its own subway system. Home to both Frederick Douglass and Susan B. Anthony, the city was the epicenter of both the Abolitionist Movement and the Women's Movement. In contrast to the nineteenth century, today Rochester's economy is in a major recession with corporations such as Kodak and Xerox either downsizing or leaving the area or both. The city is more racially segregated and it has high crime rates. Therefore, nineteenth-century Rochester serves as a sharp contrast to present-day Rochester, causing some people to view this earlier period as a better time to which they long to return. As such, the "Silver League" game can be viewed as an extension of the community's well-being and offers a chance for Rochesterians to reflect upon and reminisce about a "happier" time in the region's history.

However, although the rhetoric of nostalgia created by the game serves as both cultural and collective community nostalgia, it is also a counter-narrative steeped in an *idealized* past that may distort how audiences view the region's history and the origins of "base ball." Although Rochester as a city may have been more prosperous and progressive in the nineteenth century, it was still a time in which racial segregation was the rule and women were second-class citizens. After the Civil War, teams became segregated along class lines; as Astifan suggests, the game became demanding: "those who had occupations that allowed the time, energy, and flexibility needed to meet the game's increasing demands for perfection ("Part Two" 4). Further, as the sport continued to evolve after the Civil War, teams became completely racially segregated ("Part Two" 7–9). Therefore, although the reenactment game is played according to the 1866 rules, the rhetoric of nostalgia created by Silver League Base Ball seems to be for an even earlier pre-Civil War game.

Moreover, this idealized past of "base ball's" history in the region is often framed in terms of innocence and/or is viewed as a "simpler" time that was devoid of corruption. However, as Priscilla Astifan reveals, "base ball" was *not* viewed as innocent during the nineteenth century because "the attitudes of the public about baseball had to be persuaded to change from the image of recreation as immoral idleness to healthful pastime" ("Baseball in the 19th Century" 6). In other words, the game that is so beloved today is a romanticized version because it was originally considered as a waste of valuable time.

Since "base ball" was an amateur sport in the past, it is also seen as more "pure" because it was played for fun without the gambling or high salaries of today. The very nature of an amateur's game is such that it creates the notion of innocence, because "base ball" was supposedly removed from the taint of professionalism that we so often associate with today's game. However, as soon as it was discovered that money could be made from the sport, it became professionalized and commercialized such that some nineteenth-century players received salaries and audiences were charged to see the games (Astifan, "Part Two" 11–20). Also, as is the case today, the game was not without the corruption of gambling because, as Astifan explains, "though still in its early years, the game had already lost its innocence. Gamblers frequently visited the games and probably began to bribe umpires and players. Players conduct was eroding also" ("Baseball in the 19th Century" 21).

Another nostalgic notion surrounding "base ball's" history in the region is that games were family-friendly. However, as Priscilla Astifan explains, "as baseball continued to develop, old problems persisted.... Unruly truant boys still hung around ball fields and distracted the players by throwing sticks, stones and bunches of grass at them…. And nearby residents continued to object to an activity that broke their windows and tainted the restful nature of their urban green spaces with noise, profanity, rowdyism, intemperance, and blatant gambling" ("Part Two" 10). As such, the games were perhaps not family-oriented, innocent, or as safe as one might assume. Again, the rhetoric of nostalgia is based on an idealized version of a past that skims over and/or omits those historical facts that may not seem pleasant.

Additionally, the rhetoric of nostalgia that is created about both the region's past and the history of "base ball" can be extended to and compounded by the nostalgia that already surrounds the sport on a national level. That is to say, players and spectators in Silver League Base Ball tap into the nostalgia and mythologies surrounding baseball as a sport because, as Brian Neilson says, "baseball more than any other sport, has lent itself to the metaphorical exploration of American life" (30). In other words, there is a whole nostalgia for baseball that is often linked to American culture.

Many see baseball as demonstrating our roots as a nation and as "American as apple pie." It is frequently positioned as our favorite national pastime and a reflection of the American spirit within films such as *The Natural* (1984), *Field of Dreams* (1989), and *A League of Their Own* (1992), to name a few. Christian Messenger in "Baseball and the Meaning of America" parallels this point claiming that "baseball narrative which possesses times for its own ends, not in submission, possesses history itself and speaks to every level of our experience" (4). Therefore, in presenting an idealized narrative linked to the history of the sport as a whole, Silver League Base Ball also operates politically as a "site of struggle" over meanings associated with the sport's role in American culture today.

As a text, Silver League Base Ball operates as a counter-narrative to the modern sport by acting in opposition to contemporary baseball's professionalism and commercialism. That is to say, unlike other sports entertainment experiences, this nostalgia is not explicitly rooted in consumption. The vicarious nostalgic performances of "Silver League" and the games themselves could be viewed politically as a form of resistance and counter to trends in baseball and consumption as a whole. While baseball today is a professional sport in which players receive large salaries and the game is managed as a business, Silver League Base Ball is a way for players and spectators to enjoy an amateur experience simply for fun.

Further, in many modern ballparks, tickets are expensive, which prevents many people from attending the games whereas in the past prices were more affordable. As Kenneth Marcus laments in "Baseball Stadiums and American Audiences": "baseball today is transforming itself into a middle and upper-class pastime for audiences, especially families, willing to spend enormous sums to enjoy a nostalgic experience at the ballpark" (165). Even within those stadiums that simulate older ballparks, through size and aesthetics, the cost of tickets is high and they are steeped in consumption. As George Ritzer and Todd Stillman reveal in "The Postmodern Ballpark as a Leisure Setting: Enchantment and Simulated De-McDonaldization": "There is a long list of things that have imploded into the postmodern ballpark in order to make it more spectacular and enchanted...shopping malls and concourses...food courts...video arcades...museums that offer things like team memorabilia... amusement parks...plenty of ATMs to pay for all of this" (103–04) .

In contrast, although there is a cost involved in attending the Genesee Valley Country Village and Museum to view the game and to obtain refreshments, these costs are minimal and so allow more people from various classes to attend the events. Therefore, although the text has competing political and social implications on a local level, we can directly view vicarious nostalgic performances in Silver League Base Ball in contrast with mainstream nostalgic experiences that are rooted in consumption.

Works Cited

Aden, Roger C. "Nostalgic Communication as Temporal Escape: *When It Was a Game's* Reconstruction of a Baseball/Work Community." *Western Journal of Communication* 59.1 (1995): 20–38.

Altobelli, Joe. Foreword. *Silver Seasons: The Story of the Rochester Redwings.* By Jim Mandelaro and Scott Pitoniak. Syracuse, New York: Syracuse UP, 1996. xi–xiii.

Astifan, Priscilla. "Baseball in the 19th Century." *Rochester History* 52.3 (1990): 1–24.

———. "Baseball in the 19th Century: Part Two." *Rochester History* 62.2 (2000): 1–23.

Bauman, Zygmunt. "From Pilgrim to Tourist—or a Short History of Identity." *Questions of Cultural Identity.* Ed. Stuart Hall and Paul duGay. London: Sage, 1996: 18–36.

Bial, Henry, ed. *The Performance Studies Reader.* London: Routledge, 2004.

Blunt, Alison. "Collective Memory and Productive Nostalgia: Anglo-Indian Homemaking in McCluskieganj." *Environment and Planning D: Society and Space* 21.6 (2003): 717–38.

Carlson, Marvin. *Performance: A Critical Introduction.* London: Routledge, 1996.

Chase, Malcolm, and Christopher Shaw. "The Dimensions of Nostalgia." *The Imagined Past: History and Nostalgia.* Ed. Malcolm Chase and Christopher Shaw. Manchester: Manchester UP, 1989. 1–17.

Coontz, Stephanie. *The Way We Never Were: American Families and the Nostalgia Trap.* New York: Basic, 2000.

Davis, Fred. *Yearning for Yesterday: A Sociology of Nostalgia.* New York: Free, 1979.

Della Dora, Veronica. "The Rhetoric of Nostalgia: Postcolonial Alexandria between Uncanny Memories and Global Geographies." *Cultural Geographies* 13.2 (2006): 207–38.

Dickinson, Greg. "Memories for Sale: Nostalgia and the Construction of Identity in Old Pasadena." *Quarterly Journal of Speech* 83.1 (1997): 1–27.

Giddens, Anthony. *Modernity and Self-Identity: Self and Society in the Late Modern Age.* Stanford: Stanford UP, 1991.

Goffman, Erving. *The Presentation of Self in Everyday Life.* New York: Doubleday, 1959.

Goulding, Christina. "Romancing the Past: Heritage Visiting and the Nostalgic Consumer." *Psychology and Marketing* 18.6 (2001): 565–92.

Gronbeck, Bruce E. "The Rhetorics of the Past: History, Argument, and Collective Memory." *Doing Rhetorical History: Concepts and Cases.* Ed. Kathleen Turner. Tuscaloosa: U of Alabama P, 2003.

Harvey, David. *The Condition of Postmodernity.* Malden: Blackwell, 1990.

Jameson, Fredric. *Postmodernism, or, the Cultural Logic of Late Capitalism.* Durham: Duke UP, 1991.

Kirshenblatt-Gimblett, Barbara. "Performance Studies." *The Performance Studies Reader.* Ed. Henry Bial. London: Routledge, 2004. 43–51.

Lamude, Diane. "A Cultural Model of Nostalgia and Media Use." *World Communication* 19.2 (1990): 38–40.

Lyotard, Jean-Francois. *The Postmodern Condition: A Report on Knowledge.* Minneapolis: U of Minnesota P, 1984.

Mandelaro, Jim, and Scott Pitoniak. *Silver Seasons: The Story of the Rochester Redwings.* Syracuse: Syracuse UP, 1996.

Marcus, Kenneth. "Baseball Stadiums and American Audiences." *Telos* 1.143 (2008): 165–70.

Mergen, Bernard, ed. *Cultural Dimensions of Play, Games, and Sport.* Champaign: Human Kinetics, 1986.

Messenger, Christian. "Baseball and the Meaning of America." *Humanities* 15.4 (1994): 13–19.

Meyers, Oren. "Advertising, Nostalgia and the Construction of Commodities as Realms of Memory." *Proceedings of the International Communication Association Annual Meeting.* New York: International Communication Association, 2005.

Neilson, Brian J. "Baseball." *The Theater of Sport.* Ed. Karl B. Raitz. Baltimore: Johns Hopkins UP, 1995. 30–69.

"19th Century Base Ball Field." *Genesee Country Village and Museum.* Genesee Country Village and Museum, n.d. Accessed on 1 May 2008. <http://www.gcv.org/attractions/baseball/>.

Parry-Giles, Shawn J., and Trevor Parry-Giles. "Collective Memory, Political Nostalgia, and the Rhetorical Presidency: Bill Clinton's Commemoration of the March on Washington, August 28, 1998." *Quarterly Journal of Speech* 86.4 (2000): 417–37.

Putnam, Robert. *Bowling Alone: The Collapse and Revival of American Community.* New York: Simon, 2000.

Raitz, Karl B., ed. *The Theater of Sport.* Baltimore: Johns Hopkins UP, 1995.

Ritzer, George, and Todd Stillman. "The Postmodern Ballpark as a Leisure Setting: Enchantment and Simulated De-McDonaldization." *Leisure Sciences* 23.2 (2001): 99–113.

Schechner, Richard. *Performance Studies: An Introduction.* 2nd ed. New York: Routledge, 2006.

———. "Performance Studies: The Broad Spectrum Approach." *The Performance Studies Reader.* Ed. Henry Bial. London: Routledge, 2004. 7–9.

Smith, Kimberly. "Mere Nostalgia: Notes on a Progressive Paratheory." *Rhetoric and Public Affairs* 3.4 (2000): 505–27.

Smith, Phillip. *Cultural Theory: An Introduction.* Malden: Blackwell, 2001.

5

■ Bull Riding and the Performance of Masculinity

□ Luke Winslow

I grew up in Seattle, Washington and I was eight years old when the Seattle Seahawks football team drafted a fiery linebacker from the University of Oklahoma named Brian Bosworth. "The Boz" left an indelible impression on me as much for his on-the-field play as his off-the-field performance. He was brash, arrogant, and outspoken. He was suspended for the last football game of his college career for steroid use and was later kicked off his own team by his own coach. Much to my parents' dismay, in my eyes "The Boz" was the epitome of manhood. He played linebacker, rode a Harley, and shaved lines on the side of his head that he filled in with paint that matched his team's colors. When the Seahawks drafted him, I covered my room with his posters, bought his #55 Seahawks jersey and even shaved lines on the side of my head and filled them in with blue and green paint, just like the Boz. I didn't have very much time to enjoy him, however. His career in the NFL lasted only three years and he is probably best remembered for being run over by Bo Jackson at the goal line. He has since been widely regarded as a bust. In 2004, when ESPN named him the sixth biggest flop of the last twenty-five years, I had to wonder why, as an eight-year-old boy, I liked him so much. It wasn't as if he was that good at playing football. There were a lot of players who were much better. It was that he was very good at "performing" football.

My childhood experience with The Boz helps illustrate this chapter's central question: how does performance in sport shape masculinity? Sports are enormously important in the lives of most boys—both the teams in which they participate and the Brian Bosworths they admire from afar. Sports are often the institution that fathers use to initiate their sons into manhood (Messner 9). And the influence sports have on masculine formation doesn't end when boys turn into men and hang-up their cleats. The ideology of sports impacts not only those who actively participate, but also the millions who act as audience members to the performance of sport. As spectators, seeing how masculinity is performed in sports coaches attitudes in the audience. Watching sports, for many men, is not just a bonding activity, identity creator, or stress reliever, but also a site of masculine affirmation and inscription. My personal experience with Brian Bosworth illustrates this well. I had no personal experience with the The Boz; I had never met him. But I still used him as a measuring stick, or rating system, to construct a hierarchy of masculinity. I compared The Boz's occupation, The Boz's mode of transportation, and The Boz's hairstyle to my own and that of other men in order to find what men should look like and act like.

Football is not the only sport that can influence how an audience thinks about masculinity. Young boys and grown men alike look to all different kinds of sports and games to find out how to perform manhood. One such sport that I will look at more closely in this chapter is bull riding. Although it is true that most American men don't reaffirm their manhood by riding bulls, watching bull riding at a rodeo or on television provides a rich example of idealized masculinity. Just as The Boz was about more than football, bull riding is about much more than riding bulls. There is an important performative dimension to the sport that yields insight into how masculinity is represented in popular culture.

In this chapter, I look to *Ty Murray's Celebrity Bull Riding Challenge*, a reality television program that aired on CMT in the summer of 2007 and featured nine celebrities learning how to ride bulls with retired rodeo star Ty Murray, to demonstrate the relationship between masculinity, sports, and performance. The program features Stephan Baldwin (actor), "Cowboy" Kenny Bartram (professional motocross rider and X-Games competitor), Dan "Nitro" Clarke (former American Gladiator), Jonny Fairplay (reality television star), Leif Garrett (singer), Josh Haynes (Ultimate Fighter), Rocket Ismail (former professional football player), Francesco Quinn (actor), and Vanilla Ice (rapper). These nine celebrities train together for ten days at Ty Murray's ranch in Stephenville,

Texas, before the Pro Bull Riders Jack Daniels Invitational in Nashville, Tennessee, where they will be expected to ride a level-seven bull for eight full seconds.

Ty Murray and fellow Hall of Fame bull rider Cody Lambert are intent on schooling the stars in two areas: first, on the finer points of bull riding such as proper chute procedure, how to mount the bulls, and how to fall and get out of the way, and second, Ty and Cody also offer the stars some very vivid lessons in manhood. The show was said to be unlike other reality programs because the celebrities are not in competition with each other—if possible, all will be able to ride their bull in Nashville—but that does not mean the show is without competition. Beneath the surface, there is an important struggle being waged over who can best emulate Ty's idealized version of masculinity. From that struggle, audience members learn not only who is on top of the masculine hierarchy, but also why.

For this reason, this program is a wonderful example of the way gender ideology is constructed through sport and performance. Although few American men have any direct experience with the sport of bull riding, many use it, and other sports just like it, to make sense of the masculine hierarchy that dominates politics, the workplace, and the home.

■ Power, Performance, and Popular Culture

We can confidently say two things about power: first, some people have more power than others, and second, power can come in various forms. The power that separates some people from others is determined not only by muscle size or weapon type. Part of the reason so many attend school is to get a degree. With that degree comes power because our society stretches people along a continuum of power based on intelligence (which is often correlated to education). Gender is another factor that, in our society, can determine how much power you have. Compared to men, women in our society are relatively disempowered: they earn lower salaries for the same jobs, fewer women have prestigious occupations, and women suffer more than men from issues such as poverty, illiteracy, employment discrimination, gendered division of labor, and violence, sexual and otherwise (Brummett 5; Butler, *Undoing* 9; Judge and Livingston 994). These facts force us to question how this unequal and unjust hierarchy of power is being constructed. Although it is alive and well in some places, outright sexism has not only gone out of fashion but is also against the law, so that's probably not how unequal power systems are constructed and maintained. And it's not as if young males are all taken aside at a certain age and initiated into certain mysteries of dominance meant to keep women down (Brummett 5). For an answer to this question, we return to the second thing we know about power: it can take more than one form.

One of those forms is more obvious and direct, such as legal mandates and the threat of physical force used to uphold them. The second type of power is indirect, more subtle, but often just as powerful. This type of power is known as hegemony, a system of thought that allows one group to enjoy dominance over another often without using physical force. Hegemony theory was developed most notably by an Italian revolutionary named Antonio Gramsci who, while being confined to prison by Benito Mussolini's fascist regime, developed the concept to explain how the powerful in society can impose their will on the powerless (12; see also Hoerl 358; Meân and Kassing 129). Gramsci recognized that power is often exerted in obvious forms, such as police clubs and fire hoses, but not always. Often, power comes through in invisible or taken-for-granted forms that prop up systems of domination in a way that requires little or no physical coercion. He labeled those power struggles hegemony.

To use female disempowerment as an example, Gramsci would say that even in the days of the Nineteenth Amendment, *Row v. Wade,* and Title IX women are hegemonically disempowered by deep systems of oppression that often appear natural. These days, these systems of oppression are modeled for us, coached in us, and urged on us through the power relations that appear in popular culture. It is in our most popular music, movies, and magazines—in the moment-to-moment struggle of our everyday experiences—that important social and political battles such as these are being waged (Lipsitz, "Listening" 620; Mukerji and Schudson 1). The systems and artifacts that are widely shared amongst the population are sites of struggle that determine who has power and who does not. And it is for this reason that we need to be aware of the power in popular culture

At this point, you may be asking yourself if this complex form of power can really come from a reality television show about bull riding. If you are suspicious, you are not alone. Historically, not everyone has agreed with these claims about hegemony and popular culture. Some have argued that real power is confined to the church pulpit or Capital Hill and that television programs and popular magazines only distract the masses from the "real" political work being done in "more important" places (Lipsitz, *Time Passages* 17). That more people voted for the 2004 *American Idol* winner than for the U.S. president, or that people care more about where 50 Cent's scars are than where the Sudan is, can be used as evidence to highlight how distracted we are from the "real" power struggles. Others dismiss popular culture as trivial entertainment—nothing more and nothing less. Instead of manning the picket line or writing a letter to the editor, one can turn on the television and get sucked into imaginary solutions to life's real problems (Eagleton 3). Still others discount the power of popular culture saying that popular texts consist of hegemony from above, and no contestation from below (Adorno 107; Macdonald 40). As popular culture becomes more and more commodified and world-spanning corporations such as Disney, Sony, and News Corp. dominate the global cultural market, the broad totalizing force of media monopolies becomes more and more important (Denning 161).

I would imagine you have heard various forms of these arguments before. Many people still think of popular culture as either a distraction, trivial entertainment, or a one-way hegemonic force. But if we keep in mind what we know about power, these arguments can be refuted.

First of all, the rhetorical management of public business is not confined to traditional avenues of power. Political struggle certainly comes through when we enter the voting booth or man the picket line, but many of us actively participate in the day-to-day management of public affairs as spectators. When we watch reality television, listen to rap music, or flip through the pages of *People* magazine, we are being taught important lessons about power almost as if we were in a classroom. The lessons we learn not only teach us who is on top of our power hierarchies but also explain why those people are there.

But because spectatorship is a hegemonic process, audience members can also be taught how to struggle against oppressive structures. Popular culture in particular can be a unique site of contestation for audience members who have nowhere else to turn. Because traditional avenues of power are not open to all of us, many on the margins locate sites of struggle in the consumption of popular culture. When the rapper Eminem mimics an obsessed fan in the song "Stan" he makes this point well. He writes, "I can relate to what you're saying in your songs so when I have a shitty day, I drift away and put 'em on cause *I don't really got shit else* so that shit helps when I'm depressed I even got a tattoo of your name across the chest" (emphasis added). This fan listens to Eminem's music not merely for entertainment or to pass the time; the fan finds agency here that he cannot find anywhere else. The music serves a function for the disempowered youth who thus finds courage and control in the artifact , just as a young black man may find the strength to face another day at school by watching *Remember the Titans* or a young girl may find the power to stand up to an abusive boyfriend by reading *Ms.* magazine.

Popular culture is not empty distraction or "mere" false consciousness but rather a transformational work on social and political anxieties (Jameson 141). This argument might seem like a stretch if you spend your evenings watching *Family Guy* or Will Ferrell movies, but I would argue that despite the seemingly thin nature of a lot of popular culture, powerful life lessons can still come through. Popular culture affects politics by constructing for audiences meaning that directly and indirectly influence power relations. Systems of control and domination are propped up by popular culture, and thus it is here where control and domination can be resisted and changed.

In the next section, I will provide support for this argument by examining how performances of gender in popular culture can influence audience members' attitudes toward gender norms. Popular culture has the power to teach spectators how males and females should look and act and in so doing, popular culture constructs gender norms used to evaluate the worth of another person. This process simplifies the complexities of gender, resulting in hierarchies of power based upon how well one performs a particular gender role.

■ Gender and Performance

Gender can be a misleading object of study. On one hand, the inevitable sexual differences between men and women should produce neat and tidy categories that should be able to explain gender relations. John Gray sold millions of copies of *Men Are from Mars and Women Are from Venus* under this premise. On the other hand, because we have no essential identity that precedes social intercourse, the meaning made out of sexual difference is really not that neat and tidy at all (Jaggar 63; Walsh, Fürsich, and Jefferson 124). Humans actually have a relatively small number of divinely or biologically fixed genes, and so gender is more usefully studied as a complex confluence of social and symbolic signs and practices carried out in language. For example, if I were to buy a large 4X4 truck with a shapely female on the mud flaps and rubber novelty testicles hanging from the back, that truck would serve as a symbol used to connect my mode of transportation to a set of gendered meanings. The truck would do so much more than get me from work to school to home; the truck would be a symbol to myself and others about who I want to be as a gendered being and who I want others to see me as. And because our day-to-day lives are full of symbolic actions such as these, gender is best understood as a discourse that begins with "communication" in the narrow and traditional sense but expands to a larger symbol system that constructs and organizes cultural practices (Goffman 2; Scott 379).

Bull riding is a prime example of a cultural practice directly and indirectly linked to gender. I'll show you how bull riding assumes a distinctly gendered practice in the next section. First, let me try and explain why.

For the spectator, bull riding tells a simple and comforting story. The contingency and complexity that should arise out of sexual difference is mediated in a sport where men are men and women are women. Bull riding is one part of a larger narrative that works hard to fuse the gaping hole between our physiological sexual differences and our socially constructed gender representations. This is one of the reasons gender is such a dominant theme in our popular movies, television programs, magazines, and music. What a "man" or "woman" looks like, acts like, and buys makes for rich content in a variety of popular cultural texts ranging from *Maxim* magazine to The View. To the spectators, simple explanations bring comfort in a world where life is usually neither simple nor comforting (Hart 96).

The savvy rhetorical critic can detect these misleading explanations not only by looking for what is simple or comforting but also by noticing how those explanations serve to construct hierarchies of power. Gender in particular is simplified for the spectator when it comes through as a cultural narrative formed around a singular, monolithic, and idealized version of gender. The pattern is important to be aware of because it has a profound impact on our social arrangements. Among the facts of our cultural life in the United States is one of the most potent influences on social formation: how well one fulfills gender norms. Alison Jaggar claims that an individual's sex is the single most influential factor in determining her social position, her life experiences, her physical and psychological constitution, her interests, and her values (250). Gender structures every aspect of human nature and social life. When a doctor holds up a newborn baby and pronounces it a boy or a girl, she is also determining, to some extent, the type of life that baby will live, the job that baby can have and how much money that baby will be paid. It should be revealing if referring to the doctor in this hypothetical scenario as "she" sounded odd to you.

Social organization is predicated upon not only whether we are male or female, however. We are also ranked on how well we fulfill the idealized gendered expectations put forth in our cultural narratives. If James Bond gets the girl, then the one who can best emulate James Bond will also get the girl and also be able to return a pair of pants, ask a professor to reconsider a grade, or get a desirable job. The most appropriate gender performance is what really determines social organization. When you can perform idealized gender seamlessly and naturally, you are socially rewarded; when you cannot, you initiate a set of punishments, both obvious and indirect, that in the end makes you appear to be less human (Butler, "Performative" 423).

Judith Butler, an icon in the humanities, was one of the first to conceptualize gender as a kind of doing: an incessant activity performed without one's knowing and without one's willingness. Gender as performance eschews stable subjectivity—that is, performing gender constitutes who one is as an illusion created by our performances (Butler, *Bodies*). It is important to note that performance theory is not saying that gender is not real; only that it is real only to the extent that it is performed. And when we perform the same gendered play everyday of our lives, the repetition and ritual of it can make it seem to be natural and taken-for-granted.

These acts not only aid in the construction of identity but also have a rhetorical effect by locating us within regimes of power. Brian Bosworth and Ty Murray can become icons of masculinity because they do the best job performing the expected gender roles. This is what I meant earlier when I argued that successfully fulfilling gender expectations positions us within a hierarchy of power (Butler, *Gender Trouble* 41; Whitehead 17).

One of the best ways to anchor the idea that gender is performed is by looking at drag queens. I would imagine that most of us don't cross-dress on the weekends, but don't let that distract you from the larger point: that in a maybe more subtle or socially accepted way, we perform our gender just like drag queens do. When you get your hair cut or choose a certain cut of jean over another, you are performing your gender—a performance that has nothing to do with your reproductive organs.

Having said this, we are faced with this question: how do we successfully and unsuccessfully fulfill gendered expectations? In the next section, I provide an example of idealized masculinity by looking closely at *Ty Murray's Celebrity Bull Riding Challenge*, a wonderful example of how certain performances of gender can be elevated above others. I hope to support two arguments in this next section. First, that popular culture can have a profound impact on social organization, and second, that performing masculinity in a socially approved way can have a profound impact on an audience. More specifically, I argue that gender binaries are reinforced in this text as the prestige of the sport and that those who do it are forcefully and completely aligned with one gender and forcefully and completely distanced from another. Don't worry if you haven't seen the program; although it is available on Amazon to watch, not many people originally saw it on CMT. As you read, it is more important that you use my analysis of the program to raise your awareness of the many other representations of idealized gender that come through in popular discourse—whether they occur in *Sex and the City, Flavor of Love,* or *Monday Night Football*—so you will be better able to identify, critique, and resist unjust hierarchies of power.

■ Bull Riding and the Performance of Masculinity

Ty Murray's Celebrity Bull Riding Challenge is able to tell the spectator a simplified gendered story by tugging or aligning the traits that we commonly associate with the most masculine with the sport's top performers. In the program, bull riding is an explicitly masculine sport as the performance of masculinity and the performance of bull riding coalesce. "Courage" is a reoccurring example. Because of the inherent danger that comes with riding bulls, it seems like you can't be good at bull riding without courage. Stephen Baldwin, in the first episode calls bull riding "the toughest, most dangerous sport on the planet" ("We Just") and Ty Murray, after several celebrities get hurt, says, "At the end of the day, that's bull riding. Things like that can and do happen" ("Vanilla Ice"). The viewer learns that courage, toughness, and physical strength have the most impact on whether one can successfully ride the bull. Other, less explicitly masculine traits, such as technical proficiency, agility, or ability to take coaching, are downplayed. Of course, a person could be gentle, humble, dependent, emotional, and passive and still be an excellent bull rider, but those supposedly feminine traits would disrupt the coalescing of masculinity and bull riding.

Another example of this tugging process occurs when courageous and tough performances are aligned with male and female anatomies. On the program, the best bull riders have "balls" and the worst are "pussies." In the first episode, Hall of Fame bull rider Cody Lambert introduces the sport by saying, "Bull riding never has been, and never will be a sport for pussies. You can die doing this; it's very dangerous, no matter what kind of protection you have" ("We Just"). Lambert couldn't say "pussy" because the program was on basic cable, so he was censored. In its place, the word "wussy" or "wuss"—a combination of wimp and pussy—is often used as a euphemism for female genitalia. When actor Francesco Quinn first explains his desire to be on the program he says, "Most people think that actors are pansy-ass wussies. Hey, most of them are, but I don't like to live my life like that" ("We Just"). He makes a similar alignment after a poor, one-second ride when he explains, "I went off like a little girl" ("The Injuries"). Notice the connection here: bull riding to masculinity (or the antithesis of masculinity) to anatomy and back again.

Conversely, the best compliment you can receive as a bull rider relates to the male anatomy. In the first episode, 2005 Professional Bull Riding champion Justin McBride visits the ranch to show the celebrities how bull riding is done. After a particularly successful ride, Vanilla Ice refers to his performance as "Very ball worthy" ("We Just"). However, testicular fortitude can be used also as a cutting insult—the last thing you want to be is lacking in balls. After Leif Garrett and Stephen Baldwin have to go home because of injuries and several of the other stars express their own fears about getting hurt, Ultimate Fighter Josh Haynes tells the camera, "Some of these guys need to look inside themselves and dig down deep and find their manhood" ("A Concert"). Not having the requisite balls means that you are not only a poor bull rider, but an incomplete, ineffectual man as well.

The traits required of a bull rider and the performative dimensions of masculinity work so forcefully and so completely that masculinity becomes synonymous with courage and toughness. A great example of this is the term "Man up!" that has turned into a somewhat common cultural idiom. The term is often used as encouragement, as in when someone is not acting as courageous or tough as he should be. To "Man up!" is to be courageous as the two terms are pushed together to mean the same thing. The same connection happens consistently on the program. Cowboy Kenny Bartram tells the viewer, "To be a bull rider, you're going to have to man up" ("A Concert"). During Ty's final pep talk to the celebrities before their ride in Nashville, he says, "When you get in the chute you have to be tough. You have to say, 'I'm gonna' step up and I'm man enough and I'm gonna' do what it takes to ride this bull" ("The Final").

The coalescing of masculinity and bull riding is also evidenced by uncovering the "best" and "worst" masculine performances. Keeping in mind the title of the program, it should come as no surprise that Ty Murray does the best job of assuming the most valued traits and, therefore, puts on the best performance of masculinity. He can be the authority figure and the idealized man because his masculinity is exclusive—only he adequately assumes the masculine traits while the rest of the celebrities are left trying to mimic his performance.

The audience member comes to know Ty as the "King of the Cowboys" because of his success as a bull rider. He won the World All-Around Rodeo Champion seven times despite a career plagued by injuries. He has used his success in the arena to construct a lucrative cowboy ethos outside of it, making several appearances on television programs and commercials including a seat at the "Man Table" making "Man Laws" in Miller Lite beer commercials. And even if an audience member were to know nothing of Ty's résumé and have to make judgments based on surface appearances, Ty would still stand out from the celebrities. He doesn't look or talk like any of the others. He has a Texas accent and dresses the part of a cowboy. He wears a cowboy hat, a large belt buckle, starched pearl-snapped collared shirts with a tin of snuff in the breast pocket, and tight boot-cut Wranglers over his cowboy boots. The viewer can quickly gather that Ty's cowboy style is the most prestigious because one of the first activities the celebrities do is go to RP's Western Outlet and "get hooked up Texas style," in Nitro's words ("A Concert"). The stars leave the store with shopping bags full of boots, belt buckles, and hats. In addition to being occupationally successful and having a cowboy style, Ty Murray is the model man because he is the only person who is portrayed as someone sexually potent. Ty's girlfriend, the singer Jewel, is prominently featured in the series as the stereotypical sex object. In the first episode, she acts like the Vanna White of the mechanical bull and later sings her hit single "You Were Meant for Me" as the men give her a standing ovation.

The result of Ty's occupational achievement, cowboy style, and sexual potency is an exclusive image of the ideal man. His iconic status is quickly accepted by all the celebrities, even Vanilla Ice, Stephen Baldwin, and Rocket Ismail who have some social status themselves. Josh Haynes, the UFC fighter, illustrates Ty's exclusive status well when he says, "When Ty walks in, the whole room lights up and everyone's like, 'Oh man, Ty's here. Let's go talk to him'" ("The First"). Jonny Fairplay adds, "Ty's the kinda' person you can't let down. When you meet that guy you wanna' make him proud. He's the best and you wanna' be the best you can be" ("The Final"). Although the explicit goal for each celebrity is to be able to ride a level-seven bull by the end of the program, the more implicit goal is to assume and emulate Ty's version of masculinity.

The performance of masculinity operates by inversion, so knowing what is masculine comes only through knowing what is not. In this case, we know only that Ty's occupational achievement, cowboy style, and sexual potency vault his performance of manhood above that of all the others by comparing his performance with the least masculine and most effeminate. Enter Jonny Fairplay.

Jonny Fairplay is the "least celebrated celebrity" (he finished third on the reality television program *Survivor*) and he consistently represents the antithesis of Ty's masculinity. He lacks the courage needed to excel as a bull rider, he has the hardest time adopting the requisite style, and he is the most effeminate of the group.

Of the nine celebrities, Fairplay is the most visibly fearful of the bulls. Ty summarizes his initial feelings after the first day by saying, "Half [of the celebrities] were looking up to it, half were thinking 'what did I get myself into?'" As he says this, the camera pans Fairplay's visibly grieved face as the prospect of riding a bull is presented ("We Just"). Fairplay even admits in the first episode, "I am scared, I am. I am scared senseless" ("We Just"). Ty takes it upon himself to watch out and protect Fairplay above and beyond the other eight celebrities. Jewel admits that Fairplay is "a little fragile so Ty felt protective of him immediately" ("A Concert"), and in another episode, Ty refers to Fairplay as "my egg and I'm trying to get him home from the supermarket" ("Vanilla Ice").

Second, Fairplay is the least reluctant to model Ty's cowboy style and when he does, he mocks it in an over-the-top, "campy" sort of way. When the celebrities visit RP's Western Outlet the first day, Fairplay buys a set of extravagant and effeminate light blue chaps with long frilly laces ("We Just"). He adds to his campy look an ironic mustache and a rainbow colored headband to contain his bright red curly hair. Before Fairplay's final ride in Nashville, he jokingly tells Ty that people are going to think Ty came out of retirement because he and Fairplay look so much alike. Ty responds sarcastically, "Yeah, minus the headband and the long curly red hair" ("The Final").

Finally, according to the dominant heterosexual norm, Fairplay is portrayed as the least sexually potent. He takes on a flamboyant style. He chooses his bull on the first day, Likity Split, because "the name is a little sexual, kinda like me" ("We Just"). Later he admits that his only athletic experience is two years of jazz dancing. When he puts that to use after a short ride in the second episode, he is quickly reprimanded by Ty: "There is no Terrell Owens-end zone dancing here" ("A Concert").

Ty Murray's Celebrity Bull Riding Challenge is a wonderful example of how important performance is to masculinity. Once again, don't let the outlandish nature of the sport distract you. The performances exemplified in this text works on a more subtle, but just as powerful, level in our day-to-day activities. There are tons of Brian Bosworths, Ty Murrays, and Jonny Fairplays scattered throughout our popular discourse. Some are used to influence our expectations of how men should look and act, some are used to influence our expectations of how women should look and act. Others go beyond gender, influencing our expectations of the rich or the poor, black or white, educated or not. And it is in this tugging—this aligning—that our expectations collide with hierarchies of power. I'll spend a few moments now connecting performance and masculinity to sports, so as to better demonstrate how bull riding fits within the larger theme of this book, before I conclude with a discussion of some possible implications.

■ Performativity and the Rhetoric of Exclusion

The larger connection that can be made between masculine performativity in bull riding and performativity in other sports and games can be found in the rhetoric of exclusion. Historically, the rhetoric of exclusion has been a dominant method for constructing the masculine identity; to know masculinity is to know what masculinity is not. Kenneth Burke used this idea to help explain how we define God. "God" is hard to define: most would say they can't literally see God, hear God, or touch God, but because God plays such a massive role in so many people's lives, many feel the need to define Him. Burke points out that we circumvent the difficulty of defining God by talking about what God is not: God is immortal (He doesn't die), God is invisible (He can't be seen), and so on. We may not know what God is, but we know what God is not.

We do the same with masculinity: we may not really know what being a man is, but we know what being a man is not. The rhetoric of exclusion offers men a category in which they can define themselves against what they most fear becoming. Often this means men define themselves against the effeminate, usually women or gay men. This is done by separating what is masculine from what is feminine and dividing the traits that can be connected to each group into dichotomous binaries. On the grade-school playground, no insult stings young boys the way "sissy," "faggot," or "pussy" does. These words sting because they move the boy from the masculine and valued to the effeminate and devalued. If the stereotypical women is gentle, humble, dependent, emotional, weak, tender, submissive, modest, compassionate, sensitive, and passive, then men can perform masculinity by being the antithesis of those traits: forceful, aggressive, dominant, strong, strong-willed, ambitious, hardy, competitive, dominant, and courageous. But it is important to note that femininity is not all that men use to define themselves against. The rhetoric of exclusion can make "outsiders" of men who are the wrong color, the wrong social class, from the wrong part of the country, or the wrong height or weight or wear the wrong clothing depending on what needs to be devalued.

Terrance Real provides a wonderful example of the rhetoric of exclusion in his research on the development of the masculine identity in young boys (130). Real points out that for most boys, the achievement of masculine identity is not an acquisition so much as a disavowal. When girls and women are asked to define what it means to be feminine, they answer with positive language: to be compassionate, to be connected, or to care about others, and so on. Boys and men, conversely, when asked to describe masculinity, respond with exclusionary language. They do not talk about being strong as much as not being weak. They do not list independence so much as not being dependent. They do not speak about being close to their fathers so much as about pulling away from their mothers. In other words, being a man really means not being a woman. Real concludes that, as a result, boys' acquisition of gender is a negative achievement. Their developing sense of their own masculinity is not so much, as in most other forms of identity development, a steady movement toward something valued as a repulsion from something devalued. Masculine identity development turns out to be not a process of development at all but rather a process of elimination, a successive unfolding of loss.

This is where performativity in sports and games becomes important. There is little subtlety about what is valued and what is not valued in the gymnasium or on the athletic field (Real 167). Although for children, sports may start out as fun and egalitarian, with everyone getting some playing time and a trophy at the end of the year, most quickly take to heart Vince Lombardi's misquoted sports cliché: "Winning is not everything, it's the only thing." As children progress in athletics, it becomes more and more common for a few star performers to be elevated and everyone else to filtered out and excluded. What separates the stars from the losers and the included from the excluded is often closely associated with traditional masculine traits. Words such as "courage," "toughness," and "tenacity" that have no ontologically grounded sexual origins at all are tugged or aligned with the best performers. Indiana University men's basketball coach Bobby Knight used to put tampons in his player's lockers when they failed to properly perform these supposedly masculine traits. When NFL wide receiver Terry Glenn injured his hamstring—causing what his head coach, Bill Parcells, insisted was a mild strain—and missed the entire exhibition season, Parcells responded to a question about Glenn's training camp performance with, "She's making progress." What Parcells and Knight, two extreme models of traditional masculinity in their own right, were attempting to do in these examples is align the best traits, the traits that are supposed to be the fabric of winners and high achievers, with a masculine gender identity and subsequently align the losers and low achievers with a feminine identity.

The larger implications of the rhetorical tugging that equates valued traits with masculinity and devalued traits with femininity stretch far beyond reality television shows about cowboys and movie stars. "Courage," for example, is just one trait that can be conflated with masculinity. Being courageous can be a good thing, of course, but think about how dangerous this connection can become when traits such as "leadership" "rationality," and "assertiveness" are connected to males and "humbleness," "passivity," and "submissiveness" are connected to females. Keep in mind that these traits are deeply embedded in a fundamental structure of capitalist production that rewards individual achievement and competitiveness over relational intelligence and ability to get along with others (Hennessy and Ingraham 5). This leads to the glorification of whatever has been defined as masculine and to the disparagement of whatever has been defined as feminine (Jaggar 250–51). Falsely aligning words such as "courage" and "toughness," or "leadership," "rationality," or "emotional," with one gender and distancing those labels from the other gender is not a harmless semantic coincidence. The words we use have the power to reflect and create reality and in this example, these words create a reality that unjustly elevates one type of person over another.

■ Conclusion

In this chapter, I have used *Ty Murray's Celebrity Bull Riding Challenge* to show how masculinity is performed through a rhetoric of exclusion. Audience members watching the program are taught important lessons about masculinity by way of inversion; the most masculine performs the set of traits that puts the most distance between him and the effeminate. I offered the conflation between courage and anatomy as well as the contrast between Ty Murray and Jonny Fairplay as evidence. I'd like to close by discussing why any of this matters to you.

These findings are important even if you aren't into bull riding, masculinity, or sports because they yield insight into more important questions about who has power, who doesn't, and why. Studying masculine performance in sports suggests several important lessons that can equip you to see the rhetorical and performative dimensions of your everyday existence more richly. More specifically, I hope this chapter has provided for you a more accurate understanding of gender, a more complete explanation of the role performance plays in living out that gender, and a heightened awareness of the way these performances can position us within regimes of power.

Ultimately, I hope you are left with an improved understanding of how this hierarchy operates through gendered performances in sports and popular culture. An understanding that sports and popular culture can be a site of containment or resistance and that if a texts screams, "There is no need to look over here; there is no rhetoric going on over here," it is probably worth a second look. Hegemonies are hidden, that is what makes them hegemonic. And when they are well-disguised, it takes a savvy critic to root them out—a critic willing to dig into shows such as *Extreme Makeover: Home Edition* to think about the way they not only entertain but also influence; a critic who works like an anthropologist when he or she looks at James Bond films because beneath the sexist, racist, and reactionary surface, the films can provide audiences with the possibility of additional meanings that tell a larger story than itself—to open up these texts of everyday living that go beyond culture to the politics of culture, to show how Ty Murray, or Paris Hilton, or Barack Obama's meaning is chained out beyond themselves.

My conclusions challenge the notion that the "great speech," the important essay, and the pivotal book are the only places where important public business is managed. Our lives are given meaning in the rhetoric of the everyday, and power is shaped in everything from a presidential debate to a short-lived reality television show.

Works Cited

Adorno, Theodor W. "Culture Industry Reconsidered." *Popular Culture: A Reader.* Ed. Raiford Guins and Omayra Zaragoza Cruz. London: Sage, 2005.

Brummett, Barry. *Rhetoric in Popular Culture.* 2nd ed. Thousand Oaks: Sage, 2006.

Butler, Judith. *Bodies That Matter: On the Discursive Limits of "Sex."* New York: Routledge, 1993.

———. *Gender Trouble: Feminism and the Subversion of Identity.* New York: Routledge, 1990.

———. "Performative Acts and Gender Constitution: An Essay in Phenomenology and Feminist Theory." *Feminist Theory Reader: Local and Global Perspectives.* Ed. Carole R. McCann and Seung-Kyung Kim. New York: Routledge, 2003. 415–27.

———. *Undoing Gender.* New York: Routledge, 2004.

"A Concert by Jewel and Vanilla Ice." *Ty Murray's Celebrity Bull Riding Challenge.* CMT. Nashville, Aug. 17, 2007.

Denning, Michael. *Culture in the Age of Three Worlds.* London: Verso, 2004.

Eagleton, Terry. *Ideology: An Introduction.* London: Verso, 1991.

Eminem. "Stan." *The Marshall Mathers LP.* Aftermath/Interscope, 2000. CD.

"The Final Ride in Nashville." *Ty Murray's Celebrity Bull Riding Challenge.* CMT. Nashville, Sept. 14, 2007.

"The First Big Test." *Ty Murray's Celebrity Bull Riding Challenge.* CMT. Nashville, Sept. 7, 2007.

Goffman, Erving. *The Presentation of Self in Everyday Life.* New York: Doubleday, 1959.

Gramsci, Antonio. *Selections from the Prison Notebooks.* Ed. and Trans. Quintin Hoare and Geoffrey Nowell Smith. New York: International, 1971.

Hart, Roderick P. *Modern Rhetorical Criticism.* Boston: Allyn, 1997.

Hennessy, Rosemary, and Chrys Ingraham, eds. *Materialist Feminism: A Reader in Class, Difference, and Women's Lives.* New York: Routledge, 1997.

Hoerl, Kristen. "Cinematic Jujitsu: Resisting White Hegemony through the American Dream in Spike Lee's Malcolm X." *Communication Studies* 59.4 (Oct. 2008): 355–370.

"The Injuries Are Adding Up." *Ty Murray's Celebrity Bull Riding Challenge.* CMT. Nashville, Aug. 24, 2007.

Jaggar, Alison M. *Feminist Politics and Human Nature.* Totowa: Roman & Littlefield, 1988.

Jameson, Fredric. "Reification and Utopia in Mass Culture." *Social Text* 1.1 (1979): 130–48.

Judge, Timothy A., and Beth A. Livingston. "Is the Gap More than Gender? A Longitudinal Analysis of Gender, Gender Role Orientation, and Earnings." *Journal of Applied Psychology* 93.5 (2008): 994–1012.

Lipsitz, George. "Listening to Learn and Learning to Listen: Popular Culture, Cultural Theory, and American Studies." *American Quarterly* 42.4 (1990): 615–36.

———. *Time Passages: Collective Memory in American Popular Culture*. Minneapolis: U of Minnesota P, 1990.

Macdonald, Dwight. "A Theory of Mass Culture." *Popular Culture: A Reader.* Ed. Raiford Guins and Omayra Zaragoza Cruz. London: Sage, 2005. 39–40.

Mean, Lindsey J., and Jeffrey W. Kassing. "I Would Just Like to Be Known as an Athlete": Managing Hegemony, Femininity, and Heterosexuality in Female Sport." *Western Journal of Communication* 72.2 (Apr. 2008): 126–144.

Messner, Michael A. *Politics of Masculinities: Men in Movements.* Thousand Oaks: Sage, 1997.

Mukerji, Chandra, and Michael Schudson. *Rethinking Popular Culture: Contemporary Perspectives in Cultural Studies.* Berkeley: U of California P, 1991.

Real, Terrence. *I Don't Want to Talk about It: Overcoming the Secret Legacy of Male Depression.* New York: Scribner, 1997.

Scott, Joan W. "Deconstructing Equality-Versus-Difference: Or, the Uses of Poststructuralist Theory for Feminism." *Feminist Theory Reader: Local and   Global Perspectives.* Ed. Carole R. McCann and Seung-Kyung Kim. New York: Routledge, 2003. 378–90.

"Vanilla Ice Gets Inked." *Ty Murray's Celebrity Bull Riding Challenge.* CMT. Nashville, Aug. 31, 2007.

Walsh, Kimberly R., Elfriede Fürsich, and Bonnie S. Jefferson. "Beauty and the Patriarchal Beast: Gender Role Portrayals in Sitcoms Featuring Mismatched Couples." *Journal of Popular Film & Television* 36.3 (Fall 2008): 123–132.

"We Just Started and We're Already Losing Stars." *Ty Murray's Celebrity Bull Riding Challenge.* CMT. Nashville, Aug. 10, 2007.

Whitehead, Steven M. *Men and Masculinities: Key Themes and New Directions.* Malden: Polity, 2002.

6

■ Performing Perfection, or, How to Be a Ninja Warrior

□ Jaime Wright

Forget about perfection. There's nothing more boring than perfection.

—*Geoffrey Tennant ("Playing the Swan")*

We like heroes. Heroes do good, heroic things—they save babies from frozen lakes, they pull people out of fiery towers, they win contests of physical strength and intellectual challenge. Heroes are the center of most cultural stories and, as some have said, the hero's appeal defies cultural lines (Campbell 30). Every culture, suggests Campbell, has heroes because heroes do good, heroic things. On a slightly different note, another interesting aspect of heroes (aside from their doing-good heroic actions) is rhetorical, and this basic rhetorical foundation for heroic stature stands on two assumptions: (1) a hero works toward perfection and (2) working toward perfection is unquestionably good.

Heroes win. They are strong. Forceful and forthright, heroes can do things with their bodies (and, occasionally, their minds) that others, mere mortals, cannot do. Heroes are epic—and we worship them for this timelessness. But, most heroic depictions are face with a question: what, in the end, do heroes *do* with these perfect, heroic capabilities? Because, when we get right down to it, we cannot have a hero without some sort of war. An engagement of strategy, a technique of attack and defense, a performance of capability—each of these elements must be present in a heroic performance; they are the part and parcel of a hero's actions. A hero is defined by the actions she takes and the results she achieves in a moment of conflict. As we will see in the different definitions proposed for hero (in literature, in philosophy, in culture), conflict is the foundational element of heroic construction; and war is the performative endpoint of conflict. So, on a variety of different levels, a hero does not exist outside of war.

Discussions of violence and its effects on culture abound. Whether we (and children) are being abused, shaped, or harmed by a constant barrage of violent images in various mediated forms is a major concern for politicians, pundits, and social scientist. Typically, social science's categorizations of violence include many different situations:

> There are some commonalities across those definitions [of violence]. The studies reported here typically use definitions of violence that focus on acts of physical aggression of one fictional character against another fictional character...Most of these definitions also count accidents and acts of nature as violence, because these acts are conscious constructions of the writers and producers of television show. Most of these definitions also count acts of physical aggression in humorous and fantasy contexts...Also, most definitions do not require the victim to show harm from the physical aggression in order for it to count as violence. (Potter 222)

Violence, in this definition, requires an *act against* someone or something. The acts in these definitions of violence are read rhetorically—for the results they create, the audiences they shape, the cultural pictures they paint. Not included in this definition is the energy and praise created by the acts performed, the hero-worship they create. When the good guy beats the bad guy, literally and figuratively, the good guy acts heroically. The performance of domination is a performance of violence—regardless, as Potter mentions, of the effects such acts may have on the people at the receiving end. And performing violence perfectly is, at best, problematic.

Typically, we think of perfection, then, as the desired result of any effort. However, when we imagine a war, what would a perfect war look like? Total destruction of the enemy? Complete annihilation of the opposing perspective? If we consider war to be a zero-sum game, then a perfect war means the winner takes all. The winner, in that scenario, is the hero—brought to the forefront of the conflict by forces of nature, fate, or circumstance and poised to prove his heroic constitution by demonstrating perfect mastery of the skills needed to achieve victory. In this violent conflict, the hero's perfect performance would thus result in a devastation, an erasure; the destructive goals of violent perfection, then, make heroic performance of perfection dangerous, and worthy of some pause.

In this chapter, we're going to reevaluate the symbolic performance and cultural significance of heroes by placing heroic performance in the context of sport, specifically, the televised sporting competition titled *Ninja Warrior*. Rather than thinking, as mentioned in the first paragraph, that heroes are perfect and that perfection is an unquestionable good, let's think about the value of heroic imperfection. Heroes are created to demonstrate something about the culture they represent; heroes are signifiers of truths the culture holds dear. Therefore, heroes tell us something about a culture that we might not otherwise understand. Heroic qualities, embodied and performed by different cultural heroes (contemporary heroes often take the shape of sports figures), affect and shape cultural mores—highlighting and drawing attention to the values of a culture, as well as to the ends and purpose to which those values might be put (Butterworth, "Purifying the Body Politic" 148). This chapter explores these unspoken assumptions, these rhetorical undercurrents, in the function of heroic, warrior worship. Since modern-day heroes often take the form of popular sports figures and celebrities (such as Tony Romo or Derek Jeter), the framework for this rhetorical analysis will focus on the performance of athletes in a televised world.

Classically, a perfect warrior is a monster, a death-dealing, inhuman machine. With that observation in mind, let us ask the question "Is perfection what we seek in our heroes?" Instead of mindlessly assuming the cultural benefit of perfection, we shall study the rhetorical construction of heroes, the tug-of-war between heroic achievements and heroic perfection, and a cultural example of heroic imperfection in action. To that end, the chapter is arranged in the following way: first, I explore some of the literature addressing heroes and the performance of heroic perfection as it occurs in sporting events (for themselves and for the culture); next, I examine the theoretical and historical links between *perfection, death,* and *heroes;* and finally, I present a case study of hero worship, a brief rhetorical analysis of *Ninja Warrior.* In the conclusion, we will revisit our opening quotation, examining the symbolic value and cultural significance of perfection as it relates to heroism.

■ Rhetorically Constructing a Hero

Hero is a word used in epic tales, in descriptions of beloved mentors, and in Saturday morning cartoons. These examples are only hints of the pervasive presence of heroes in human society. Human beings admire, analyze, and discuss heroes in almost every aspect of life, both real and imagined. Mental images of Achilles, Wonder Woman, Joan of Arc, and Jean Valjean create lives for us to live vicariously and elucidate ideals we strive to achieve. In *The Denial of Death,* Ernest Becker considers some of the reasons for our human hero worship:

> When we appreciate how natural it is for man to strive to be a hero, how deeply it goes in his evolutionary and organismic constitution…In our culture anyway, especially in modern times, the heroic seems too big for us, or we too small for it. Tell a young man that he is entitled to be a hero and he will blush. We disguise our struggle…But underneath throbs the ache of cosmic specialness, no matter how we mask it in concerns of smaller scope…the urge to heroism is natural, and to admit it honest. (4)

Becker's "urge to heroism" is a human one. Specifically addressing cultural concerns, he mentions the distance many people feel from heroism—the notion that regular human beings are "too small" to be heroic—which, some might suggest, could stem from contemporary thoughts relating the heroic to the perfect. In Becker's work, though, the heroic is an instinct, an innate reaction to the inevitability and cruelty of death. Rather than striving to reach the end, which is how many define the notion of perfection, heroism is a fight against such certainty, a struggle to evade the stillness of perfection.

Of course, examples of heroes in sport performance abound. As Barthes notes in "The World of Wrestling," the function of sports heroes is to reiterate and remind the attending audience of the cultural truths and mythological foundations of their surroundings—he writes that wrestling, unlike, boxing, is a spectacle, a construction of moments designed to tell certain elemental tales. It is not the passage of time in which an audience is interested (as they might be in a sports performance of, say, football or baseball, in which the participants are engaged in contests of excellence). Rather, an audience member watches wrestling (and I will argue later, *Ninja Warrior*) in order to see the play of cultural conclusions performed:

> A boxing-match is a story which is constructed before the eyes of the spectator; in wrestling, on the contrary, it is each moment which is intelligible, not the passage of time. The spectator is not interested in the rise and fall of fortunes; he expects the transient image of certain passions. Wrestling therefore demands an immediate reading of the juxtaposed meanings, so that there is no need to

connect them. The logical conclusion of the contest does not interest the wrestling-fan, while on the contrary a boxing-match always implies a science of the future. In other words, wrestling is a sum of spectacles, of which no single one is a function: each moment imposes the total knowledge of a passion which rises erect and alone, without ever extending to the crowning moment of a result.

Thus the function of the wrestler is not to win: it is to go exactly through the motions which are expected of him. (24)

In this excerpt, the wrestlers perform the role of hero (or villain, as the case may be) for the audience gathered to watch them. As opposed to more traditional sports performances, in which heroes are organically performed and the outcome is important, performances of heroism in wrestling and *Ninja Warrior* are dependent upon the scene in which they occur, the backdrop against which they struggle. For wrestlers, the backdrop consists of off-stage historical character construction and mythological themes of competition; in *Ninja Warrior,* the offstage character construction is a part of the contest but the real competition is against the backdrop of time and self. The competing warriors perform heroic acts in a sporting context of self-will and elemental struggle.

Stories of heroic actions call readers to recognize heroes within the narratives. These heroic identifications also, Becker might argue, call the readers to act as heroes, a process that is something natural and human. Rabbi David Wolpe writes, "Images of heroism stir emulation: watching the hero, we wish to be as strong, passionate, grand as the depiction on the page or screen" (74). The more like a hero one sounds, the more like a hero one acts, and the more likely one's story will be heard, received, and remembered.

There are many different conceptions of the term "hero," and that is, perhaps, significant. The rhetoric used to portray and illuminate actions of heroic individuals varies depending on the context in which they are found. "We must pause to remind ourselves of the different models of a hero, for confusion about heroes and uncertainty about true strength are a legacy of our times" (Wolpe 75). Rabbi Wolpe aptly pinpoints the need for further examination of hero conceptualization and echoes Becker's observations that current approaches to life frequently obscure a clear understanding of the human need for heroes. In the following section, I provide four different attitudes toward the word "hero." Often, in these different attitudes, rhetorical details (such as masculinity versus femininity, domination versus submission, and action versus intellect) come to light. These nuanced differences in concepts of hero will figure prominently in the *Ninja Warrior* analysis—how perfection, performance, completion, and action relate to rhetorical conceptualizations of the heroic. We must remember that the concept of hero cannot be divorced from the language in which it is described and with which it is created. As Victor Brombert, in *The Hero in Literature,* asserts, "the question of the hero cannot be isolated from the total experience of man [*sic*]" (11). Thus, a clarification of some popular conceptions of hero, as well as their connotations, must be made in order to comprehend fully the influence that heroic language might have in the realms of the personal, the political, and the cultural.

The challenge to writers, rhetoricians, and philosophers since time immemorial has been to understand the "total experience" of humanity. Stories of ordinary people (or not so ordinary people) who became heroes have been a constant companion to this search. "The very absurdity of life makes heroism inevitable. Millennia have not reconciled man [*sic*] with death. Man's questioning of his destiny, no matter what form that questioning may take, is thus fundamentally a challenge to fate, an affirmation of his will and of his prerogative. It is heroic by its very nature" (Brombert 21). Using words such as "challenge," "affirmation," "destiny," and "will," Brombert calls to mind the most central concepts of heroism: battle and struggle. Heroes, after all, are the people capable of fighting insurmountable forces, forces such as death and fate. Heroes are innately connected with these existential and ontological concerns. They are also innately connected with manhood. The rhetorical construction of heroes, for Brombert, is inseparable from a masculinized language of action and domination.

Heroes engage in life-defining and death-defying battles. The first adheres to a violent or glorious ideal of heroism. This ideal informs our modern appreciation of classical heroes such as Achilles and Joan of Arc. Heroes are assumed to have a special kind of power, granted to them by some sort of supernatural powers, that separates the heroes from other human beings. The power is commonly displayed in battle, because battle provides the most searching tests not merely of strength and courage but of resource and decision as well. The greatest heroes are primarily men (emphasis on *men*) of war. But even in battle what really counts is the heroic force, the assertive spirit that inspires a man to take prodigious risks and enables him to surmount them successfully or at least to fail with glorious distinction (Bowra 27). Bowra's masculinized heroes dedicate their lives to action. They are not considered failures when they meet the ends of their lives in the battles that consume them. In fact, they are usually admired more for those deaths: "It is somehow *right* that great warriors should die, as they have lived, in battle, and refuse to surrender to powers stronger than themselves" (50, emphasis added). Echoes of this notion of a "fitting" or "right" end can be seen as both heroic and rhetorical. They call to mind images of decorum and propriety, ideals intimately related to rhetorical models such as the one described in

Lloyd Bitzer's often-referenced "The Rhetorical Situation." As we see in Barthes's discussion of wrestling, mythological and historical constructions of hero are set against a background of action and completion. Heroes perform the fitting role within contexts of conflict—as in a sporting situation, heroic performance is designed to demonstrate certain cultural truths, about courage, about action, about right and wrong.

The second kind of hero is contained within a more introverted and intellectually inclined rhetoric. In this perception, the hero "has to overcome, to learn, and through that learning to grow. The growth is not without pain and the learning is not without loss" (Wolpe 73). This definition is a product of our times and pertains to the performance of heroes in sport as well. The narrative structure of "good guy versus bad guy" or the "hero versus elements" places the hero-subject in time and space; each action and reaction becomes a part of the greater whole. So, when a Ninja Warrior is portrayed working out in his private practice arena, or contemplating a difficult task, or suffering a loss, his actions, as thought-oriented and introverted as they may seem, are still heroic performance writ large. As both Wolpe and Becker remark, there is a distinctive flavor to contemporary thought that, while recognizing the heroic qualities admired by the ancients, is forced to reconcile those qualities with a different set of struggles. "For most of us, heroism is an attribute of action...we assume that a hero is one who can manage feats of physical courage and stamina to astound others...Although we recognize the existence of emotional and spiritual courage, these are less often the attributes we associate with heroism" (Wolpe 75–76). In both schools of thought, struggle is a constant heroic trope. However, each school interprets the struggle differently; the visible actions taken by the hero to confront challenges are appraised from divergent points of view, as are the results of such struggles. Further, I suggest that these qualitative differences are attributable to the friction that exists not only between action and intellect, but also between idealized images of masculinity and femininity. In the testimonies of survivors, there are echoes of heroic struggles with emotional and spiritual courage. As we begin to understand the underlying and gendered assumptions associated with classical definitions of heroism, we may begin to see the difficulties arising in classifying the actions of different genders in response to Nazi ideology.

Philosophers and social scientists such as Ernest Becker in *The Denial of Death* and Joseph Campbell in *The Hero with a Thousand Faces* examine influences the aforementioned definitions of heroes may or may not have on the actions, thoughts, and language of regular human beings. They assert that the characteristics demonstrated by heroes in literature are present in the minds of all humans and that these concepts drive us to achieve nobility and honor.

Becker writes: "heroism is first and foremost a reflex of the terror of death. We admire most the courage to face death; we give such valor our highest and most constant adoration" (11). Here again we see the intimate connection between heroes and insurmountable forces. Rhetorical creations of heroism become answers to the human fear of death. Because of the great divide between human beings and other animals, because we know that we will end, we provide ourselves with examples to emulate: in the face of our mortality, we look to heroes who survived that knowledge and managed to live valiantly in the shadow of death. Becker, echoing the second school of literary thought, provides heroism with a more spiritual definition: a hero is a person who is not heroic through violent action but through conscious spiritual and emotional effort: "How can the person take his private inner being, the great mystery that he feels at the heart of himself, his emotions, his yearnings, and use them to live more distinctively, to enrich both himself and mankind with the peculiar quality of his talents?" (72). Becker's ideal of heroism is linked to a battle with fate that is not fought only on a bloody field of war.

Another rhetorical element innate to the definitions and concept of hero is the quest. Linked to the active focus on heroic conceptualization, Campbell describes the monomythic (cross-cultural) hero as created by the quest s/he pursues. The details of the quest may vary; there are myriad ways in which a hero can answer the call to adventure. However, the major steps of the quest are as follows: a call to adventure, helpers of some kind, challenges (or tests), flight from the ferocious and/or seducing enemy, return, and the sharing of a boon (the elixir) for the benefit of society. Each of these steps must be met in some way for the hero to achieve what is ultimately his goal: to give some gift to society that is worthy of remembrance. Where Becker and Brombert provide us with a definition of the characteristics of "hero," Campbell describes a veritable "how-to" list. Without each of these steps, he argues, a hero does not exist.

Finally, Michael Hyde, in his more recent discussion of heroes, draws a careful line (echoing Daniel Boorstin) between the hero and the celebrity, suggesting that the difference between these two mediated constructions has mostly to do with intent and longevity. Heroes, first of all, act according to conscience: "The genuine hero answers the call of conscience, not for egotistical reasons, but rather for the sake of something other than self" (188). Without considering the possible responses to or reception of her actions, the hero jumps into the frozen lake to save the drowning child. All else is beside the point. The second difference, according to Hyde, is the issue of longevity. Whereas a hero is established over the course of time (after folks have had some space to think about the deeds done), a celebrity only fades. In our over-mediated world of managers and agents, heroes may still exist, but they are of the "unsung" variety (189–90). Much like the previous conceptions of hero, Hyde's image focuses on action, results, intent, and time—the difference in his definition has to do with the notion of media and celebrity. In discussions of heroic performance in sports, both of these concerns feature prominently. Whether a hero, mediated or not, can continue to maintain a heroic air and to perform heroic achievement in the flurry of attention he receives is a perennial question—one that is fundamental to the relationship between performed perfection and heroic imperfection.

In the previous passages, I examine a wide range of perspectives brought to bear in definitions and expectations of heroes. Although the term "hero" connotes a variety of different meanings, let's look at some pervasive heroic themes. First, without mortality, there is no hero; a hero confronts death. In sports and performance, the hero's confrontation with death is perhaps less obvious but is there nonetheless—witness the violence with which football players play (Butterworth, "The Politics of the Pitch" 184). Their bodily sacrifices and force are the reasons audiences flock to watch the games. Another example, more performative, might exist in NASCAR—spectators watch the races, wishing for (and hoping against) fiery crashes. Recognizing one's own mortality, accepting that fate, and acting in the face of certain doom—all of these actions comprise the heroic model.

Second, a hero wages war. Heroes are connected with performed action, active rather than passive approaches to fate. To be a hero, one must struggle, combat, fight, contesting the very nature of mortality and/or humanity itself. The ritualistic qualities of sports performances shape, and are shaped by, cultural understandings of what is heroic and how the hero acts within certain spaces and social contexts (Grano 452). The contested nature of sports—especially in sporting events including face to face combat, such as boxing, or carefully planned strategy, such as baseball—demonstrates the heroic performance of war in sports. Third, a hero controls. This performance of control is visible in all of the previously mentioned sporting events—control against others (car racing, football, baseball)—as well as self-control (golf, gymnastics, swimming, bicycle racing). Each of these sports performances requires controlled action in the face of uncertain situations, situations comprised of other human beings (an opposing team) or elemental scenery (a racetrack, a steep hill). A hero controls some aspects of himself or his surroundings; he must exert enough of his will so that he is not subsumed by the enemy he faces. These three things constitute a traditional view of heroism: a confrontation with death, a battle for the odds, and a control over some aspect of self.

■ Rhetorically Constructing Perfection

Now that we have seen some of the sports and performance demonstrated in historical definitions and concepts of heroes, let's look at the relationship between heroes, perfection, and violence. In *The Call of Conscience,* Michael Hyde describes the "symbolic construction of heroes" as the "most *positive* rhetorical event of the euthanasia debate" (186). This positive event becomes a system—a way to measure the interaction of action and conscience—for any human being inclined to heroic activity. He writes,

> A hero system records and directs courageous and virtuous behavior; it provides instructions for understanding what human greatness is and thereby what it takes for a finite being to live on after death in the hearts and minds of others. A hero system...speaks of the possibility of being immortal and thus "god-like."
> (187–88)

Heroes, again, do not work without the leering inevitability of death; mortality and heroism go hand in hand. In each of Hyde's case studies, the looming specter of death drives each person—to court, to computer, to work, to care, to kill. The intimate connection between Hero and Mortality is always foregrounded—the heroic struggle would not be heroic without the undeniable and unavoidable immanence of death.

In these cases, choice and control are key. At the beginning of this chapter, I examined traditional conceptions of heroes—the tragic warriors and the stoic fighters—who make up the cultural, intellectual framework allowing heroes to be, as Campbell posits, monomythic. There is one story, Campbell argues, and Hyde agrees. Each of these cases paints a similar picture of hero. Holes in these similar heroic depictions, however, refer us to the original question of this chapter: what, in the end, do heroes *do* with these perfect, heroic capabilities? It's easy to see the benefits of heroic construction in a discussion of courtrooms and classrooms, basketball courts and rugby fields; in normal social situations, an ethics of caring for others is not assumed to be a luxury—it's an obligation and heroic, to boot. Again and again, observations about the thin line between heroism, perfection, and death can be seen. Heroes do not exist without violence, death is the culmination of perfect violence, and death is the perfect end.

So, do those connections, innate as they seem to be in heroic rhetorical construction, seem to be slightly out of line with the cultural assumption that heroes are, always and automatically, to be worshipped? In an article exploring the depiction of "heroic masculinity" within contexts of spinal cord injury and recovery rhetorics, Susan L. Hutchinson and Douglas A. Kleiber question the automatic assumption that heroism overtly masculinized and aggressive is always a good thing. Instead, they write, it can do harm, physical and emotional, to people it is intended to bolster:

> We have concerns...about unreflexively adopting a heroic approach to recovery from SCI (spinal cord injury) and emphasizing heroic efforts in the rehabilitation process.... The distance these images put between the person featured in the success story and the reader with a disability highlights the extend to which many men may feel they do not or cannot live up to this heroic ideal. Of more concern is the extent to which the *narrowness* of the pathway for transcendence of SCI...may limit men's understanding of successful adjustment. (50, original emphasis)

This excerpt demonstrates the physical and emotional danger presented by the violent perfection often associated with heroic action. The authors are not excluding the benefit of heroic rhetoric; instead, they emphasize the dangers of such a narrow definition of recovery.

Reflecting on these rhetorical constructions of heroes and their cultural implications is the responsibility of both critic and consumer. By emphasizing concepts like "choice" and "control" without question, we fail to notice the careful, steady violence of certain rhetorical constructions. In *This Republic of Suffering,* Drew Gilpin Faust details the cultural connections between death and social control during the American Civil War. The nation, she writes, was changed not only by the magnitude of death but also by the ease with which Americans on both sides slipped into the murderous mindset required during a war:

> Far from finding reluctance about killing among his comrades, H. C. Matrau of the Union's Iron Brigade explained to his parents how military training seemed only to enhance an innate brutality. A month of drilling in bayonet attacks led him to conclude, "It is strange what a predilection we have for injuring our brother man, but we learn the art of killing far easier than we do a hard problem in arithmetic." Surprised at this discovery, Matrau began to revise his understanding of human nature and its capacities. Many soldier's found that society's powerful inhibitions against murder were all too easily overcome. (38)

The practical difficulty of killing another human being, when placed against the theoretical difficulty facing a student of arithmetic according to a soldier-in-training, pales in comparison. The actions, the functions, the work of defense and offense—are all much closer to the surface than social mores would have us believe.

Then, in a discussion of heroes, whose very words and actions become models for emulation—where life and death are not theoretical or distanced— the responsibility of these unquestioning assumptions about the value of a cultural hero worship becomes of the utmost importance. The rhetorical construction of heroes and its immediate conflation of "the heroic" with "the perfect" deserve some more scrutiny. It is not necessarily a bad thing to hero worship. Heroes, as I say in the beginning of the chapter, do heroic things. However, we might benefit from a pause in our adulation; when we praise the life-affirming efforts of Joni Eareckson Tada (pro-life euthanasia activist) or the death-defying agility of Makoto Nagano (the only competitor to complete *Ninja Warrior*'s gauntlet twice), we are valuing a war—with inevitability, with certainty, with the end. As Diane Davis eloquently observes in "Addressing Alterity," her discussion of hermeneutic rhetoric (the violent, virulent implications of translation and appropriation), interpreting the *said* and suffering the *saying* hold different (sizable) theoretical implications.

> Rhetoric's hermeneutic dimension allows subjects to get things done in the world, and this work is, of course, imperative. But this work, by definition, requires appropriation and assimilation; it can account for the "other" that overlaps with the Same, which means that it *cannot* account for the other at all, cannot attend to radical alterity—it can only undergo it, suffer it as an interruption, a rhetorical rupture. (208, original emphasis)

The constant suffering of difference, the mutability of the *saying,* is a work against appropriation. Recognizing our weird drive toward teleology—as Davis does, and as Faust does—Kenneth Burke discusses the human being's obsession with naming. We are, he writes famously, "rotten with perfection" (3–24). Every symbolic action, every move, is designed to freeze a particular moment, to name a particular situation. As Edward Appel observes,

> For human beings, material nature and its motions are not "good enough" or "bad enough" in themselves. The mere satisfaction of physical needs is never the sole motive of the symbol-using animal. The question of "whether" these needs are met is always accompanied by the transcendentally moral query, "How?": "How well?" Or "How badly?" (52)

Like the writers discussing heroes, Appel and Davis refer to human interaction at its most basic level—a level never very basic at all.

But even in the middle of these discussions of humanity's ongoing motives and purposes, Burke recognizes the value of mutability. To finally perfectly name a situation is to kill the negative, the basic driving force of human symbolic action. Davis suggests that we, as readers and critics, attend to the assumptions made about what it is to *know* someone else. And Appel reminds us that human beings are never completely satisfied with the superficial functioning of the universe in which we dwell. How, you may ask, can these two seemingly diverse observations come together? In a discussion of heroes—the search for perfection, in all its philosophical and historical glory, is haunted by the impossibility of stillness. Humanity's discussion of (and obsession with) heroes becomes a substitute, an imperfect surrogate; heroes, by their heroic actions, rather than performing perfection, demonstrate the constant practice of living, the repetitious rupture of the *saying,* and the life-giving certainty that nothing is certain, except that we all have the capability to be heroic. Which is only to say, really, that we write books such as this, watch shows like *Ninja Warrior,* or go to weddings only because we are all innately driven by the drive to be heroic—not perfect.

■ Rhetorically Constructing a Warrior

War is a perennial favorite of popular audiences; we are seduced by warriors.[1] Adjectives like strong, muscular, true, fast, determined, and elite are used to describe and shape the ideology of warrior-worship because often it is easy to see the possibility of performed perfection in the scenery of war, the mighty clash of warriors—the good guys are strong and forthright, the bad guys are devious and sneaky, and the background is filled with innocents waiting to see what fate holds in store for them. A cult of perfection, centered on the rhetoric of warriors, becomes a bodily performance, a spectacle of endurance.

In this chapter, I explore the performance of such a bellicose perfection. The popular performance of perfection demonstrates two things: (1) a hero works toward perfection and (2) working toward perfection is unquestionably good. In this link between perfection and the symbolic, the perfect body is described and proscribed by both physicality and (the potential for) violence. Performed perfection is all about potentiality—the potential for violence (between individuals), the potential for balance (between mind and body), and the potential for war (between individuals, between bodies, between minds).

In keeping with performed perfection as an act of war is the Japanese television show *Ninja Warrior.* Makoto Nagano, a commercial fisherman from Japan, is a modern-day Ninja Warrior. He is one of many to attempt a televised obstacle course, designed to separate the *real* Ninjas from the wannabes. *Ninja Warrior,* appearing frequently on the American channel G4, is a popular program.[2] The show is a spectacle of endurance, a series of physical feats designed to weed out all competitors. Over the last eight years, 1,700 competitors have attempted the course (Hibberd). So far (and as of March 5, 2007), Makoto Nagano and Kazuhiko Akiyama are the only two people to pass the test—which makes sense because, after all, perfection is rare.

Ninja Warrior is designed to showcase perfection performed—the performance of physical feats, the concentration required to complete those tasks, and the (implied) goal of achieving performed perfection in order to engage in acts of violence. This chapter, therefore, explores *Ninja Warrior*'s presentation of bodily and bellicose perfection. The entire set up of the show showcases the bellicosity of performed perfection. Mythically and historically, ninjas are a special subset of the samurai class—the extensively trained, elite warrior class of classical Japan. Ninjas were the samurai trained in espionage. And, along with their martial and physical training, they learned mind control—over themselves and the people they were sent to fight. The myth of the ninja has achieved monumental popularity in the American cultural imagination, which may explain *Ninja Warrior*'s omnipresence on G4. The mystification and mythologizing of this mystical, Eastern Other feeds into American audience's expectations that the ninja, historically an imperial tool of espionage, is in fact a contemporary manifestation of perfection—both mind and body must come together flawlessly for the competitors to actually *become* Ninja Warriors.

To analyze the heroic rhetorical construction of Ninja Warriors, I look to the audience—by studying the audience's discussions and observations, we can see the cultural function of these Ninja Warriors. Therefore, I investigate four separate websites: http://ninjawarrior.us/ (a homemade fansite, showcasing minute examinations of the various obstacles), http://en.wikipedia.org/wiki/Ninja_warrior (a fairly thorough history of the show—depicting its Japanese origins, detailing its most successful competitors, and noting the different competitors), http://www.g4tv.com/ninjawarrior/index.html (G4's official site), and http://www.imdb.com/title/tt1014786/board/threads/ (the message boards on IMDb.com dedicated to discussions of the show). Two of the websites are openly fansites: the first is ninjawarrior.us (http://ninjawarrior.us/) and the second site is a message board on The Internet Movie Database containing discussions about the show and its contestants (http://www.imdb.com/title/tt1014786/board/threads/). Both of the fansites are designed to discuss, debate, and praise the show and its contestants. G4's website is corporate, and I include it only for specific details about the show and its presentation. The Wikipedia entry is, of course, partially a fansite (who else would provide an entry about *Ninja Warrior* than a fan?), but it also includes helpful information about the background (including specific histories of the "All Stars," its Japanese origins, and its Americanization).

In this section, then, I rhetorically analyze these sites, looking for the following two things: how "hero as perfect" is problematized, either deliberately or accidentally, or how the competitors are categorized, alternately, as "heroes" or "humans"; and the ways in which differentness, Eastern or otherwise, get mentioned. Descriptions equating warriors with heroes, allusions to the fictional/symbolic function of ninjas in the Western mindset, and the Americanization of the show might be able to provide us with concrete demonstrations of both of Hyde's observations (about the human longing to be perfect/heroic), as well as Davis's concerns about symbolic violence and appropriation. The Other is not so other when we see him through a lens of sameness—however, if the sameness is a drive toward perfectability, there is some value to such a comparison. Perhaps there are different valences to appropriation; recognizing similarities in the Other that equate to a search for goodness and goodwill, as opposed to dangerous otherness, could be cause to value rhetorical heroic constructions.

First, let's look at some of the ways in which "hero as perfect" gets problematized in audience discussions of *Ninja Warrior*. What I mean by such a problematization has to do with the notion that our desire to emulate our heroes stems from their imperfectability. By noticing their mistakes and gaffes, we see heroes as both something Other and something similar. For example, in the discussion boards on IMDb.com, there is a thread centering around the actions, off-course, of Makoto Nagano, "a 36-year-old fisherman living near Kagoshima and the second man to ever complete the course" ("Sasuke"). Under a thread titled "Nagano 'What the hell?'" doughgirlsass writes,

> When I saw him smoking I really wanted to kick him in the nards. I was so incredibly mad! I could never be in as great shape as him and I don't smoke!!!!! I have respiratory problems and I wish I could do half the things that mofo can do and he freaking smokes!!!!! I don't idolize him anymore, and he also seems smug. I'm disappointed in him. ("Board")

Doughgirlsass, in this observation, attends to two elements of Nagano's personality—his physical capability, which seems to go with the warrior appearance, and his performative responsibility, which may or may not go with his warrior appearance. Her anger is directed toward the opposing tug of the warrior's perfectability and his human reality. In a response to doughgirlsass, megapedestrian says, "Nagano has been smoking all along. A lot of people smoke in Japan (and by a lot, I mean almost 50% of the men). The Japanese aren't all crazed about the health hazards, they even have cigarette vending machines. The Japanese are generally healthier than westerners, too" ("Board"). Megapedestrian's suggestion is a defense, of Nagano and of difference. In his response, he seems unconcerned with Nagano's imperfect smoking habit, and he alludes to the different cultural expectations that might allow for some space between a Western specimen of physical perfection and a Japanese one.

Another response, touching simultaneously on the normalness of Nagano and his heroic achievements, comes from jonm_89:

So your mad at nagano because you're out of shape and he is in shape, you aren't aloud to smoke but he does?

Nagano is just a regular person, he has flaws and he has positives, its what makes him so cool, he seems like a nice guy, but afterall, he is on a fishing boat most of the time, how happy would you be? ("Board")

His attack on her perspective focuses on the comparison between her actions/physicality and Nagano's, as well as the metaphysical status of their respective physical locations. The first question is more than a slap on the wrist—how dare you, out-of-shape message-board writer, question the actions of someone like Nagano? And the second observation, stepping back a bit, seems to allow for some personal motivations aside from culture, as we see in the first response. Nagano, who spends most of his year on a commercial fishing boat, might have reasons behind his actions that relate to his location in life, not just his physical performance on *Ninja Warrior.*

The Wikipedia entry on *Ninja Warrior* is mainly a list of deeds performed and the people who performed them. The separate competitors are divided by successes (the All Stars), nationalities (different national athletes competing over the years), entertainers (the Japanese performers who go on the show in order to increase or maintain their celebrity appeal), and "Other Notable Competitors" (the first to compete, people in different professions who have done surprisingly well, the only woman to have completed the first stage). Each of these categories is filled with descriptions of the physical status of each competitor, some personal history, and descriptions of their performance on different stages of the course. Occasionally, if the personal background is pertinent (especially in the lists of the All Stars), the entry includes lengthier biographical details. There is a fair balance between the heroic performance of the competitors and their heroic achievements.

In discussions of the All Stars, the Wikipedia entry mentions unique situational elements related to either the on-show performances or the pre- and post-show training. For example, in the entry for Bunpei Shiratori, a particularly harrowing performance is described: "During the 15th Competition, Bunpei overcame heat exhaustion to complete the First Stage and advance to the Climbing Bars (Bridge of Destiny) in the Third Stage; temperatures that day were reportedly at 100 degrees Fahrenheit" ("Sasuke"). After describing this impressive physical achievement, the entry goes on to discuss Bunpei's individual kindness and training: "He has built a full-sized model of the course in his backyard known as the Shiratori Shrine, where he trains. He invites the other Sasuke All-Stars to train there, and even invited the first G4 American Ninja Challenge finalists, Colin Bell and Brett Sims, to his course in 2007" ("Sasuke").

Along those same lines, workout regimes and planning are another interesting audience-centered aspect of these sites, indicating a (performed) desire to participate in the actual competition. On the NinjaWarrior.us site, members are invited to include their own workout routines. Wikipedia and the IMDb.com discussion board both include some mention of each athlete's training—one of the most frequently cited is Nagano's. Implied in all of these discussions is the assumption that each member, if only they worked out hard enough, practiced enough, knew enough about the competition, and had the right amount of luck/timing, could become a Ninja Warrior. The repeated attempts by so many of the competitors adds to this idea: only two people have completed all the stages and yet many of the athletes return again and again. These assumptions and repetitions reinstate the humanity of each competitor, as well as the admirable determination they maintain to achieve performed perfection.

Finally, there is an intriguing connection between the life histories of various competitors and their heroic aspirations. One of the contestants, Toshohiro Takeda, used his Ninja Warrior fame to stump for Japan's firefighting recruitment in 2006 ("Sasuke"). Another contestant, Katsumi Yamada, has allowed his dedication to (obsession with?) the competition to get in the way of his connections with family and work ("Sasuke").

■ Conclusion

In this chapter, we have explored the rhetorical construction of heroes as it relates to sports and culture. First, we examined historical conceptions of heroes according to poets and philosophers, considering the ways in which heroes work to alter and maintain cultural first assumptions and the ways in which human beings are "wired" to desire heroism. Next, we problematized the innate connection between perfection and hero. Rather than worshipping the mindless physicality of a hero such as Achilles, whose almost complete bodily perfection fed his emotional bankruptcy and bloodthirsty hunger for immortality, we might do better to praise the actions and deeds of Hector, a hero who performed valiantly in the face of doom for culture and family.

Also, there might be a link here between the concerns voiced by Diane Davis about rhetorical appropriation and the praise heaped on heroes by Michael Hyde. Because, even in all the fan discussion of the warriors' humanity, there is still an understanding of difference, performatively and imaginatively. The most dangerous aspect of these rhetorical relations is the Westernization of the Eastern Other. In the process of making Ninja Warrior into a G4 juggernaut, the constructors of the show play on audience assumptions of similarity and cultural appropriation of things that "Look" Eastern. *Ninja Warrior,* as cultural item and as performance of culture, becomes yet another example of what Salazar notes is the tension between different conceptions of *ethos* in athletic heroism—the function of *ethos* as an extension of an *ethnos* (membership in a particular community) and *ethos* as a demonstration (or performance) of the moral self (361). Further, audience members watching the show often seem to imagine themselves consuming some easily knowable aspects of Japanese culture, through the lens of *Ninja Warrior.*

With such considerations in mind, we interrogated the cultural function of a particular TV show: *Ninja Warrior.* The heroic and human depictions of the contestants provide us with some interesting material for discussion, as it relates to sports, rhetoric, and culture. The rhetorical construction of heroes and the philosophical study of perfection are intimately related. Heroes are fascinating to us—for reasons related to both entertainment and performance. The reason why we love Batman more than Superman (Batman's vigilantism is more human than Superman's perfect performance), why Ironman is so intriguing (his flaws make him seem more real), why Gollum is actually the hero of *The Lord of the Rings* (he is the greatest lover and ultimate destroyer of the One Ring, despite all his efforts to the contrary), and why romantic comedies often end with a kiss (if the union is, in fact, a perfect culmination of love, then what else is there to watch?).

Heroes are not perfect; they are imperfectly heroic. They make mistakes— huge, ghastly mistakes. After the mistakes, heroes must sacrifice large parts of themselves to rectify the situations, saving the world and the culture in the process. We need heroes to be imperfect, so that we ourselves can strive to emulate them. *Ninja Warrior* is a careful demonstration of this imperfect performance. In the repeated attempts (and failures) of all of these athletes to reach the end of the obstacle course, the cultural proportions of heroic achievements take a bodily form.

Works Cited

Appel, Edward C. "Implications and Importance of the Negative in Burke's Dramatistic Philosophy of Language." *Communication Quarterly* 41.1 (1993): 51–65.

Barthes, Roland. "The World of Wrestling." 1957. *Steel Chair to the Head: The Pleasure and Pain of Professional Wrestling.* Ed. Nicholas Sammond. Durham: Duke UP, 2005. 23–32.

Becker, Ernest. *The Denial of Death.* New York: Free, 1973.

Bitzer, Lloyd. "The Rhetorical Situation." *Philosophy and Rhetoric* 1.1 (1968): 1–14.

"Board: 'Ninja Warrior' (2007)." *IMDb.com.* Internet Movie Database, n.d. Accessed on 22 Aug. 2008. <http://www.imdb.com/title/tt1014786/board/threads/>.

Bowra, C. Maurice. "The Hero." *The Hero in Literature: Major Essays on the Changing Concepts of Heroism from Classical Times to the Present.* Ed. Victor Brombert. Greenwich: Fawcett, 1969. 22–52.

Brombert, Victor. "Introduction: The Idea of the Hero." *The Hero in Literature: Major Essays on the Changing Concepts of Heroism from Classical Times to the Present.* Ed. Victor Brombert. Greenwich: Fawcett, 1969. 11–21.

Burke, Kenneth. *Language as Symbolic Action: Essays on Life, Literature, and Method.* Berkeley: U of California P, 1966.

Butterworth, Michael L. "The Politics of the Pitch: Claiming and Contesting Democracy Through the Iraqi National Soccer Team." *Communication & Critical/Cultural Studies* 4.2 (June 2007): 184–203. *Communication & Mass Media Complete.* EBSCO. Jamaica, NY: St. John's University Library. Accessed on 18 Feb. 2009 <http://jerome.stjohns. edu:81/login?url=http://search.ebscohost.com/login.aspx?direct=true&db=ufh& AN=25049331&site=ehost-live>.

———. "Purifying the Body Politic: Steroids, Rafael Palmeiro, and the Rhetorical Cleansing of Major League Baseball." *Western Journal of Communication* 72.2 (Apr. 2008): 145–161. *Communication & Mass Media Complete.* EBSCO. Jamaica, NY: St. John's University Library. Accessed on 18 Feb. 2009 <http://jerome.stjohns.edu:81/ login?url=http://search.ebscohost.com/login.aspx?direct=true&db=ufh&AN=32 746869&site=ehost-live>.

Campbell, Joseph. *The Hero with a Thousand Faces.* Princeton: Princeton UP, 1949.

Davis, Diane. "Addressing Alterity: Rhetoric, Hermeneutics, and the Nonappropriative Relation." *Philosophy and Rhetoric* 38.3 (2005): 191–212.

Faust, Drew G. *This Republic of Suffering: Death and the American Civil War.* New York: Knopf, 2008.

Grano, Daniel A. "Ritual Disorder and the Contractual Morality of Sport: A Case Study in Race, Class, and Agreement." *Rhetoric & Public Affairs* 10.3 (Fall 2007): 445–473. *Communication & Mass Media Complete.* EBSCO. Jamaica, NY: St. John's University Library. Accessed on 18 Feb. 2009 <http://jerome.stjohns.edu:81/login?url=http:// search.ebscohost.com/login.aspx?direct=true&db=ufh&AN=28066237&site=eh ost-live>.

Hibberd, James. "More 'Warrior' for G4." *Television Week* 5 Mar. 2007: 2–4. Hutchinson, Susan L., and Douglas A. Kleiber. "Heroic Masculinity Following Spinal Cord Injury: Implications for Therapeutic Recreation Practice and Research." *Therapeutic Recreation Journal* 34 (2000): 42–54.

Hyde, Michael J. *The Call of Conscience: Heidegger and Levinas, Rhetoric and the Euthanasia Debate.* New York: U of South Carolina P, 2000.

"Ninja Warrior." *G4.* G4 Media, Inc., n.d. Accessed on 22 Aug. 2008. <http://www.g4tv. com/ninjawarrior/index.html>.

"NinjaWarrior.us: A Community of Sasuke Enthusiasts." *NinjaWarrior.us,* n.p., n.d. Accessed on 22 Aug. 2008. <http://ninjawarrior.us/>.

"Playing the Swan." *Slings and Arrows: Season 1.* Writ. Susan Coyne, Bob Martin, and Mark McKinney. Dir. Peter Wellington. Movie Central. 8 Dec. 2003. DVD. Acorn Media, 2008.

Potter, W. James. "Adolescents and Television Violence." *The Changing Portrayal of Adolescents in the Media since 1950*. Ed. Patrick Jamieson and Daniel Romer. Oxford: Oxford UP, 2008. 221–49.

Salazar, Philippe-Joseph. "Rhetoric on the Bleachers, or, the Rhetorician as Melancholiac." *Philosophy & Rhetoric* 41.4 (Nov. 2008): 356–374. *Communication & Mass Media Complete*. EBSCO. Jamaica, NY: St. John's University Library. Accessed on 18 Feb. 2009 <http://jerome.stjohns.edu:81/login?url=http://search.ebscohost.com/login. aspx?direct=true&db=ufh&AN=35665026&site=ehost-live>.

"Sasuke (TV Series)." Wikipedia: The Free Encyclopedia. Wikimedia Foundation, Inc., 22 Aug. 2008 Accessed on 22 Aug. 2008. <http://en.wikipedia.org/ wiki/ninja_warrior>.

Wolpe, David J. *In Speech and in Silence: The Jewish Quest for God*. New York: Holt, 1992.

Notes

1. Stars such as Chuck Norris and Sylvester Stallone are some of the people who benefit from this cult of perfection. While Norris stumps for political candidates, and Stallone offers up yet another *Rambo* movie, other folks are trying to capitalize on the notion that strength in simulated war is equivalent to performed perfection. *American Gladiators* is back—as of spring 2008, a new roster of amateur athletes will be competing with certain chosen gladiators in various feats of strength and agility. *Pros vs. Joes*, a similarly constructed show on Spike TV, pits "average Joes" against professional fighters and athletes. There are many other shows revolving around the antagonistic competition between different kinds of strongmen.

2. Twice a day, except on marathon days when *Ninja* is the only program shown for hours at a time.

7

■ *Rollergirls*

Superhero Rhetoric in Post-Feminist Television

❑ Alexis Carreiro

Today, we live in the age of the "superwoman"—a post-feminist, pop culture concept that attempts to explain how empowered, contemporary women can "have it all." Television series such as *Sex and the City, Lipstick Jungle,* and *Desperate Housewives* revolve around the "superwoman" concept. "Superwomen" have successful careers and beautiful babies, lean boyfriends and fat bank accounts, good friends and bad attitudes. They do not need to choose between these categories because they can have it all (or at least, that is the goal.) But how did we get here? And what can *Rollergirls*, a 2006 reality television series, reveal about the relationship between performance, the superhero myth, and the failure of post-feminism? Post-feminism is embodied in the superhero myth, and the failure of the myth to empower here shows post-feminism's failure overall.

■ The Failure of Post-Feminism

Invisibility is a common superhero power. In comic books and movies, the power of invisibility is associated with spying, stealing, and getting away (with a heroic act or a villainous crime) unnoticed. Invisibility is one of the best ways for a superhero to keep his or her secret identity a secret. However, invisibility is only a superpower when the person wielding it already has a strong visible presence elsewhere. Invisibility on its own accord is not about power—but a lack of it.

Invisibility and powerlessness are at the heart of the feminist project. Feminism's historical trajectory (often conceptualized as three "waves") began with women's political invisibility and impotence. Until the year 1920, women were not allowed to vote. Early feminist activists fought to make women visible within the political landscape. The First Wave's key tenets include women's suffrage, the right to own property, and the opposition to chattel marriage. The First Wave established feminism's basic principle that gender should not impede anyone's personal or civil liberties. The Second Wave refers to the feminist movement between the late 1960s and 1970s. During this time, feminism was a social and political movement that championed Equal Rights—political, professional, and personal—and challenged sexist power structures. Second Wave feminists rallied against pornography and championed abortion rights, domestic policy, and collective sisterhood. However, despite its emphasis on equality, not everyone equally benefited from it. The Second Wave fostered rigid, essentialist binaries between male and female, masculine and feminine, and feminine and feminist. It privileged an essentialist perspective about "women"—a biologically inclusive yet culturally exclusive term usually conflated with the white, middle-class, heterosexual women primarily at the movement's forefront. As a result, it ostracized and further marginalized women of different races, classes, and sexual orientations. Third Wave feminism emerged in the 1980s (alongside the MTV generation) as a reaction against the Second Wave. The Third Wave challenged the essentialist assumption that individuals naturally behave according to their biologically sexed bodies: "men/male/masculine" (strong, tough, aggressive, powerful, etc.) and "women/female/feminine" (sensitive, emotional, seductive, demure, etc.). Instead, it suggested that individuals learn how to perform gender (via attitude, body language, clothing, hairstyles, etc.) according to rhetorical symbol systems (language, media, and culture) and traditional, social norms. It also rejected the essentialist idea that "women" were a unified group of people with similar histories, beliefs, and agendas. It sought to politically mobilize young women, disrupt rigid binaries, and fostered a community of inclusivity (multi-class, multi-racial, multi-gender, multi-sexual) rather than exclusivity. In addition, Third Wave feminists began "appropriating the male gaze, embracing multiple identities, and re-claiming sexual pleasure" (Owen, Stein, and Vende Berg 125). They also embraced mass media and popular culture as part of the political, feminist project.

Post-feminism emerged alongside Third Wave feminism. However, post-feminism (as the prefix implies) refers to the idea that modern society has moved beyond feminism. Post-feminist discourse assumes that feminism, for the most part, has already succeeded. It assumes that women have already achieved equality so that the collective, political feminist project is no longer necessary. Instead, it emphasizes individual lifestyle choices as a way to politicize pleasure, such as personal style, consumer purchases, and pop culture preferences (as a result, post-feminism is also referred to as "free market feminism," "commodity feminism," "attitudinal feminism," and "lifestyle feminism"). This, however, is one of post-feminism's major failures. It offers females the superficial appearance of destabilizing patriarchy—as "consumers, but not political agents" (Owen, Stein, and Vende Berg 10). For example, "grrrl/girl power" is a key characteristic of both Third Wave feminism and post-feminism. During the Third Wave, "grrl power" emerged alongside the 1990s, punk rock, Riot Grrrl movement. "Grrrl power" emerged as a "model of hybridity and contradiction vital to the 'kinderwhore' aesthetic propounded by Courtney Love…. Love's performance of 'ironic femininity' is highlighted as decentering dominant configurations of both patriarchal femininity (across the Madonna/whore binary) and feminist identity" (Munford 145). The Riot Grrrl ethos supported the concept that "the personal is political" and encouraged Third Wave feminists to produce their own grrrl-centric music. Post-feminism has since co-opted "Grrrl power" into "girl power"—a watered-down consumer version of its punk predecessor devoid of the sexual politics or cultural critique (think Spice Girls and Britney Spears). In film, young action heroines also reflect the "girl power" mantra. The girlie action hero is symbolically male (tough, aggressive, powerful) and sexually idealized (think Angelina Jolie in *Lara Croft: Tombraider* or Cameron Diaz in *Charlie's Angels*). Most importantly, she (like post-feminism itself) never threatens patriarchy (Stasia). She only looks like she can. According to Christina Lucia Stasia, "as 'strong' as she is, she is ultimately there for (male) pleasure" (178). This is another of post-feminism's key failures. It attempts to co-opt and re-appropriate the male gaze but instead just reproduces it. It reinforces hegemonic patriarchy under the pretext of individual, female empowerment. Rather than situate itself within a larger anti-hegemonic project, post-feminism separates itself from feminism and consequently undermines it. As a result, with its insistence on individual versus collective resistance, post-feminism (and the media texts that support it) does little to affect institutional structures that continue to oppress women.

Rollergirls' failure as post-feminist television is important to consider here because of television's ideological work as public discourse within contemporary, American society. According to Brundson and Spigel, "reality and lifestyle TV are, of course, ripe for this kind of analysis because, while scripted, they are primarily about the performance of self" (4). Television is a symbolic site of popular and cultural contestation. It is an ideological institution and its texts are rhetorical, performative symbols. They are cultural artifacts created in specific historical contexts that reflect, reinforce, and challenge the social values in which they are produced and consumed. The critic's (and the audience's) role is to interpret how a television text manipulates the symbols within it and how it functions as an ideological tool for socio-historic, audience consumption. According to Robert C. Allen,

> The ways in which we make sense of and take pleasure from even the most inconsequential moments of television are worth thinking about because—if for no other reason—the aggregate of those moments constitute a good portion of millions and millions of people's waking hours…. Moreover, examining the pleasures and meanings of television we watch "for fun" might shed some light on other aspects of our everyday lives: how narratives work, how our notions of masculinity and femininity are constructed, how and why different cultural products appeal to different groups of people, and, most generally and most importantly, how we make meaningful and pleasurable the numerous and enormously diverse symbol systems we encounter everyday. (4)

Extending this idea to feminist television criticism, Bonnie Dow suggests that it is important to examine "television's role in mediating social change, in reproducing assumptions about women's 'appropriate' roles, and appealing to and constructing a subjectivity for women as a television audience" (xix). Every television text makes claims about the characters within it and assumptions about the audience members who watch it. Unpacking and analyzing these claims is critical in today's media-saturated culture. Feminist television criticism is necessary in order to understand how hegemony operates within mass media, what it looks like, and how we (the audience) participate in it (Brundson and Spiegel 12). It enables viewers to recognize how television represents patriarchy and how we in turn re-produce or reject it in our own lives. In short, it gives viewers the necessary tools to participate in emancipatory feminist politics. According to Owen, Stein, and Vende Berg,

> Emancipatory politics…*requires* history—a narrative of oppressions and the struggle against that oppression. Postfeminism and other hegemonic forces reduce feminist claims of a history of oppression to a self-indulgent whining over "victimization." The rejection of victimization is a rejection of memory, a symbolic cleansing that crafts a future utterly dissociated from the past. Hegemonic representations play a significant role in this dissociation. (128, original emphasis)

Post-feminism's assumption that we are beyond feminism eradicates the history of women's oppression and returns feminism to its roots. It once again renders invisible women's unequal power within society. It obscures the various ways that women (of all race, class, and sexual preferences) do not have equal wages and representation in the workforce. It conceals the need to resist against gender discrimination and sexual violence. In short, post-feminism (and the media texts that support it) hides hegemonic patriarchy in plain sight and undercuts the need for feminism itself.

Feminist television criticism, therefore, is a necessary corrective. It makes visible what post-feminist television texts attempt to obscure. Here, it highlights how post-feminism is embodied in the superhero myth and warns against the mistake of turning real feminist politics into reality television fantasy.

■ Heteronormative Superheroes: *Rollergirls* as "Superwomen"

Feminism's return to invisibility (again, a common superhero power) coincides with the post-feminist concept of the "superwoman."[1] According to Coppock, Haydon, and Richter,

> If the claim to a "post-feminist" society is underpinned by any one principle it is that women have "made it," or they have the opportunity to "make it." The proposition that woman can decide on their priorities and "go for them"—career, motherhood, world traveler, etc.—is at the heart of the image-makers' construction of the "superwoman." (4)

Coppock, Haydon, and Richter's conceptualization of the "image-maker" is important to consider here. It highlights the idea that post-feminist media texts are commodities within the capitalist marketplace. Post-feminist media texts are produced primarily for profit, not just for politics. Post-feminist media texts and profitable brands—like The Pussycat Dolls (the burlesque show, the pop music group, and the television series) and *Sex and the City* (the television series and film)—present the image of "liberated" (politically, sexually, and financially) female protagonists within sexually idealized bodies for male and female audiences. Women want to be them and men want to be with them. Post-feminist media texts offer the audience (television consumers) an idealized version of the contemporary "superwoman"—because this image sells.

Rollergirls, a 2006 reality television series highlighting several skaters from the Texas Roller Derby (TXRD) Lonestar *Rollergirls* league, is the latest post-feminist text to offer an idealized version of the "superwoman." It rhetorically explores the question "Does 'feminist' equality require a rejection of femininity, or is it dependent upon it?" (Levine 375). The answer here is both. *Rollergirls* attempts to prove that these women can have it all by complicating the relationship between femininity and fighting; appearance and aggression; gender, sexuality, performance, play, and sport. The roller derby skaters dress in highly sexualized costumes and use pseudonyms on the track—such as Venis Envy or Sister Mary Jane. Each episode juxtaposes the skaters' public, traditionally feminine identities off the roller derby track (as sweet, loving girlfriends and mothers) with their disguised, transgressive identities on it (violent, aggressive, sexualized, punk-rock skaters). As a result, it extends the "superwoman" mythology to an ironic extreme. The dual identity theme (masked/unmasked) rhetorically frames the women as "superheroes" within the text. *Rollergirls'* superhero narrative mimics post-feminism "superwoman" rhetoric. Yet, it fails to support that rhetoric. It argues that women can have it all—but not at the same time. Instead, they must chose between the two sides (their dual, superhero identities) and perform only one at a time.

Rollergirls—like the majority of mass-media texts that support consumerism and capitalism—reinforces heterosexist ideology. In fact, heteronormativity is at the center of *Rollergirls'* superhero rhetoric. It refers to the basic presumption that everyone is traditionally masculine or feminine and (unless otherwise noted) desires a heterosexual lifestyle complete with marriage and children. In order to better understand *Rollergirls'* superhero rhetoric, it is first necessary to understand how the reality show itself rhetorically constructs heteronormative ideology. For example, casting is a particularly important rhetorical device. In 2006, there were approximately sixty skaters in the TXRD roller derby league from which *Rollergirls'* producers could cast in the series. The racially and sexually diverse skaters (in their twenties to forties) within the overall TXRD league represented a wide range of physical characteristics such as tall, tattooed, sexy, fat, scrawny, pierced, unattractive, short, feminine, butch—and almost everything in between. Yet unlike the racial, sexual, and physical diversity presented within the TXRD league itself, the featured *rollergirls* were primarily slender, attractive, white, heterosexual women in their mid-twenties to early thirties. As such, they rhetorically work together to perform the standard, sexy, heteronormative image of a female "roller derby skater." Within the thirteen-episode series, *Rollergirls* emphasizes six skaters: Sister Mary Jane, Lux, Venis Envy, Miss Conduct, Punky Bruiser, and Cha Cha. The names themselves are performative. They are playful, poignant, and suggest a spunky, if not defiant, type of femininity. Each of these skaters are featured (and named) within the series' introductory credit sequence each week. They are also featured on A&E's *Rollergirls'* webpage ("Meet the Girls"). Five additional skaters (Witch Baby, Chola, Jailbait, Lunatic, and Catalac) are also emphasized throughout the series and on the webpage but are not predominantly featured during the introductory credit sequence. The prominence of these eleven skaters throughout the series casts them as the reality television show's principal characters. They drive the action and emotional arc of each episode.

Heterosexuality is a major theme within the television series. In fact, eight out of thirteen episodes highlight the skaters' heterosexual relationships. During the series, *Rollergirls* emphasizes four (out of six) of the featured skater's heterosexual relationships. The first episode introduces the audience to featured skater Venis Envy and her long-term boyfriend Palmer ("The Rookie"). *Rollergirls* also chronicles the relationship between featured skater Lux and her boyfriend Frankie. During the series, he tattoos her image on his arm and they also move in together. One episode highlights Catalac's return to roller derby after battling ovarian cancer ("The C Word"). It explores her relationship with her husband and emphasizes her pride in being a mother. The series also follows Sister Mary Jane and her boyfriend Clay as they discuss marriage and eventually move to Hawaii together. These deliberate casting and editing choices rhetorically support *Rollergirls'* heteronormative ideology.

The *Rollergirls'* website also supports the series' deliberate heteronormative construction. The Arts and Entertainment channel used the *Rollergirls* website as a way to market the reality television show. As such, the website is a complementary text and a rhetorical tool designed to brand the series. According to the website,

> Every non-scripted *Rollergirls* episode follows the women as they square off against each other on the track and then face everyday challenges with boyfriends and bosses off-track. Some have kids. Some are married. Some just want a body-busting wild time…. A 21st-century sports phenomenon, *Rollergirls* captures the rich detail of the league's over-the-top antics and adrenaline-drenched performances that are inspiring all-girl teams across the country. Like any great sports story, *Rollergirls* is rife with hotshots and hellions, rebels and rascals, the unsung and the underhanded—first-class competitors all. It's just that these sassy stars sport fishnets beneath their shin guards. ("About the Show")

The website accomplishes its objective to brand *Rollergirls* as a heteronormative text in two ways. First, the words "boyfriends," "married," and "kids," in the series' description, undercut any suggestion that the featured *Rollergirls* might be gay, bisexual, or anti-marriage. Instead, it foregrounds their heteronormative identities. Second, the description "body-busting wild time" and the emphasis on the skaters' fishnet clothing highlight their physical appearance alongside (or perhaps secondary to) their athletic abilities. Here, *Rollergirls* makes no claim to be about roller derby itself. It is about the league's "over-the-top antics." In short, it is a reality show about performance. It is a sexualized spectacle produced for a heteronormative (female and male) audience. Like the majority of sports coverage of female athletes, *Rollergirls* succumbs to sexually objectifying its female athletes. However, unlike traditional sports coverage, *Rollergirls* sexually objectifies its roller derby skaters under the guise of female empowerment.

Rollergirls, like most post-feminist media texts, offers a superficial version of feminism. It is a highly stylized and heterosexualized, feminist performance—but the performance is a guise. The performance offers a pseudo-feminist image, not real feminist indignation. The style lacks substance because post-feminism lies only on the surface but not beyond it. It provides "girl power sound bites…[and] offers girls the encouragement to do anything without providing them with the knowledge or tools to do so" (Stasia 180). It offers individualized empowerment in lieu of the collective activism necessary to affect real, institutional change. Over and over again, *Rollergirls* reveals a "superwoman/girl power" mentality. By all accounts, there is nothing these women, or rather, these girls, cannot do. They are smart, professional women off the track and wild, sexy, hellions on it. They are loving girlfriends, wives, and mothers off the track and angry, violent, roller derby brutes on it. The website's claim that the skaters are "inspiring all-girl teams across the country" suggests that *Rollergirls* is an empowering text for fans and female roller derby athletes in the United States. However, only one episode specifically deals with this issue ("Big Time").[2] Beyond that, the text focuses on the individual league, the individual skaters, and their highly personal, heteronormative lives in Austin, Texas. As a result, *Rollergirls* is a heteronormative performance of the post-feminist aesthetic evacuated from real feminist politics.

The emphasis on the skaters' heteronormative, dual identities sets the stage for the skaters' superhero performance within the series. On the surface, it appears to challenge the traditional masculine/feminine binary (tough, strong, and powerful versus soft, nurturing, and emotional) but it reproduces it instead. According to the website, "Sister Mary Jane lives quite a double life. By day, she's a special education teacher in an elementary school. At night, she becomes a competitive powerhouse in the rink" ("Sister Mary Jane"). In fact, throughout the series, several skaters use the "superhero" metaphor as a strategy to resolve the dissonance between their traditionally feminine personas outside the game and their masked personas as aggressive, violent, and competitive roller derby athletes. During the "Punky Needs a Life" episode, Sister Mary Jane (Ashley, who skates for the Catholic school girl-themed Holy Rollers team) contemplates leaving roller derby to move to Hawaii with her boyfriend. She asks, "You know I'm a school teacher by day and a roller derby girl at night…. Who will I be without being Sister Mary Jane?…Am I gonna miss being a superhero for an hour out of my month? Like, that's a pretty powerful feeling." Johnna ("Witch Baby" on the Rhinestone Cowgirls team), also reinforces the superhero metaphor. According to Johnna, "That is what roller derby gives you. The knowledge that you are, in fact, a superhero. And you don't have to wear the cape. But you do get to wear the tights" ("No Pain, No Jane"). Janelle (who skates for the Rhinestone Cowgirls team as "Lux") works as a maternity nurse in Austin. In the "Undefeated" episode, Janelle says, "I'm not Lux at work, obviously.... You can't completely get the two personas out of each other. I mean, Janelle is my real person but Lux is still inside me somewhere." In the "Rollerball" episode, Lux's boyfriend Frankie also acknowledges her dual identity. According to Frankie, "I like the idea of your dual personality thing. It's like I have two girlfriends. There's Janelle, the nice baby nurse who goes to work at the hospital and Lux is the evil roller derby queen who beats up people." Having a dual identity is a key, superhero characteristic. For Superman, it's Clark Kent. For Batman, it's Bruce Wayne. For Wonder Woman, it's Diana Prince. In fact, the *Rollergirls'* overall superhero narrative mimics Wonder Woman's mythology beyond mere secret identities. The narrative similarities include the inaugural maternal storyline, the emphasis on their flashy and functional costumes, and their athletic prowess.

Wonder Woman debuted in print in 1941 (Muir 550). In the inaugural comic book storyline, Captain Steve Trevor, an army pilot, crashes into the remote and female-inhabited Paradise Island. The Queen of the island (the Amazon Queen) creates an Amazon Special Olympics to locate the toughest Amazon woman capable of transporting Captain Trevor back to the United States but forbids her own daughter from entering the competition. Princess Diana, however, wants to prove herself to her mother and disguises herself to hide her true identity. She competes against her mother's will (and against her Amazonian sisters) in a series of dangerous and physically demanding tests— and wins. After she wins, the Queen learns Diana's true identity. Instead of punishing her, she grants Diana with super powers and bestows her with the "Wonder Woman" title (Daniels 24).

Rollergirls' inaugural episode ("The Rookie") mimics the *Wonder Woman* narrative. It centers on the skater Venis Envy (Melissa) and her rookie bout as a member of the Putas del Fuegos (Whores of Fire). It highlights her mother's impending visit to Austin to watch Venis's roller derby debut. A central thread within "The Rookie" narrative is Venis's desire to gain her mother's approval through her athletic performance on the track. It explores Venis's apprehension regarding roller derby's extreme physicality. In the episode, Venis wonders if she will be strong enough to accomplish the task of winning for her team. She fears she will let her sisters down if she is not strong enough to win. However, like Diana Prince before her, Venis does receive her mother's blessing at the end of her exhausting and dangerous physical trial. Throughout the episode, Venis states her immense love and respect for the all-female roller derby league and declares her pride in being part of it. Throughout the series, the skaters discuss the importance of having an all-female space of their own in which to bond, support, and physically challenge one another. As a result, the Texas Lonestar roller derby league rhetorically functions as a modern-day Paradise Island. Both Wonder Woman and *Rollergirls* treat female-centric space as sacred.

Fashion is also central to the narrative similarities between Wonder Woman (or superheroes, in general) and *Rollergirls*. When Wonder Woman first appeared in print, she wore a tight, sexy, red bustier with short, blue and white bottoms. This outfit protects her from harm and also gives her special powers. When used against a male antagonist, her golden lasso compels him to tell the truth. Her bracelets are made of "feminum" and protect her against speeding bullets. Like the stage name Venis Envy (or Witch Baby or Helena Handbasket), Wonder Woman's "feminum" bracelets are a clear indication that her superpower is directly related to her female gender (Muir 552). When Wonder Woman appeared on television in 1975, she morphed from Diana Prince into Wonder Woman by spinning in circles, with her arms outstretched. A flash of white light marked her final transition. Once the transition was complete, Wonder Woman stood with her hands on her hips for a few seconds before rushing off to fight crime. On A&E's *Rollergirls*, the narrative also centers on how their clothing functions as a source of power. Like Wonder Woman, they wear wrist guards to protect them when they fall and also spin in circles (on a banked track) in their highly sexualized, form-fitting roller derby outfits. The roller derby clothing, however, appears less as uniforms and more like costumes. Each team has a different and themed costume. The Holy Rollers look like naughty Catholic-school girls. They wear plaid mini-skirts and tight white shirts. The Rhinestone Cowgirls wear mini-denim shorts and tight red shirts. The Putas del Fuegos wear black tops and bottoms. Some members from every team also wear fishnet stockings. The costumes are part of roller derby's sexualized and transgressive spectacle.

The costumes (the highly stylized makeup, clothing, and stage pseudonyms) are a critical part of the skater's superhero performance. They disguise, or mask, the skater's "citizen" identity off the track. According to Danny Fingeroth, author of *Superman on the Couch*, "The mask is recognized as bestower of power as well as disguiser of identity" (51). This mask gives the skaters the freedom to transgress social codes of appropriate feminine ("good girl") behavior. It gives them the freedom to publicly perform socially inappropriate behavior such as fighting, swearing, tackling, shoving, spitting, elbowing, punching, and the like. It lets them honor their aggression, show off their athleticism, and exhibit their sexuality all at the same time. According to Sister Mary Jane, her citizen identity (a special education elementary school teacher) is totally separate from her roller derby identity and that is one of the reasons she loves roller derby. According to her, roller derby is "just this really cool thing where you can be entirely yourself, and be completely feminine, and athletic, sexy and threatening at the same time" ("No Pain, No Jane"). For example, the "No Pain, No Jane" episode shows that whenever Sister Mary Jane performs well for her team during a bout, she raises the back of her skirt to the opposing team and the audience and flashes the "No Pain, No Jane" slogan written across the back of her underwear. The gesture is meant as an insult to the opposing team. It signifies her very public "kiss my ass" sentiment to the opposing team, yet it also functions as a moment of burlesque for the audience who witnesses it. As a rollergirl, Ashley can "get away with" this type of exhibitionism but not as a special education, elementary school teacher. Therefore, assuming the "Sister Mary Jane" character during bouts is a useful strategy for Ashley to employ in order to transgress the boundary between appropriate and inappropriate public, female behavior. The skaters' transgressive performances on the roller derby track, however, are only episodic ruptures within the otherwise "contained" series' text.

Editing is a key aspect of *Rollergirls'* contained superhero construction. Each individual episode is edited according to the classic, three-act structure. *Rollergirls'* three-act structure unfolds as a citizen-superhero, skater-citizen (public-private-public) story arc. The first act reveals the "A" and "B" plot. The roller derby match functions as the "A" plot. Almost every episode begins with a title card that announces a pending roller derby match.[3] The "A" plot's central tension centers on which team will win the roller derby match. Each episode also includes a "B" plot. The "B" plot centers on a central conflict (or theme) for the skaters off the roller derby track; it is often some aspect of their heteronormative, "citizen" identity. The second act contains each episode's main action. It follows the character (or characters) into a roller derby match and reveals their citizen/superhero transformation. In fact, almost every episode includes a montage segment of the girls getting into costume. The montage segment shows them walk up to the arena in their everyday, citizen clothing and then change—literally into their costumes (hair and makeup) and figuratively into their superhero stage personas. This scene functions as their "Clark Kent/Superman" phone booth moment. However, they do not tear open their shirts to reveal a giant "S" on their chest. Instead, their transformational moment occurs in several close-up shots of key players pulling up their fishnet stockings, putting on makeup, and forcefully pushing their feet deep into their shiny, black roller skates. In this moment, the skaters are both the subjects and the objects of the text. According to Ringrose and Walkerdine, this dual identity "both consumes itself into being and is the object of consumption" (231). In *Rollergirls*, Ashley becomes Sister Mary Jane, Janelle becomes Lux, and Melissa becomes Venis Envy. The second act emphasizes the skaters' aggression, violence, athleticism, strength, power, and competitiveness. In short, it represents their symbolic masculinity. It highlights the various ways the women perform outside traditional gender norms and, as a result, transgress them. The second act resolves the episode's "A" plot once the roller derby bout is over and a winner is declared. Finally, the third narrative act centers on the women's return to their "citizen" identity off the roller derby track. Like her cinematic equivalent, when the girlie action hero "successfully completes her male-directed mission: she is returned to the private sphere" (Stasia 177). *Rollergirls'* third act shows the women back in their "citizen" clothing as they resume their traditionally feminine, heteronormative identities (girlfriend, wife, mother, nurse, etc.). Once again, the girlie protagonist does not threaten patriarchy. She only looks like she can.

It could easily be argued that *Rollergirls* simply mirrors the performative nature of roller derby itself, but that would obscure the series' deliberate ideological construction. *Rollergirls'* three-act story structure (citizen-superhero skater-citizen) is a rhetorical narrative strategy. The series' first and third acts privilege the women's traditionally feminine identities off the track as girl-friends, wives, and mothers—not those on the track as aggressive, athletic, powerful women. The women's superhero identities do not "spill" into the first or third acts. As a result, their feminine transgressions are rhetorically contained in each episode's second act. This frames their female transgressions on the track as a momentary aberration. *Rollergirls'* rhetorical structure ideologically restricts the characters' superhero identities in the middle of the narrative as a way to isolate their feminine transgressions. It contains their feminine "misconduct" within the heternormative spaces off the track and, as a result, undermines transgressive behavior that does not adhere to conventional notions of femininity.

The second act's citizen/superhero transformation scene (the Clark Kent/Superman montage) undermines the skaters' feminine misconduct on the roller derby track. It is a rhetorical tool for the television audience. It persuades the audience to read the women in costume on the track and highlights the match itself as a performance. It highlights the women's transgressive behavior on the roller derby track as a performance; as an aberration to their "real" identities. It suggests that the women are in disguise on the roller derby track—but not in real life. This rhetorical strategy normalizes the women's' more traditional "non-performed" feminine identities off the roller derby track. It de-emphasizes the artificiality of the characters' traditionally feminine, civilian clothing and disguises the various ways women perform femininity in their everyday lives—in padded push-up bras, high heels, "natural" makeup, trendy hairstyles, and coy gestures. It disguises how women perform traditional femininity in their everyday lives and actively participate in contemporary patriarchal culture. In short, highlighting the women's performance and costumes on the track but not off it hides hegemonic patriarchy in plain sight. As a result, *Rollergirls* undermines its own radical feminist potential. Instead of deconstructing hegemonic patriarchy on and off the track, it simply disguises it. *Rollergirls* is a post-feminist, television text that masquerades as a show about collective female empowerment. Ultimately, however, *Rollergirls* naturalizes women's performance of traditional femininity off the roller derby track and neutralizes their feminine transgressions on it.

■ Post-Feminism and the Superhero Myth

On the surface, *Rollergirls* deconstructs essentialist Second Wave binaries. However, in its ironic attempt to mock these binaries (Madonna/whore; feminine/masculine), it reproduces them instead. Its contradictory message critiques traditional femininity as it simultaneously replicates it and empowers women as it sexually objectifies them. *Rollergirls'* superhero rhetoric, combined with its punk-rock aesthetic, reflects the danger in conflating post-feminism or "lifestyle, attitudinal feminism with the hard political and intellectual work that feminists have done and continue to do...the danger is in believing that image is equal to politics and material change" (Dow 214). As a result, *Rollergirls* undermines its own radical feminist potential. Instead of simultaneously representing the roller derby athletes as strong, smart, nurturing, complex, sexy, powerful, violent, vulnerable, aggressive and complicated, it splits them in two and turns them into superheroes instead.

The dual identity is at the center of the superhero myth. In his book *Superman on the Couch*, Danny Fingeroth asks "What fantasy does the double identity appeal to?" According to Fingeroth,

> Perhaps...it is to allow us to believe that, deep down, we are or could be so much more than we appear. "If only they knew how special I am," we think. Don't we all have secret identities, those sides of ourselves we feel we dare not risk revealing? The secret identity is where our fantasies and ambitions take hold and ferment. We eagerly seek the time when we can give free rein to the "superhero within." (50)...The fantasy is a large part of what draws people to these heroes in the first place. After all, if a hero's identity is a secret then that cute guy or girl you've glanced at across a crowded room may just think you are a Woman of Wonder or a Super Man. Maybe that possibility even gives you the momentary illusion/fantasy/thrill that you could indeed be super-powerful. Of course, the illusion and the fantasy are fleeting and momentary and then all parties remember that this is the real world and that there are no superhumans. But maybe...just maybe. (60–61)

The superhero myth hits at the core of our trust in faith and our love of magic. It relies on the assumption that we all have the potential to be more of who we really are, more of the time. It appeals to our desire to believe in something bigger than ourselves and to the dream that (maybe, just maybe) we are special. It offers the fantasy that by splitting ourselves into two separate identities, we can become more whole. But the fantasy is an illusion. The myth is a lie. It suggests we can achieve more, that we can be more, by becoming less. It falsely assumes that disintegration brings integration. In short, it is at odds with living a whole, holistic life.

Part of the Third Wave feminist project highlights how patriarchy pulls society apart; how it forces men and women to perform arbitrarily gendered roles; how it assigns power and powerlessness to these roles. It illustrates how patriarchy splits people into "his" or "hers," "masculine" or "feminine," and prevents them from realizing their holistic potential as whole human beings. It resists rigid essentialist binaries ("this" or "that") because they are exclusive; not inclusive. The "superwoman" concept emerged alongside the Third Wave to explore how women could "have it all"—at the same time. It explores how women might integrate their complex identities, desires, and demands into one coherent self. Although the "superwoman" image is often idealistic (and perhaps unrealistic), it moves the Third Wave one step away from the exclusive binaries that fracture women's identities and one small step closer toward holistically restoring them. In contrast, *Rollergirls'* superhero rhetoric reifies essentialist binaries and takes two steps backwards. It applies superhero mythology to the "superwoman" ideology and encourages its audience to view the skaters' disintegrated, dual identities as a sign of post-feminist empowerment. This reality show relegates its "real" characters into the realm of fantasy and make-believe. It suggests that becoming a superhero (with separate, dual identities) is the only way modern women can reconcile the complex (and often contradictory) demands society puts upon them. Post-feminism is embodied in the superhero myth, and the failure of the myth to empower here shows post-feminism's failure overall.

The concept of "girl-power" or "superwoman" as a form of feminist empowerment is flawed at best because it conflates a post-feminist aesthetic with real feminist politics. However, it is important not to lose sight of the political significance of female-centric television texts. According to Stasia, "Although girl power, within mainstream hegemonic popular culture, is a severely diluted and over-simplified form of feminism, it is not necessarily anti-feminist" (182). In fact, almost any series that stars female athletes and explores the complex demands placed upon them is a productive feminist text in today's male-dominated television landscape. In the United States alone, sports (a $60 billion-plus industry) occupy a strong visible presence on

American television (Fuller 3). Despite its strong presence, however, female athletes are largely absent—largely invisible—from national sports coverage. Based on research by Duncan, Messner, Williams, and Jensen, Greta L. Cohen states that "females constitute 53% of the population and receive only 5% of the sports coverage" (174). *Rollergirls* is an important site for cultural and political analysis because it represents a shift in media coverage of women athletes and women's sports. It is, by no means, a perfect text. However, it takes up the basic feminist project to make women more visible in the cultural landscape and offers the audience critical moments of feminine transgression not seen elsewhere on television. As a result, it opens the door for future television series willing to take a chance on female athletes—and female transgression. *Rollergirls* may not revolutionize the television (or cultural) landscape overnight, but it offers a potential (although not necessarily "super") model for future series.

Works Cited

"About the Show." *aetv.com.* A&E Television Networks, n.d. Accessed on 1 Apr. 2007 <http://www.aetv.com/rollergirls/rg_about.jsp>.

Allen, Robert C., ed. *Channels of Discourse Reassembled.* 2nd ed. Chapel Hill: U of North Carolina P, 1992.

"Big Time." *Rollergirls: The Complete Season One.* Arts and Entertainment Home Video. Go Go Luckey Productions, 2006. DVD.

Brundson, Charlotte and Lynne Spigel. *Feminist Television Criticism: A Reader. 2nd Ed.* New York: Open University Press, 2008.

"The C Word." *Rollergirls: The Complete Season One.* Arts and Entertainment Home Video. Go Go Luckey Productions, 2006. DVD.

Cohen, Greta L., ed. *Women in Sport: Issues and Controversies.* Newbury Park: Sage, 1993.

Coppock, Vicki, Deena Haydon, and Ingrid Richter. *Illusions of Post-Feminism: New Women, Old Myths.* Washington, DC: Taylor and Francis, 1995.

Daniels, Les. *Wonder Woman: The Complete History.* San Francisco: Chronicle, 2000.

Dow, Bonnie. *Prime-Time Feminism: Television, Media Culture, and the Women's Movement since 1970.* Philadelphia: U of Pennsylvania P, 1996.

Fingeroth, Danny. *Superman on the Couch.* New York: Continuum International, 2004.

Fuller, Linda K., ed. *Sport, Rhetoric, and Gender: Historical Perspectives and Media Representations.* New York: Palgrave, 2006.

Levine, Elana. *Feminist Media Studies* Volume 8, No. 4, 2008. 375–389.

"The Love Boat." *Rollergirls: The Complete Season One.* Arts and Entertainment Home Video. Go Go Luckey Productions, 2006. DVD.

"Meet the Girls." *aetv.com.* A&E Television Networks, n.d. Accessed on 1 Apr. 2007 <http://www.aetv.com/rollergirls/rg_meet_the_girls.jsp>.

Muir, John Kenneth. *The Encyclopedia of Superheroes on Film and Television.* Jefferson: McFarland, 2004.

Munford, Stasia. "Wake up and Smell the Lipgloss: Gender, Generation, and the (a) Politics of Girl Power." *Third Wave Feminism: A Critical Exploration.* Ed. Stacy Gillis, Gillian Howie, and Rebecca Munford. New York: Palgrave, 2006. 142–53.

"No Pain, No Jane." *Rollergirls: The Complete Season One.* Arts and Entertainment Home Video. Go Go Luckey Productions, 2006. DVD.

Owen, Susan A., Sarah R. Stein, and Leah R. Vende Berg. *Bad Girls: Cultural Politics and Media Representations of Transgressive Women.* New York: Lang, 2007.

"Punky Needs a Life." *Rollergirls: The Complete Season One.* Arts and Entertainment Home Video. Go Go Luckey Productions, 2006. DVD.

Ringrose, Jessica and Valerie Walkerdine. *Feminist Media Studies* Volume 8, No. 3, 2008. 227–246.

"Rollerball." *Rollergirls: The Complete Season One.* Arts and Entertainment Home Video. Go Go Luckey Productions, 2006. DVD.

Rollergirls: The Complete Season One. Arts and Entertainment Home Video. Go Go Luckey Productions, 2006. DVD.

"The Rookie." *Rollergirls: The Complete Season One.* Arts and Entertainment Home Video. Go Go Luckey Productions, 2006. DVD.

"Sister Mary Jane." *aetv.com.* A&E Television Networks, n.d. Accessed on 1 Apr. 2007 <http://www.aetv.com/rollergirls/rg_cast_crew.jsp?index=1&type=actor>.

Stasia, Christina Lucia. "'Wham! Bam! Thank You Ma'am!': The New Public/Private Female Action Hero." *Third Wave Feminism: A Critical Exploration.* Ed. Stacy Gillis, Gillian Howie, and Rebecca Munford. New York: Palgrave, 2006. 175–84.

"Undefeated." *Rollergirls: The Complete Season One.* Arts and Entertainment Home Video. Go Go Luckey Productions, 2006. DVD.

Notes

1. The term is often used in a heteronormative context. It usually refers to how women balance the traditional demands of raising a family with managing their careers. However, not all women (straight, bi, or gay) choose to do both. My emphasis here on the "superwoman" as an inclusive concept is in no way meant to exclude those women who fall outside its traditional definition or who choose not to participate in this particular endeavor. Rather, it is meant to highlight how *Rollergirls* extends the "superwoman as superhero" concept as a post-feminist narrative strategy.

2. The episode focuses on the first interstate roller derby battle in thirty years between the TXRD All-Star team and the Arizona Renegade Rebels. According to the rollergirls, the ultimate goal is to take roller derby to a national level.

3. Only two episodes do not include a roller derby bout within the narrative: "Searching for Ann Cavello" and "Rollerball."

8

■ Going All in on the Global Market

The Rhetorical Performance of Neoliberal Capitalism on ESPN's *World Series of Poker*

□ **Jay P. Childers**

Anyone who has ever sat down to play a serious game of poker knows how central one's performance is to winning. Having good cards and knowing the percentage odds of potential winning hands will get one only so far. Beyond luck and math, poker is a human enterprise. Good poker players are always trying to *read* their opponents—discover *tells* that will let them know just how good their opponent's hand really is. Is she talking too much? Why does she keep rubbing her ear? Is her leaning in over the table a sign of strength or nervousness? Is she bluffing or not? Great poker players go further than simply asking these questions; great poker players learn to use this human aspect of the game to their advantage. A great poker player learns to control her nerves and to use fake tells to trick her opponents. She may hesitate before calling a bet in order to seem nervous when she knows she has the best hand. She might raise big to seem confident when she is not. And the better she has learned her opponents' behaviors the better she will be able to misdirect them. Playing a game of poker is then very much rhetorical dueling, players performing against one another in the hopes of persuading each other to make a mistake. It is, of course, this performative aspect of poker that makes it so challenging and also what has helped it become such big business.

In recent years, poker has certainly emerged as big business for media. The driving force behind poker's growth are young amateur players who have found learning poker increasingly easy due to "the plethora of books, blogs, and DVDs now easily accessible, and the rapid growth of poker online" (Poker 32). Indeed, online poker has become so popular that it "had worldwide revenues of around $15 billion in 2006" (Poker 32). In addition to online poker, the game has also found a great deal of success on television. According to 2007 tracking, poker was "the third most watched sport on television in the United States, after car racing and American football" (Poker 33). And no show in the United States has been more popular than ESPN's coverage of the annual Las Vegas World Series of Poker tournament that routinely draws audiences of more than one million viewers. ESPN's televised serial broadcast *World Series of Poker* (*WSOP*) has become television's preeminent celebration of poker.

ESPN's *WSOP* does a great deal more, however, than simply offer coverage of the Las Vegas tournament. As a much celebrated piece of mediated popular culture, the *WSOP* helps the viewer make sense of the changing economic structures of the twenty-first century. That is, the *WSOP* offers its viewers "mediated symbolic equipment to help them confront certain real life problems" (Brummett 247). The show does this by presenting the viewer a particular view of rhetorically performed poker play through its use of narrative structures, thematic frames, and discursive cues. That is, the *WSOP* represents a rhetorical site of struggle hidden behind the dramatic entertainment of men and women betting literally millions of dollars in competitive card play. Given the *WSOP*'s popularity, its ideological discourse is compelling and powerful and more than worthy of critical analysis.

Through an ideological analysis of ESPN's coverage of the 2007 World Series of Poker's No Limit Texas Hold'em Main Event, I argue here that the show advances a neoliberal global capitalism worldview—*a system that promotes the international realization of a free market, competitive capitalism in which the state is no more than a facilitator and the individual is prized over larger collective organizations*. To make this argument, I start by defining further what a neoliberal global capitalistic worldview means. Next, I briefly explain the rules of No Limit Texas Hold'em and offer a brief history of the World Series of Poker tournament. Then I turn my attention to an ideological reading of *WSOP* focusing on the performative aspects of the Main Event emphasized by the show's production and editing. As a complete text, I will ultimately reveal the *WSOP*'s neoliberal, globalized, capitalistic rhetorical performance, which certainly supports the global media market ESPN and its parent company, Disney, work within.

■ Neoliberal Global Capitalism

Neoliberalism is the belief that society works best with the least amount of state intervention (Hardt and Negri 167). As a response to the social welfare system imposed during the Progressive movement through the Johnson administration's push for the Great Society, neoliberalism represents a return to more classical notions of liberalism as they were espoused by Adam Smith. This is the point Nancy Auerbach makes when she suggests that "neoliberalism is…a revived form of economic liberalism, as both concepts share critical common core market-oriented ideas and directives" (27). The emphasis in these original conceptions of liberalism centered around individual autonomy. As Charles Taylor has argued, the two underlying assumptions that guide modern liberal thinking in the United States are (1) that egalitarianism is preferred to social hierarchies and (2) that individual rights take precedence over collective rights (60–61).

While neoliberalism shares the basic assumptions of egalitarianism and individual rights, it is more concerned with creating the governmental and market forces necessary to make such basic tenets a reality. By focusing upon the system, neoliberalism can be understood as ideological. This is the point Auerbach makes when she notes that neoliberalism is a "mental model [that] tells members of society how an industrial market economy works" (47). As an ideology, neoliberalism, Colin Hay has recently argued, can be characterized, among other things, as a system that is confident "in the market as an efficient mechanism for the allocation of scarce resources," believes "in the desirability, all things being equal, of a limited and non-interventionist role for the state," and defends "individual liberty" (54). Neoliberalism is then the ideologically constructed relationship between the people, the government, and the market in such a way as to promote free-market capitalism.

Although free-market capitalism is the dominant economic system in the United States and many other Western nations, it is not the only viable form of capitalism. Economic theorist Michel Albert argues just this point when he suggests that capitalism has "two faces, two personalities" (18). For Albert, there is the overly individualistic and competitive American version of capitalism and one that has German roots and more recent Asian manifestations that emphasizes more on collective concerns. More recently, a group of economists has identified four different versions of capitalism—entrepreneurial, big-firm, state-directed, and oligarchic. Although all four of their categories offer important insights, particularly relevant to the argument below are entrepreneurial and big-firm capitalism. Entrepreneurial capitalism, what they identify as the current dominant US model, emphasizes the greatest individual autonomy and market access. It rewards those individuals willing to take great risks and offers only limited forms of punishment for those whose risky ventures fail (Baumol, Litan, and Schramm 7–8). In contrast, big-firm capitalism, which is historically emblematic of the United States, emphasizes the importance of established, dominant companies to monitor the marketplace with as little regulation from the government as possible. Although there are certainly rules to which these companies must adhere, the assumption is that such established firms have already proven their viability and will continue to work within acceptable limits in order to sustain themselves. Put together, these two models, entrepreneurial and big-firm, represent the recommended capitalistic synthesis the authors believe should be promoted internationally.

At the international level, the advance of capitalism is understood in terms of globalization, the increasing interconnectedness of nations, companies, and individuals. While some argue that globalization is an expressly sought after goal of a few international interests, such arguments seem to miss the historical progression that international trade and travel have followed over the past several centuries. That is, with the increased speed and ease of international travel and the creation of global communication networks, globalization has been inevitable. But how nations engage a globalizing world and to what extent such a shift is celebrated or derided remain contentious issues. Whether one wants to think of globalization as a way to describe an inevitable shift or prescriptively as a system advocated through the interests of powerful economic controllers, it is, nevertheless, extremely difficult to argue against the thesis that the world has seen in recent decades a growth in globalization.

Globalization is, of course, not new. Explorers have been sailing the world for millennia and nations have risen and fallen through economic and military conquests of global proportions for centuries. What has happened in recent decades is a recognition of the "widening and deepening of the international flows of trade, capital, technology, and information within a single integrated global market" (Petras and Veltmeyer 49). What has accompanied these increasingly strengthened transnational networks is the emphasis on capitalism and the communications needed to advance capitalism on a global scale. So connected are globalization and capitalism today that it has led some to talk of global capitalism as one idea. Noting what he calls a 500-year march of globalization, William Robinson has suggested the following:

Today we are in the early phases of the fourth epoch of capitalism—globalization—highlighted technologically by the microchip and the computer—symbols of the "information age"—and politically by the collapse of twentieth century attempts at socialism and the failure of a whole generation of Third World national liberation movements to offer an alternative to world capitalism. (5)

According to Robinson, globalization and capitalism have merged so that the former can be understood today only through the latter's growing influence of control over the world market.

As one can easily see, neoliberalism, capitalism, and globalization are individual concepts with clear relationships to one another. Neoliberalism is an ideological system suited to the advancement of capitalism, and globalization has led to the increasing hegemonic hold capitalism has on the world market. Each concept can still be understood autonomously, but all three have become integrally connected with one another. In this connection, a neoliberal global capitalism is, moreover, an ideological system promoting a set of power relations that, as noted above, emphasize an individualized free-market, competitive capitalism on a global scale. Whether these power relations are positive or negative is an important question but not one within the scope of this chapter. What is important to note is that this ideological system has become increasingly dominant in Western public culture, and it can, therefore, be found manifested in many forms of popular culture. What I argue below is that the *WSOP*, one representative of the broader popular culture, ideologically models the neoliberal global capitalistic system through the ways in which it presents the performance of poker.

■ No Limit Texas Hold'em

Texas Hold'em has become one of the most popular casino card games in the world. With its roots traced back to Texas during the early twentieth century, Texas Hold'em (originally simply Hold'em) made its way to the Las Vegas casinos in the 1960s. As the more traditional draw poker allowed for only two rounds of betting, some in Las Vegas found Texas Hold'em's four rounds of betting and increased need for strategy more enticing. As poker great Crandell Addington notes, No Limit Texas Hold'em was popular among players long before it became a staple of Las Vegas casinos, but the casinos, led by Sid Wyman of the Dunes in 1969, eventually saw the need to draw in the high-stakes players for business (77–78).

What distinguishes Texas Hold'em from the more traditional draw poker popularized by Westerns and other film genres for decades is that all the players share five community cards that are revealed to everyone at the table. A hand of Texas Hold'em begins with each player being dealt two cards—the only two cards each player is dealt—known as the hole cards. After each player looks at her own cards, a round of betting follows. Next, the dealer places three cards face up on the table; these initial three community cards are referred to as "the flop." These cards are considered community cards and open to be played by all of the players. After these three cards, another round of betting ensues. This is followed by a fourth community card, "the turn" card, and a third round of betting. Finally, a fifth community card, "the river" card, is placed face up and this is followed by the fourth and final round of betting. In the end, each player has her own two cards and the five community cards, and her goal is to create the highest five-card poker hand.

While Texas Hold'em is usually played with blinds (set amounts of money that two players must put in the pot before ever seeing even one card) to force play and preset betting limits that cannot be exceeded, No Limit Texas Hold'em allows any player, at any given betting opportunity, to go "all in." To go all in literally means that a player puts all of her chips at risk in the pot during a hand. No Limit play, therefore, raises the risks and rewards available to each player on each and every hand. Such excitement has much to do with ESPN's *WSOP*'s popularity.

Although the World Series of Poker has become clearly identified with ESPN, the popular poker tournament actually began in 1968. Even from the beginning, the World Series of Poker was a series of tournaments that included, among other poker games, five-card draw, seven-card stud, and Texas Hold'em. This tradition continues today with the 2007 World Series of Poker offering fifty-five different game variations, but No Limit Texas Hold'em has always been the most celebrated game at the tournament. In 1971, the World Series of Poker ended with the first Texas Hold'em Main Event and the winner that year, Johnny Moss, was voted by his peers to be the World Champion of Poker. He beat out five other players. While the popularity of the World Series of Poker grew over the years, the number of entrants in the Main Event did not exceed one hundred players until 1982. Even as recently as 2003, the Main Event drew only 839 entrants. But by 2007, with the help of ESPN's coverage, 6,358 players sat down at the Main Event, which lasted twelve days and had a total prize pool of almost $60 million. The winner's prize was $8.25 million.

■ ESPN's World Series of Poker

With over six thousand players and twelve days of poker play, one can surmise that ESPN filmed thousands of hours of the Main Event. Each day a featured table equipped with nine small cameras to let viewers see each player's two hole cards was filmed for the entirety of the day. In addition to the featured table, camera operators moved around the rest of the tables following the action and individual players throughout the tournament. Outside of actual poker play, at least three dozen players were filmed being interviewed about their lives and poker strategies. Ultimately, these thousands of hours of footage were edited down to sixteen episodes (each approximately forty-five minutes, totaling twelve hours) focused on the individual performances of only a small number of players. How ESPN edited all of this footage into a series of narratives for viewers to follow reveals the rhetorical choices that create the neoliberal global capitalistic ideological discourse underlying the *WSOP*.

■ Neoliberalism

At its core, neoliberalism is one type of relationship between the individual and the government, and it prefers to limit the extent of government interference in the lives of individuals. In poker, the analogous relationship is between the individual players and the house. Held at Harrah's Las Vegas Rio Hotel and Casino, the World Series of Poker tournament most certainly had house and tournament controls in place to deal with the thousands of entrants and millions of dollars. How ESPN's *WSOP* chose to portray these controlling forces reveals, however, that they delegate these central performers to unimportant, often invisible roles. What the viewer is left with, then, is the sense that the poker games being played have little to no governance.

Managing thousands of card players and millions of poker chips requires a good deal of planning and infrastructure. This begins with the simple fact that each table requires a dealer, whose job it is to oversee the players, deal the cards, count chips, and keep the play moving forward. Despite the hundreds of dealers required at the Main Event and their central role in each and every hand dealt, dealers are very rarely shown speaking. In fact, dealers are rarely shown at all. For the most part, all the viewer ever sees of the dealers are his or her hands dealing the cards or pushing chips around. On the few occasions when a player does make some kind of playing error that the dealer would normally correct, it is the other players who are most often shown enforcing the rules. In the few instances when cameras do focus on dealer's bodies and faces, they do so because a player has stood up and is talking to the dealer, usually pleading with the dealer to give him the card he needs to complete his hand. Even in these moments, the dealers remain silent and unobtrusive.

In addition to the dealers, the Main Event is literally policed by officials who are there to keep players in order and oversee the dealers. These officials are meant to make sure that everyone follows the rules and no one becomes unruly. Despite their continuous presence around each of the tables, these officials are never mentioned on *WSOP*. Only once during the sixteen episodes is one ever heard talking. In Episode 11, the show offers a montage of players on "tilt," which is used to describe a player who is losing badly and unable to stay focused and keep his emotions under control. During the montage, one of the officials is shown forcing an unruly player to leave his table and take a thirty-minute break to calm down. Outside of this one instance, the World Series of Poker officials are seen only in the background walking around observing but never interfering with the poker play.

The only continuous sign of external forces are the announcers. In much the same way a baseball game is covered by two announcers, the *WSOP* is narrated by two men—Lon McEachern and Norman Chad. McEachern offers play-by-play analysis; Chad is the color commentator tending more often towards humor and player biography. While these men are rarely shown, their voices can be heard throughout the show offering the viewer both pertinent information and entertainment. They do not, however, have any influence on the games being played nor do they ever talk about the dealers and officials.

Instead of demonstrating the many ways in which the poker players are constrained by the tournament rules and its officials, the *WSOP* portrays the tournament and the players as being overseen by an invisible hand. This invisible hand is, of course, what Adam Smith, the great-grandfather of neoliberal thought, argued maintained an open-market system of economic exchange. Smith argued that, instead of depending on the public good and governmental intervention, it is "by pursuing his own interest [one] frequently promotes that of the society more effectually than when he really intends to promote it" (423). It is this concept of the invisible hand that guides many supporters of neoliberalism. Neoliberalists believe that the capitalistic market can take care of itself and, therefore, governmental institutions must be restrained (Roy, Denzau, and Willett 8). Given the *WSOP*'s lack of focus on the governing institutions at the World Series of Poker Main Event, the viewer cannot help but get the impression that the tournament is governed, if at all, by an invisible hand and the players are the ones in charge.

■ Globalization

Despite the fact that the World Series of Poker takes place each year in Las Vegas, Nevada, and only one-fourth of the players are born outside the United States, the *WSOP* emphasizes the integral performative role of international players. In doing so, it place the neoliberal governing structure within a global context. This focus is so central to the *WSOP* that it begins with the opening credits. In the opening minute of Episode 1, the viewer hears a voice-over state that the World Series of Poker is the "Greatest Tournament in the World." Just seconds later, professional poker player Annie Duke suggests that what makes the World Series of Poker so exciting is that it is "the one that the world looks at." The very next shot is of fellow professional poker player Phil Helmuth saying that whoever wins the Main Event gets the title "World Champion of Poker." And finally, the opening credits also show international scope with a past winner wrapped in an Australian flag, dancing next to a poker table and chanting "Aussie, Aussie, Aussie!" Following the opening credits, the announcer states that the 6,358 players in the main even represent the "World's Best." Regardless then of the actual number of international players and the appeal of the tournament overseas, the *WSOP* wants its audience to view the show as a globalized event from the very beginning of the series.

In addition to these opening moments, the *WSOP* repeatedly reminds the audience of the international players. The *WSOP* does this primarily through two techniques. The first global emphasis can be found at the featured table. At the center of the tournament floor, the featured table offers the fans in attendance video screens to watch and the television viewers cameras with which to see the hole cards of the players (an important feature of the television spectacle, since it allows the viewer to feel in on the action). The featured table of nine players is so central to the *WSOP* that it is actually separated from the other tables and players. What is important to note about the featured table is that the players are chosen arbitrarily; they do not represent the chip leaders or the more well-known poker celebrities. So the fact that the featured table is never without at least three easily identifiable international players (most usually through their accents) reflects the intentions of the *WSOP* to emphasize the international appeal of the show.

The second way the *WSOP* emphasizes globalization is through the repeated reminders of player's origins. While many of the international players have accents that would make it obvious to the viewer that they are originally from another country, the *WSOP* announcers identify the players they focus on by country as well. This is most commonly done by simply stating a player's name and his country. So, for example, the announcers refer to players as "Nicholas Petrejov from Sweden" or "Michael Madsen from Denmark." Although many of the American-born players are also identified by their city and state of origin, these national identifiers may seem of little importance, but they are buttressed by many other moments of emphasis as well. In one such instance, South African Raymand Rhame has several winning hands in a row, to which color announcer Norman Chad offers, "We've created a South African senior citizen monster" (Episode 14). In another example, Chad notes that Philip Hilm lives in Cambridge, England, but that he is originally from Denmark, his father is from Poland and his mother is English. To this Chad adds, "He's the World Series wrapped in one person." So strong is the international emphasis on the *WSOP* that it comes as little surprise to hear Chad comment on the final nine players thusly: "Major League Baseball has its World Series, but it's a very small world—just the United States and Canada. This year at the World Series of Poker we have seen a huge international influence from the very first day, and now it is down to these nine player from seven different countries."

The players at the World Series of Poker Main Event were certainly an international crowd. And the final table was represented by a number of internationally born players, although these were only six (i.e., Denmark, England, Laos, Russia, South Africa, and Vietnam), one of which had long lived in the United States. While these are facts of the World Series of Poker, the *WSOP*'s focus on the performance of international players is a theme that runs throughout the sixteen episodes of the Main Event. This focus, moreover, works to celebrate the individual players and highlight the international playing field simultaneously. In doing this, the *WSOP* represents a globalized group within its neoliberal governing structure.

■ Capitalism

At its most basic, capitalism is an economic system in which property is privately owned and used primarily for profit. The game of Texas Hold'em can obviously be seen as a capitalistic game. Each player has her own chips, which she privately owns, and her entire goal is to gain more chips by betting her own chips against other players. As philosopher Raymond Belliotti has put it, "from a Marxist perspective, poker players are capitalist entrepreneurs writ small" (25). Capitalism is, however, more than just private property and profit. This is especially true of the entrepreneurial capitalism identified above as the dominant form of capitalism in the United States today. Entrepreneurial capitalism requires, after all, innovative skills and a willingness to take risks.

It emphasizes individual profit and "discourage[s] activity that aims to divide up the economic pie rather than increase its size" (Baumol, Litan, and Schramm 7). And entrepreneurial capitalism must be an open system to which anyone can gain access with only limited restrictions. That is, entrepreneurial capitalism must acknowledge and make manifest the rags-to-riches narrative central to the success of the system. The *WSOP* consistently and clearly demonstrates an ideological discourse that supports an entrepreneurial capitalism by focusing on performances of established skills, risk taking, and individual success.

To sit down at a table and play in the World Series of Poker No Limit Texas Hold'em Main Event each player must pay a $10,000 buy-in, a risky venture for all the players since in 2007 only 621 of the 6,358 entrants would get any money in return for their investment. Still, each player starts out with an equal financial base. Not everyone, however, is considered equal once the cards are dealt. The announcers, in fact, spend a good deal of time talking about the difference between the skilled professionals and the many amateurs. While the amateurs' successes are occasionally discussed as surprising streaks or moments of luck, the *WSOP* focuses on the skillful play of established professional poker players who routinely outperform their opponents. In Episode 11, for instance, former world champion Huck Seed is shown playing poorly. After losing several hands he is seen verbally berating himself, but the announcers describe his unfortunate play as a series of bad mistakes and not poor luck. So central is the *WSOP*'s portrayal of poker as skill over luck that Episode 5 is framed around the issue. One minute into the episode, McEachern sets the theme when he states, "in the remaining field filled with brash newcomers stand two of the game's greats including two former champions that know the dangers that lay ahead." This is followed by the two champions offering some advice on the role of luck in poker. The 2005 world champion Joseph Hachem argues, "you can only dodge so many bullets for so many days." And 1998 world champion Scotty Nguyen suggests of the final table that "you have to play good to get there. People think poker is just luck, but skill carries you on." The episode plays this theme out.

While each of the episodes spends a good deal of time focused on established professionals, Episode 5 does so by emphasizing the performative nature inherent in skillful play. Halfway through the episode, attention is turned to professional poker player Kenny Tran as he goes all in against an unknown amateur. With only one card left to be turned over and all the chips in the pot, the winning chances are shown in percentages for each player. The amateur, it is revealed, has a 77% chance of winning the hand. But when Kenny Tran takes down the pot with a surprisingly lucky card on the river, announcer McEachern calls it a "stunning win for Tran." At the end of the episode, a similar situation is shown between professional Miami John Cernuto and another amateur. This time, however, the roles are reversed. With Miami John all in and only one card left to be revealed, his chances of winning the hand are put at 93%. But when the river card gives the amateur the win, both announcers are shocked. Norman Chad suggests that the final card was such a surprise that it hurt him from the announcer's booth and then adds that he "hates to see this class act take that bad beat to end his main event." While Tran's skillful performance seems to underlie his stunning win, Miami John's loss is a bad beat in which an unknown amateur seems to do nothing more than get lucky. This emphasis on established players is the other side of the *WSOP*'s capitalistic ideology, what has been called "big-firm capitalism" (Baumol, Litan, and Schramm 79–85). That is, the *WSOP* reinforces, in addition to entrepreneurial capitalism, a belief in the importance of a limited number of established players to the game of poker.

Although the *WSOP* may downplay the role that luck plays in any poker game, it does not downplay the role of risk. Most of the featured hands that are shown during the sixteen episodes are, in fact, hands in which one of the players goes all in and puts all his chips at risk. This celebration of risk taking is, in fact, something so important to the *WSOP* series that each episode offers the Degree Deodorant-sponsored Degree All In Moment. One example can suffice to demonstrate the dramatic nature of this episodic moment. Episode 9's theme is that of age and experience. The episode spends much of its time focused on the twenty-one-year-old chip leader Dario Minieri from Italy, whom the announcer's refer to as "the whiz kid." At one point in the episode, the other players at the table with Minieri are actually shown discussing whether or not they can refer to him as kid, and later in the show older and younger players discuss the advantages and disadvantages of aggressive youth and wise experience. And throughout the show, Minieri is often shown playing hands against the much older Allen Levin, both of whom are amateur players. One of their hands is presented as the Degree All In Moment. After the flop and a couple of raises from each player, Minieri raises enough for Levin to call he would have to go all in. As the announcer Norman Chad notes, the raise "would put Allen Levin all in. A decision for Allen Levin's tournament life right here." After a few suspenseful seconds in which the camera focuses on Levin as he decides what to do, Levin says, "Call." At this point, McEachern excitedly announces that "Levin will make the call. This is the Degree All In Moment." And after Levin wins the hand and remains in the tournament, McEachern adds, "A great move for all his chips for Allen Levin. Allen Levin earns the Degree check mark and doubles up." Although any player might very well feel a surge of adrenaline when he puts all his chips at risk and this is one of the more appealing dramatic aspects of No

Limit Texas Hold'em, the *WSOP* goes out of its way to highlight and celebrate such risk taking.

In addition to emphasizing skills and risk, the *WSOP* also focuses a great deal on individual success. No Limit Texas Hold'em is, of course, an individual's game. Only one person can win each hand and only one person can win the tournament. Nevertheless, each table at the World Series of Poker Main Event consists of nine players and one dealer. Some of the players, especially the professionals, know one another and some form of group dynamic surely forms. And with over six thousand players on the first day, it is hard to imagine how the *WSOP* could emphasize individual success. But from the very start, the *WSOP* does emphasize individuals by focusing each show on one or two primary players. On day one, for instance, the focus is clearly on poker great Doyle Brunson and his decades of experience. To highlight this individualism, each episode also takes the one or two players being focused on away from the poker table. Each episode offers individual vignettes where a player is shown sitting in a chair or on a couch talking to the camera about his or her life experiences or poker knowledge. These individual vignettes resemble a cross between daytime talk shows and reality television's confessionals.

Nowhere is this individual success theme more apparent than in Episode 3, which focuses almost exclusively on Chris Moneymaker. For poker fans, Moneymaker's story is well-known, but this does not stop the *WSOP* from retelling the popular narrative. The episode begins with an explanation of what has become known in poker circles as the Moneymaker effect. As Lon McEachern narrates, "Nothing in poker is bigger than the main event. And there's one name to blame." Footage is then shown of Chris Moneymaker winning the 2003 Main Event, and this is followed by Moneymaker saying, "Everybody I talk to says, 'man, I started playing poker because of you.'" And then just seconds later McEachern adds that "players from all walks of life are here hoping to do what Chris Moneymaker did in 2003. It is almost mind boggling how many people are in this room because of that man, Chris Moneymaker." As the episode goes on to explain, Chris Moneymaker entered the 2003 World Series of Poker Main Event through an online satellite tournament win. The twenty-eight-year-old former accountant from Tennessee spent $39 for an online poker tournament and won the game, earning a seat at the Main Event. And against all expectations, Moneymaker won the Main Event. Moneymaker's win in 2003 marks a clear increase in the success of the World Series of Poker in particular and of poker in general. The Moneymaker effect can be seen most easily in the numbers of players attending the Main Event. After Moneymaker's win in 2003, the total number of entrants jumped from 839 to 2,576 in 2004 and grew to 8,773 players in 2006. That is,

Moneymaker has helped make poker a big business for the *World Series of Poker* and ESPN.

Given the Moneymaker effect, it is little surprise to find the *WSOP* spending so much time focused on him. While Moneymaker does not last very long into the tournament, the entire third episode is focused on him and his ability to play. Moneymaker's story works, of course, because it fits a well-established rags-to-riches narrative performance that plays an important role in the American entrepreneurial capitalistic ideology. This story is what Dana Cloud has called in reference to Oprah Winfrey "the success myth," which emphasizes the ability of any one individual to work hard, make sacrifices, and find monetary success in the United States (116). And to emphasize the role Moneymaker's abilities played in his winning the 2003 tournament, the *WSOP* repeatedly emphasize Moneymaker's playing skills. One of the negative issues concerning Moneymaker is that since the 2003 Main Event he has failed to even come close to winning another tournament despite turning pro. Despite these failures and Moneymaker's quick exit at the 2007 Main Event, the *WSOP* announcers do not fail to argue that Moneymaker is a talented player. Following, for instance, a hand in which Moneymaker actually loses many of his chips, Norman Chad notes that "Moneymaker's instincts were spot-on there." This comment is made, it seems, not in reference to Moneymaker's actual play but to the fact that Moneymaker himself says he is about to make a mistake before he makes it. Later, when Moneymaker is shown winning a hand, Chad argues even more strongly, "Who says this guy can't play!" So important to the *WSOP* is Moneymaker's success myth that even after he loses his chips by the end of Episode 3 going out in 4,328th place, Norman Chad ends the episode with this final statement: "Chris Moneymaker, who proved he belonged." To maintain their model of big-firm, entrepreneurial capitalism, the *WSOP* not only repeatedly retells Moneymaker's historical performance, it also repeatedly suggests that he has more than proven that risk taking and luck are not all it takes to succeed at the poker table.

■ The American Dream

While I have shown that the *WSOP* clearly offers the World Series of Poker Main Event through the ideological discursive strategies of neoliberalism, globalization, and capitalism in a variety of symbolic strategies, all three discourses can be found synthesized in the final two episodes of the Main Event coverage. As noted above, this synthesis begins with a focus on the international players at the final table. It is a fact that each player plays for himself and not his country; this does not, however, stop Norman Chad from noting at the beginning of Episode 15 that the final table "resembles soccer's World Cup." And while this international focus is central to these last two episodes, the show does not fail to emphasize the capitalistic impulse by repeatedly showing men in suits surrounded by armed guards counting out the winning prize money in the casino vault and then carrying it out onto the floor and actually stacking it up next to the final table during the last episode. As Lon McEachern notes in the opening seconds of Episode 15, everything has come down to the final table where the real "fight for fame and fortune begins." In the end, the fight comes down to two players perfectly suited to the neoliberal global capitalistic ideology, what the announcers ultimately refer to as "the American dream."

First and second place at the 2007 World Series of Poker Main Event went to two foreign-born players—professional poker player Tuan Lam and amateur Jerry Yang. Lam, originally from Vietnam, and Yang, originally from Laos, had personal stories well-suited to the *WSOP* ideological discourse and the show was not shy to exploit these narratives. As the *WSOP* reveals during the final episode, second place finisher Tuan Lam moved to Ontario, Canada, as a teenager in search of a better life. The announcers point out that Lam, having survived a refugee camp before arriving in Ontario, faced a great deal of adversity when he first moved to Canada and "could not get a job washing dishes for $3 an hour." Instead, Lam's first job in North America was mowing lawns, and his first paycheck was for $280, with which he immediately started playing poker. Lam's success in Canada, the announcers argue, stems from his hard work and a system that rewards such individual drive.

The eventual winner of the 2008 World Series of Poker Main Event was Jerry Yang. Yang, like Lam, also immigrated to North America in his youth after spending time in a refugee camp. And while Yang's humble beginnings in Vietnam are surely noteworthy, the *WSOP* emphasizes Yang's roots much more prominently than they do the reality of his time in the United States, where he has lived the majority of his life. While an amateur at poker, Yang, as the *WSOP* notes briefly, is also a certified psychologist and social worker in California. And while Yang is shown kissing a picture of his six kids each time he makes an important decision at the poker table, more important for the *WSOP*'s ideological discourse is the fact that Yang "got into the Main Event by winning the last satellite seat at his local casino. It cost him $225 to enter." And as Yang wins the final hand, Norman Chad comments that the win represents "An American dream come true for Jerry Yang." And as a parting shot, Lon McEachern offers these words about Jerry Yang's win: "He dealt with hardships his entire life, never lost faith, and persevered at this final table." Unclear as to what hardships Yang endured as a successful psychologist with a wife and six kids, the *WSOP*'s argument is clear—Jerry Yang represents their idealized American dream, one that is built upon a neoliberal global capitalism.

■ Conclusion

In this chapter, I have argued that ESPN's *WSOP* is a mediated sports spectacle that rhetorically argues for a worldview predicated upon neoliberal global capitalism. Through its representation of the 2007 World Series of Poker's No Limit Texas Hold'em Main Event, the *WSOP* offers narrative structures that emphasize the individual success inherent in free-market capitalism. The *WSOP* discursively celebrates the tournament's international players in such a way as to promote globalization as both inevitable and desired. And the *WSOP* frames (both visually and discursively) Texas Hold'em Poker as governed by nothing more than the invisible hand of neoliberalism. And in the end, I showed that the *WSOP* packages even this neoliberal, global capitalistic ideology as the American dream.

In making this argument, I would add here that the *WSOP*'s rhetorical discourse may very well be ideologically overdetermined. ESPN and its parent company Disney are both American media conglomerates with a clear global reach. ESPN is, moreover, a central component of the Disney Corporation. The *International Herald Tribune* made this point in September 2007 when it described ESPN as "the U.S. cable television network that has driven profit growth at Walt Disney for much of this decade" (Fixmer 12). As corporations, ESPN and Disney are certainly capitalistic; that is, they are both out to make as much of a profit for their stakeholders as possible. To make such profits, ESPN and Disney desire, moreover, as little state intervention as possible, as can be seen in their promotion of media deregulation policies both domestically and internationally. And despite being based in the United States, both ESPN and Disney derive a great deal of their profits from international sales and viewership. ESPN itself has international channels that include ESPN Australia, ESPN Brasil, ESPN Latin America, ESPN+ (South America), ESPN Star Sports (Asia), and NASN (Europe). It may come as little surprise that ESPN's *WSOP* promotes an ideology that benefits the company.

While it may be of little surprise, the *WSOP*'s ideological discourse is far from unimportant. What I have hoped to show is that as a mediated sports spectacle, ESPN's *WSOP* does a good deal more than entertain; it, like all popular culture, also teaches its viewers a particular way of viewing the world. And while some popular culture texts may more openly engage in such epistemological strategies, those packaged as sports may more often than not hide their larger rhetorical strategies. To allow them to do so, however, is to let them bluff you off a potentially better hand.

Works Cited

Addington, Crandell. "The History of No-Limit Texas Hold'em." *Doyle Brunson's Super System 2: A Course in Power Poker*. Ed. Doyle Brunson. Las Vegas: Cardoza, 2005.

Albert, Michel. *Capitalism vs. Capitalism: How America's Obsession with Individual Achievement and Short-term Profit Has Led It to the Brink of Collapse*. Trans. Paul Haviland. New York: Four Walls Eight Windows, 1993.

Auerbach, Nancy N. "The Meanings of Neoliberalism." *Neoliberalism: National and Regional Experiments with Global Ideas*. Ed. Ravi K. Roy, Arthur T. Denzau, and Thomas D. Willett. New York: Routledge, 2007. 26–50.

Baumol, William J., Robert E. Litan, and Carl J. Schramm. *Good Capitalism, Bad Capitalism, and the Economics of Growth and Prosperity*. New Haven: Yale UP, 2007.

Belliotti, Raymond A. "Karl Marx Meets Texas Dolly." *Poker and Philosophy: Pocket Rockets and Philosopher Kings*. Ed. Eric Bronson. Chicago: Open Court, 2006. 15–26.

Brummett, Barry. "Electric Literature as Equipment for Living: Haunted House Films." *Critical Studies in Mass Communication* 2.3 (1985): 247–61.

Cloud, Dana L. "Hegemony or Concordance? The Rhetoric of Tokenism in 'Oprah' Winfrey's Rags-to-Riches Biography." *Critical Studies in Mass Communication* 13.2 (1996): 115–37.

Fixmer, Andy. "Disney's Star Player Expected to Slow." *International Herald Tribune* 7 Sept. 2007: Finance 12.

Hardt, Michael, and Antonio Negri. *Multitude: War and Democracy in the Age of Empire*. New York: Penguin, 2004.

Hay, Colin. "The Genealogy of Neoliberalism. *Neoliberalism": National and Regional Experiments with Global Ideas*. Ed. Ravi K. Roy, Arthur T. Denzau, and Thomas D. Willett. New York: Routledge, 2007. 51–70.

Petras, James, and Henry Veltmeyer. "Globalization Unmasked: The Dynamics and Contradictions of Global Capitalism." *Globalization and Change: The Transformation of Global Capitalism*. Ed. Berch Berberoglu. Lanham: Lexington, 2005. 49–64.

Poker: A Big Deal. *The Economist* 22 Dec. 2007: 31–38.

Robinson, William I. *A Theory of Global Capitalism: Production, Class, and State in a Transnational World*. Baltimore: Johns Hopkins UP, 2004.

Roy, Ravi K., Arthur T. Denzau, and Thomas D. Willett. "Introduction: Neoliberalism as a Shared Mental Model." *Neoliberalism: National and Regional Experiments with Global Ideas*. Ed. Ravi K. Roy, Arthur T. Denzau, and Thomas D. Willett. New York: Routledge, 2007. 3–13.

Smith, Adam. *The Wealth of Nations*. 1776. Ed. Edwin Cannan. New York: Modern Library, 1937.

Taylor, Charles. "The Politics of Recognition." *Multiculturalism and "The Politics of Recognition."* Ed. Amy Gutmann. Princeton: Princeton UP, 1992.

World Series of Poker. ESPN. 21 Aug.–8 Oct. 2007.

9

■ *Lucha Libre*

Mexican Wrestlers and the Portrayal
of Politics in the Arena

□ Laura Barberena

For the funeral, it was important for people to see him in his mask as
they were not going to see Rodolfo Guzman, but El Santo, so yes,
he was buried with his mask on.
—*El Hijo del Santo [The Son of the Saint] (Rothstein)*

People need heroes. Before his death in 1984, Rodolfo Guzman fulfilled that
need for many, particularly for Mexican audiences of little economic means.
He did so not as himself, but rather as someone greater than himself. Guzman
was and continues to be one of the most celebrated wrestlers in Mexico's
Lucha Libre, loosely translated as free-style wrestling. He donned the mask of
El Santo el Enmascarado de Plata (The Saint with a Silver Mask). He was most
commonly known simply as *El Santo,* and he became one of *Lucha Libre's*
most renowned characters.

What exactly is *Lucha Libre?* Some liken it to professional wrestling in the
United States. Indeed, *Lucha Libre* does share some similarities with America's

World Wrestling Entertainment (WWE)[1]. Like the WWE, *Lucha Libre* wrestlers or *luchadores* are morally coded and narratives unfold to pit good against evil. But Mexican wrestling has a style all its own.

The free-style fighting of *Lucha Libre* brings together in a wrestling ring opponents using a combination of various popular fighting techniques or combative art forms. Wrestling, boxing, kickboxing, judo, and jujitsu are "blended with the elements of soap opera and dramatic storytelling, physical comedy, incredible athletics, suspense and intrigue" to form what is called *Lucha Libre* (Madigan 29). But what truly sets it apart from other wrestling genres, such as those of the United States or Japan, for example, is the action— it's excessively flamboyant and borders on outrageous. The *luchadores* put on a spectacle with electrifying energy, flying through the air more like circus acrobats than wrestlers. Mix this kind of over-the-top action with theatrical, dramatic performances and you begin to get a picture of what *Lucha Libre* is all about. To completely understand it, you simply must experience it live.

Why do I refer to Guzman as a renowned *character* rather than a decorated athlete? After all, he demonstrated tremendous athletic ability in the ring. He was able to throw his opponents over his shoulder and across the wrestling ring, leaping on them from atop the ropes, and use his brute strength to pin them down until the referee's hand slapped down on the mat three times and bellowed "uno, dos, tres," to signify the end of the match. In fact, virtually all of the wrestlers who perform on the *Lucha Libre* circuit demonstrate this kind of athletic agility. Mexican wrestlers harness great physical ability that is matched only by their acting skills, which is key in moving along the story narrative that unfolds and develops during the match. It is the abundance of theatrics, story telling, acrobatics, and slapstick that makes *Lucha Libre* more of an entertainment event than a sport. Yet, this sport of wrestling continues to be promoted and advertised as the reason for the gathering even though audiences essentially witness a fake competition. That is to say that the outcomes of the matches are predetermined by the industry. Dramatic storylines are developed across characters and matches that incorporate narrative cliffhangers to keep the audience hooked on the action, a ploy reminiscent of soap operas.

In a genuine sporting event, such as soccer, there is a shared understanding among the audience that a real contest is taking place and that the events that are unfolding are indeed spontaneous and not scripted ahead of time. The predetermined nature of the wrestling matches in *Lucha Libre* disqualifies it as a genuine sport. That is not to say that *Lucha Libre* doesn't emulate sport. In fact, it can be argued that it intentionally resembles sport both in form and content (Atkinson). But fundamentally, it is the performance of sport rather than a sport itself. Unlike legitimate sports, *Lucha Libre* brings together wrestlers and audience in such a way that they each take on a performative role in the event, as do the referees and announcers. And yet, in the midst of all this performance and ritual, and despite the absence of true competition, this pseudo sport remains very popular among the Mexican working class.

In this chapter, I'll argue that *Lucha Libre* creates a space for a kind of performance that is different from other types of performance genres such as speech, theater, and dance. *Lucha Libre* metaphorically wrestles with the political and social realities of the Mexican working class within the ring and invites the audience to take an active and participatory role in this performance. This invitation is different from that made by its American counterpart because of a key central element—the masked wrestlers. I'll deconstruct the masked wrestler and his/her symbolic function in the overall performance act. In addition, I'll explore the ways in which the larger symbolic function provides a unique form of meaning, allowing the audience to interpret and cope with the complex world around them, more so for members of the lower economic groups than others. To that end, I'll attempt to identify what rhetorical effects are produced from class struggle narratives, implicit or otherwise. More fundamentally, I'll explore what it means to say that *Lucha Libre* is performative and why this type of sports genre calls for a performative analysis.

■ The Art of Mexican Wrestling

Likely the first time most non-Hispanics encountered the term *Lucha Libre* was when they heard it at the movies in 2006 in the American-made film *Nacho Libre* starring Jack Black (Méndez). Few realize that the film was actually loosely based on a real Mexican wrestler named *Fray Tormenta* (Friar Storm). Father Serio Gutiérrez Benitez was an actual Mexican priest who moonlighted as a masked *luchador* in order to raise money to support his orphanage (Jones). He survived over four thousand bouts spanning twenty-three years. When his true identity was revealed and it was learned that he was actually a Catholic priest and not just a person acting like a priest, opponents grew hesitant about challenging him for fear of audience retaliation. *Fray Tormenta* was forced into retirement in 2005 (Sullivan).

Lucha Libre has actually been in existence in Mexico since the 1930s. The man who is credited for developing it there is Don Salvador Lutteroth, a successful entrepreneur and businessman born in 1897 in the small town of Colotlan, Mexico. He had attended a wresting match at Liberty Hall in El Paso, Texas, where he witnessed the crowd react loudly and positively to an American masked wrestler named "Cyclone" MacKay. Lutteroth believed that the mystery and intrigue surrounding the masked wrestlers would be well received in Mexico. Moreover, he felt that the combination of sport, wrestling, and entertainment would be embraced by the people of Mexico. He was right. Just a decade after he and his business partner, Francisco Ahumada, combined a small number of investors to start the company *Empresa Mexicana de la Lucha Libre,* the first arena exclusively built for *Lucha Libre* broke ground. The *Arena Coliseo* seated three thousand spectators. Working-class Mexicans immediately took a liking to *Lucha Libre.* Shows were sold out and patrons were turned away at the doors. By 1956, the sport had such a following that a twenty-thousand-seat arena, Arena México, was built in Mexico City (Madigan).

The first matches took place in Mexico City, but over the years, many title fights migrated north to cities such as Monterrey, Torreón, Reynosa, Nuevo Laredo, and Tijuana ("Wrestling Titles"). These cities are also home to Mexico's *maquiladora* industry that employs over a million Mexican low-wage workers. *Maquiladoras* are foreign-owned factories or assembly plants in Mexico that import materials for assembly and then export the assembled goods. These factories draw, employ, and sustain a large working class sector, which makes up *Lucha Libre's* fan base.

Though *Lucha Libre* has rules similar to those in American wrestling, the audiences and symbolism in Mexican wrestling are entirely different (Beale). In *Lucha Libre,* unlike American wrestling, heroes and villains are clearly defined and are labeled good or bad by the announcer over the loudspeaker as they enter the ring. While it is true that American wrestlers are also morally coded, it is not so explicit. Good and bad are implied by the wrestler's actions, costuming, and face makeup, and reinforced by the announcers who call the action (Oppliger 10).

In *Lucha Libre,* the good guy is known as the *técnico* or *científico* and the bad guy is known as the *rudo* (Levi, "Sport and Melodrama" 63). Matches consist of one *técnico* against one *rudo,* or teams of two or three each. The object is to win two out of three rounds to win the match. Wrestlers can be immediately disqualified if they remove their opponent's mask. The mask is central to the persona of the Mexican wrestler. With the mask comes freedom—freedom to set aside the wrestler's own real life to become a character that has its own, separate life. "The mask unleashes a part hidden deep within the Luchador's psyche that he has tried to keep hidden. Wearing the mask allows the Luchador a sense of freedom to be who he wants to be, and how he wants to act comes alive" (Madigan 60). For Mexican wrestlers, the mask is the single most important thing in their life. If the mask is removed in the ring, with it goes the mystery, suspense, and allure. If the real identity of the wrestler is revealed to the audience, his/her career is ruined. Thus, removing the opponent's mask during a bout constitutes killing the persona, a move that is, without dispute, out-of-bounds.

Over the years, *Lucha Libre* has enjoyed much success and has turned many wrestlers into national and even international celebrities. *El Santo* is easily the most iconic. Others who enjoyed similar fame include Blue Demon and *Mil Mascaras* (A Thousand Masks). Their personas transcended the ring, and they were introduced to other performance forms and new audiences. They were successful in their adaptation. *El Santo,* with the help of Blue Demon, played Mexican masked superheroes on the silver screen and took on vampires, werewolves, and other scoundrels, thus entertaining thousands of moviegoers. And, comic books called *fotonovelas* were also a huge success in promoting the masked crusaders to new fans.

Nearly seventy-five years after its introduction to Mexican audiences, *Lucha Libre* continues to draw fans to arenas. It has also captured the attention of scholars from Mexico and the United States who want to better understand the appeal of Mexican wrestling with working class audiences and uncover the relationship between this audience and the wrestlers.

■ Academic Approaches to Wrestling

Roland Barthes' essay "The World of Wrestling" is credited with establishing the field of professional wrestling studies. Academics have approached professional wrestling with a variety of critical lenses including those that are political, social, cultural, and gendered. Barthes likened professional wrestling to Greek drama, not sports. He viewed wrestling as a form of myth (Levi, "Sport and Melodrama" 58). Barthes' positioning of wrestling in the genre of Greek drama situates him as a structuralist. Barthes occupies one of two schools of thought that have taken up the performative nature of wrestling: structuralists and interactionists. Structuralists read wrestling as highly performative, with a social contract between performer and audience, where the audience understands that the matches are not "real." In this relationship, audiences can be analyzed as experiencing catharsis. Monsiváis and Blanco are two such scholars who believe that the appeal of *Lucha Libre* is a straightforward catharsis (see also Levi, "Sport and Melodrama" 62).

Levi too has examined *Lucha Libre* apart from the wrestling genre as a whole. Her interpretation of *Lucha Libre* as melodrama is also a structuralist read. Levi suggests that *Lucha Libre* is a melodrama because audiences observe the morally coded characters act out struggles between good and evil, the sport relies on the use of disguises, and it conceals structural ambiguities (Levi, "Sport and Melodrama"). These are three central features to the melodramatic mode. But, structuralists overlook an important element of *Lucha Libre,* audience participation in the spectacle.

Interactionists are scholars who recognize the co-production shared between wrestler and audience. They have been described as seeing wrestling as a social drama (Levi, "Sport and Melodrama" 58). Freedman and Webley are two such thinkers. They situate the performance of wrestling between the wrestlers and the spectators (see also Levi, "Sport and Melodrama" 58).

Although I generally agree with the interactionists, I think these scholars fall just short of understanding what happens with wrestlers and audiences at *Lucha Libre.* I believe that the audience adds an extra layer of performance that other sports don't have, thus situating *Lucha Libre* in a unique dramatic space all its own. This interaction is what makes the performance qualities of *Lucha Libre* so different from those of other spectacles. In theater and dance, the audience is expected to sit quietly and observe the action. Applause is the only accepted social norm of reaction to the performance. In *Lucha Libre,* the audience is expected and encouraged to do the exact opposite. Not only is the audience allowed to interact with the performers but also it can do so in a way in which their participation effects the unfolding of the narrative. Their interactions don't necessarily change the final outcome of the bout, but they do affect the pacing, feelings, and dialogue generated inside the ring.

The audience's dramatic interactions also contribute to the rhetorical impact of the performance. Intensity of the interactions can be strong, and the exchanges can be described as emotional and even liberating, as the crowd is allowed to speak in the space (the arena) in a way they cannot do elsewhere. They scream and shout at the *luchadores* and at each other, expressing support or disdain, devoid of any kind of censorship whatsoever. Gestures accentuate the audience's participation, making the interactions both verbal and physical. Of course, not all of the audience members participate in the performance as such, though a great majority do and, frankly, are expected to. It is part of the unwritten social contract between the wrestlers and the spectators and is essential in the performance of *Lucha Libre.* Thus the audience's involvement strengthens the rhetorical impact of the larger performance and transforms the drama into a unique performative genre.

■ *Lucha Libre:* Social Drama or Social Scene

Lucha Libre is essentially a drama about working class struggles. It is a drama about corruption and is a representation of the way in which the working class, or the proletariat, view the world (Levi, "Sport and Melodrama" 57).

The labor class is drawn to the world of *Lucha Libre* because for them this realm of leisure represents an alternative space of autonomy and community (Alamillo 5).

Lucha Libre is a mix of numerous dramatic genres. It is sport, spectacle, melodrama, theater, spoken word, dance, myth, and ritual. Moreover, the audience is part of the performance. But unlike spectacles where the audiences simply react to the performance—as in the case of football games where audience members cheer and scream, or where they enact their own separate performance, like the costumed group dancing in front of the movie theater at the *Rocky Horror Picture Show*—*Lucha Libre* blurs the lines of performance and audience. The audience is actually engaged in a performance *with* wrestlers. They affect the pace in which the scripted narrative unfolds. The audience can even add to the narrative, taking part in side plots with the wrestlers.

For instance, in a bout between *Hijo del Santo* (Son of the Saint) and *La Parka,* audience members might heckle the "evil" wrestler, *La Parka,* so as to engage in a side conversation with him. Their exchange of words would turn *La Parka's* attention away from the action of the ring and toward the audience, giving *Hijo del Santo* time to recover or strategize his next move. Often audience members try to get wrestlers to engage them with hopes to give the other wrestler an advantage. This can lure wrestlers to leave the ring and move into the seating area to confront the heckling audience members, a move that drives the crowd into a frenzy. These kinds of impromptu interactions, between wrestler and audience, allow the audience to take command of the narrative, if only for a short while.

In this respect the audience is also performing, and their relationship with the wrestlers is reciprocal. When the audience participates, it is empowering. They yell and scream, often to break the social norms that are rigidly honored outside the arena—speaking out against their employment superiors, turning violent against injustices, or standing up to public agency corruption such as that of law enforcement brought on by the *narco-traficantes* (drug traffickers). They aren't given voice in their daily lives, but they are giving voice in the *Lucha Libre* arena. As Levi notes, "Workers like to watch wrestling not because it represents capitalist relations but because it coexists with these relations yet simultaneously resists certain of their terms" ("Sport and Melodrama" 61).

There is also a great deal of ritual in *Lucha Libre* that the working class audience has come to recognize, adopt, and perform as a role in the spectacle. Commenting on this ritual, Levi writes, "With its masks, its moral text, the importance of gesture, the intimacy between performers and audience, the infinite play of secrecy and revelation, Luch Libre figured as urban ritual par excellence" ("Masked Media" 346). The ritual begins as the audience files into the arena. The announcer will almost always use a microphone to conduct the proceedings, and he is the one charged with making sure that the ritual moves along, much like a priest does at mass. He announces each match, then each wrestler. As their name is called, the masked wrestler enters the ring and completes a dance-like movement that establishes both his character (good or bad) and relationship with audience. The relationship may be combative, established by swearing at the audience accompanied with lewd gestures, or the relationship may be affable with high-fives and poses for photographs. The masked wrestler may strut around the ring, jump onto the ropes and howl at the audience, beat his chest, or simply raise his arms in the air. The audience is thus cued to participate in the ritual, to cheer or boo, depending on their affections for the particular wrestlers. Then the match begins. Throughout the bout there are interactions, vocal and physical, between the wrestlers and audience members. The referees call the matches, and whoever wins two out of three rounds wins the match. Then the next match begins and the dance-like ritual begins its second act and so on. To what extent the audience becomes engaged in the action is up to them as individuals, and this may vary from match to match or event to event. In so far as *Lucha Libre* is ritual, it allows participants to "tell themselves about themselves" (Geertz 448). Moreover, the storylines that unfold contribute to the revelations they want to make about who they are as individuals and provide commentary about their group consciousness as members of the lower class. They can identify with the *técnico* wrestler, morally coded as good, who fights the evil opponent in a world where evil cheats, breaks the rules, and conspires with the referees to win. The workers, like their masked heroes, face what appear to be insurmountable challenges in their daily lives. Yet, they continue "fighting," as do the wrestlers, in the face of these difficulties. They can draw strength from the perseverance of the characters, and solidarity from the shared desire with the spectators around them that good will overcome.

Lucha Libre, like American wrestling, can be seen as a symbolic representation of audience members' social struggles (Leverette 116). Alamillo writes this of the Mexican working class:

> Mexican working men and women drew upon cultural resources at their disposal—pool halls, sporting events, church-related events, and patriotic festivals, among others—to build ethnic solidarity, critique social inequities mobilize oppositional resistance and to some extent improve the conditions of their lives. (5)

Thus *Lucha Libre* is less of social drama and more of a social scene. Participants don't just sit and watch the narrative of the match unfold before them. To the contrary, they yell, shout, and take ownership of the epic battles.

Curiously, the bourgeois class is never mentioned as a prominent spectator in literature, scholarship, or other texts that take up the subject of *Lucha Libre*. Perhaps this is because Mexican free-style wrestling is not as appealing to this affluent sector as it is to the struggling working class. It would stand to reason then that the bourgeois are less likely to participate in the perfomative role of the audience. They are simply not called to "perform." Their lived experience or social and political narratives are not represented in the wrestling ring in a positive light.

■ *Lucha Libre* as a Bank of Signs

Analyzing the appeal of American professional wrestling, Leverette describes the narratives: "the storylines in which these dramatic battles unfold are in effect, the American audience's reading of the American social experience. Thus the matches witnessed by millions week in and week out have a *symbolic function* to reveal an audience conception of American society" (107, original emphasis). *Lucha Libre* also has a symbolic function that reveals the struggle of the Mexican working class—their political and social realities. *Lucha Libre* consists of a collection of signs that serves as a focal point for the attribution of meaning to the Mexican working class. These signs are located inside the ring and are derived from a variety of sources including the masks worn by the wrestlers, the wrestlers themselves, the referees, and, most importantly, the mythic narratives. When combined as a group, these signs serve a symbolic function and form meaning that allows the audience members to interpret and cope with the complex world around them. For these proletariat spectators, whose only asset is the labor they sell to their employer and who have little or no political power, making sense of their role in a highly commoditized, commercialized, and politicized society can be complicated. Let's examine each source of signs more closely.

■ The Masks

Masks have long been a key symbol in Mexican national culture. They are present in numerous indigenous ritual practices. Masks are most often used in performances that engage ritual combat or where participants ridicule powerful notables (Levi, "The Mask" 104). Indigenous people who constitute much of Mexico's working class have an immediate visceral connection to the mask-wearing wrestlers. *Lucha Libre's* adaptation of the mask tapped into the native cultural cues of Mexico's working class.

Although the use of masks can be found in American professional wrestling, Mexican wrestling's use of masks is different. In describing *Lucha Libre's* distinctiveness, Heather Levi writes, "The nationalistic themes that structure the *North* American version were played down and new elements of dramaturgy, movement, vocabulary, and dress were added" ("On Mexican" 179). The addition of dress, more specifically the mask, is a distinct departure from American wrestling because the masks are so prominent. Almost none enter the ring without wearing one. And, the mask is central to the enactment of struggle, as being unmasked in the ring not only demoralizes the but also ends the career of the unmasked and disqualifies the perpetrator. As José Joaquín Blanco writes, to remove a wrestler's mask is to "despoil the most cared for and coveted virginity on earth" (qtd. in Levi, "On Mexican" 183).

Antonio H. Martínez, a shoemaker in Mexico City, is credited with designing and producing the first mask used in Mexican wrestling in 1934. A wrestling boot maker, Martínez was asked to design a hood for a Cyclone MacKay, a North American wrestler who was looking to use a Masked Marvel gimmick in Mexico (Levi, "The Mask" 104). He wanted a hood, but Martínez designed a form-fitting cotton-Lycra mask made from four pieces of material sewn together with holes cut out for the eyes, nose, and mouth. This design became the template for the iconic masks worn to this day.

But the mask also has an effect on the wrestlers, transforming them into someone other than themselves. Mazer describes how the mask alters the wrestlers and how the wrestlers embody their masks:

> He refers to it [mask] as a source of power and, like Rubio, claims to be unable to wrestle effectively when not full masked and costumed. While Rubio insists that he loves his mask because he's "sexier" and "all the women" love him when he's wearing it, Frankie says that it's important to him that he is able to "do things—not just the moves" and that he feels he can act more forcefully and graceful as a wrestler and as a man when wearing his mask than when he is without it (interview 1993). And indeed, the masks of the luchadores have a striking effect. By supplanting the wrestler's face with less human images—abstractions of animals and symbols of power—what becomes visible is the idea of the man and his body in motion When Rubio and Frankie do work without their masks, they are not so much diminished as utterly transformed. (68)

As Leverette notes, "The wrestler comes to represent us symbolically. The ring comes to stand as a microcosm of the world" (123). This is indeed true for *Lucha Libre*. And, the use of masks contributes to this notion, because they keep the identities of the *luchadores* hidden. The wrestlers could actually be anyone among the audience, anyone among the working class.

The masks also serve as a mechanism for the audience to project themselves onto (and into) the struggle being enacted in and around the ring. Because they don't know the true identity of the wrestlers, the struggling laborer is given hope that someone like them, someone ordinary and of little economic means, can stand up to corruption or to a powerful nemesis. The masks allow them to escape from the harsh realities of their lives and imagine themselves as the masked wrestlers, heroes fighting for justice.

The masks also seduce the children who are to purchase the masks of their favorite wrestling characters from vendors outside the arenas. The commodification of wrestling characters allows these youngsters to play their favorite wrestler in their own living rooms and backyards—in the reality of their daily lives. In *Lucha Libre,* the mask holds great meaning for those who wear one and fosters identification for those who desire to wear one. In the face of working class realities, this identification with the wrestlers helps them to cope with and understand their social realities and offers hope for overcoming oppression and corruption. This is particularly true when the *técnico* (the morally coded good guy) wins the match.

■ The Bodies and Styles of the Mexican Masked Wrestlers

An important difference between *Lucha Libre* and American wrestling is in the body type and wrestling style of the participants. American wrestlers exude hyper-masculinity, with protruding biceps and pectorals. These characters' demonstration of power and strength in the ring is tied to the outward appearance of their bodies. These body types are acquired only with time (to pump iron) and money (having capital that allows you time away from work). Free time and disposable income are scarcities among the working class. Mexican wrestlers, on the other hand, are not bound to outward displays of muscular physique. In fact, many of the *luchadores* do not have well-defined bodies. The absence of a steroid-enhanced, body-building appearance suggests that the wrestlers are not of the bourgeois class. That is to say, because the bodies are not extraordinary, ordinary, working class individuals can see themselves as a wrestling hero or believe that a hero is among them, among their family, co-workers, or community. Moreover, *luchadores* aren't forced to rely on their bodies to display power. Because their bodies are average looking, they can turn to other tactics to win. Their less defined, less bulky bodies gives them the latitude and physical agility to be more acrobatic. Somersaults and back-flips are often incorporated into the narrative.

Furthermore, they can outsmart their opponents as opposed to physically overtake them.

■ The *Rudos* and Referees

Rudos, or heels, are the *Lucha Libre* wrestlers who are morally coded as bad. "The *rudo* is a brawler, a rule breaker: nasty, mean and unrepentant. A great *rudo* will dictate the pace of the match" (Madigan 52). They are in control of the match and usually win only by cheating. The *rudos* symbolize corruption and wealth in Mexican society. Their shenanigans incite the working class audiences, bringing them to their feet to yell and wave their fists. The audience is invited and expected to vocalize their discontent with the bad guy and the tainted match that has come to symbolize the corruption of the state.

The *rudos* are often characterized by ominous names and costumes. Their clothing usually consists of dark colors such as black or dark brown and sometimes mixed with dark red or purple. The masks of the *rudos* are often adorned with devilish horns and other such decor. Their costumes and capes are often more elaborate and adorned and can symbolize both wealth and corruption. They make rude gestures and bully the audience directly by yelling at them or indirectly by knocking over the fans' food and drinks. And, the *rudos* always pull dirty tricks in the ring, which often involve illegal procedures. For the working class spectators, these actions can represent the ways in which the elite class exploits the workers by manipulating the power structures in society, such as law enforcement, the judiciary, and the politics.

The referee is the third person in the ring and he/she is also morally coded.

They can be either *técnicos* (good) or *rudos* (bad). This element is unique in Mexican wrestling. Referees in American professional wrestling may be incompetent or dawdlers, but they rarely take part in the main action as a good or bad character. As Madigan observes of Mexican wrestling, "It is not uncommon for the referee to get caught up in the physicality of the match and take a few 'bumps' of his own" (53). When the referee is corrupt and calls the match unfairly, he comes to symbolize the corrupt authority in Mexican society, a system that prevents the working class from achieving any gains.

Referees have their own costuming that resembles that of American professional wrestling. The referees wear black and white striped shirts and black pants. Audiences can't tell if the referees are corrupt by just looking at their attire. The only way to distinguish between good referees and bad ones is to watch them call the match. If the referees are easily distracted by the *rudos* or they conspire with them, then they are considered corrupt. When corrupt referees conspire with the *rudos* the storylines seem to ignite audiences, increasing the intensity of spectator performance in the match.

The *rudos* and the referees are representations of class distinctions in the ring, and deciphering and reacting to these distinctions is part of the audiences' function and purpose at a *Lucha Libre* match.

■ Mythic Narrative

The narratives that unfold in the ring of Mexican wrestling are fairly basic and melodramatic: good versus evil. Sometimes good wins and sometimes evil wins, but the story is always the same—good fights evil and evil is relentless. Jonathon Clark gives this detailed description of a *Lucha Libre* storyline.

> The introductions for this evening's next tag-team match leave no ambiguity as to who are the good guys and the bad guys.
>
> "Presenting Team Técnico: Mistico ("The Mystic"), Volador ("The Flyer") and Misterioso ("The Mysterious One")!"
>
> Three white-masked and white-caped fighters jog buoyantly into the ring. They politely acknowledge the cheers of their fans, then huddle up for a momentary prayer. "Now, their opponents from Team Rudo: Averno, Mephisto and Olimpico!" Upon emerging onto the runway, the three black-clad wrestlers, all sporting masks adorned with devilish horns and trimmings, immediately distinguish themselves with their boorish behavior; they purposely spill fans' drinks as they pass by and gesture obscenely in every direction. Somewhat predictably, Team Rudo takes the first advantage, throttling their opponents with a variety of barely legal and illegal procedures. But just when all looks lost for the técnicos, team captain Mistico finds his second wind, and in a dizzying whirling dervish of a move, somersaults Mephisto to the mat for the three-count and the victory. (1)

In this epic battle and other narrative like it, *Lucha Libre* uses heightened parodic figures to challenge the social inequality experienced by the working class. The comic effect of these characters allows for a critique of the capitalist system without provoking the workers to engage in organized, violent efforts to overtake the system. The stories portray the workers as good, noble, and moral individuals who were victimized by corruption, while the bad are egotistical, self-interested scoundrels who break the rules to win.

Audiences come face-to-face with their working class realities in *Lucha Libre* through story and characters. Frustrations are released allowing for solidarity to take its place. Workers encounter a shared experience in the arena, and that shared experience brings them together as a community with common interests and shared aspirations for the future. The story in the ring is the story of their lives, and they are drawn to the spectacle as they are drawn to the hope that they will overcome their troubles.

■ Conclusion

Masks, characters, and narrative mix together in *Lucha Libre* to form symbolic meaning for working class audiences. The symbols and iconography have come to be so strong that they have been co-opted by other groups hoping to make inroads into the working class. Superbarrio is one such example of groups borrowing from the bank of signs created by Mexican wrestling.

Superbarrio was a popular hero created to raise awareness about housing concerns in Mexico. Annis describes Superbarrio as, "a masked wrestler, a colorful good guy sworn to oppose the bureaucracy, greedy landlords, and political hacks. Dressed in yellow tights, red cape, and mask emblazoned with 'SB,' Superbarrio led tens of thousands of people in street protests" (101). Like the *luchadores* he emulated, Superbarrio refused to remove his mask, arguing that, as in *Lucha Libre,* taking off his mask would be paramount to losing. Superbarrio managed to create a shared consciousness and a formidable political force.

But the symbolic meaning of *Lucha Libre* has been co-opted by not so noble causes as well. A recent television commercial for a chain of pawnshops featured a masked and caped *luchador* promoting cash in exchange for household items. He was framed as a hero (*técnico*) coming to the rescue of the cash-needy. The advertisers' aim was clearly to tap into the symbolic meaning of Mexican wrestlers to entice the working class to patronize their stores. Nevertheless, it is an example of how deep *Lucha Libre* penetrates and connects cultural identities.

Today, *Lucha Libre* has gone global. Matches tour across Mexico and the United States and have made their way across the Atlantic Ocean to other countries. *El Hijo del Santo* (Son of The Saint) has performed in London and throughout Europe. *Luchadores* can also be seen on the small screen. Spanish language television in the United States and Mexico carry matches regularly. Pay-per-view bouts have also sprung up on cable networks. *Lucha Libre* is big business. Masks and figurines of popular wrestlers can be purchased outside the arenas. Kids swarm to these vendors. You can even purchase capes and boots to complete the *Lucha Libre* look.

Films such as *Nacho Libre* thrust *Lucha Libre* onto the American popular culture scene. The Cartoon Network now has a program based on *Lucha Libre* called *Mucha Lucha*. *Lucha Libre* also has a strong web presence with numerous sites dedicated to the sport and the *luchadores*. Sites such as www.mexican-wrestling.org and www.unknown.com offer extensive coverage of *Lucha Libre* wrestlers. And, *Lucha Libre* still thrives at the local level, where the sport got its original footing. Matches can be seen in Mexico City, in cities in northern Mexico, along the Texas border, and in the United States in places such as San Antonio and El Paso.

The great Mexican wrestler *El Santo* is still present after death, not just through his son's wrestling career or in the legend that he has left behind, but in the hearts and minds of struggling working class Mexicans who continue to believe in what *El Santo* represented. He personified their struggle, their struggle to fight back, their struggle to persevere, and their struggle to overcome injustices. He, like *Lucha Libre,* will live on.

Works Cited

Alamillo, José M. *Making Lemonade Out of Lemons*. Chicago: U of Illinois P, 2006.

Annis, Sheldon. "Giving Voice to the Poor." *Foreign Policy* 84 (1991): 93–106. *Google Scholar*. Accessed on 3 July 2008.

Atkinson, Michael. "Fifty Million Viewers Can't Be Wrong: Professional Wrestling, Sports-Entertainment, and Mimesis." *Sociology of Sport Journal* 19.1 (2002): 47–66. *Academic Search Complete*. Accessed on 10 July 2008.

Barthes, Roland. "The World of Wrestling." *Mythologies*. Trans. Annette Lavers. New York: Hill, 1972. 15–25.

Beale, Lewis. "Who's That Masked Man and Where Did He Learn to Wrestle Like That?" *New York Times* 28 May 2006, late ed., sec. 2: 11. *LexisNexis*. Accessed on 27 May 2008.

Blanco, José Joaquín. *Un Chavo Bien Helado: Crónicas de los Años Ochenta*. México, DF: Ediciones Era, 1990.

Clark, Jonathan. "Beyond the Mask: A Night in the World of Mexican Wrestling." *Miami Herald* 16 Oct. 2004, Mexico ed., n. pag. *Jon's Mexico Page*. Accessed on 27 Sept. 2008. <http://www.geocities.com/jonclark500/stories/lucha.html>.

Freedman, Jim. "Will the Sheik Use His Blinding Fireball?: The Ideology of Professional Wrestling." *The Celebration of Society: Perspectives on Contemporary Cultural Performance*. Ed. Frank E. Manning. Bowling Green: Bowling Green State UP, 1983. 67–79.

Geertz, Clifford. *The Interpretation of Cultures: Selected Essays*. New York: Basic, 1973.

Jones, Vanessa E. "Mexican Wrestling, Mass Appeal." *Boston Globe* 11 June 2006, 3rd ed.: N9. *LexisNexis*. Accessed on 27 May 2008.

Leverette, Marc. *Professional Wrestling, the Myth, the Mat, and American Popular Culture*. Lewiston: Mellen, 2003.

Levi, Heather. "The Mask of the Luchador: Wrestling, Politics, and Identity in Mexico." *Steel Chair to the Head: The Pleasure and Pain of Professional Wrestling.* Ed. Nicholas Sammond. Durham: Duke UP, 2006. 96–131.

————. "Masked Media." *Fragments of a Golden Age: The Politics of Culture in Mexico Since 1940.* Ed. Gilbert M. Joseph, Anne Rubenstein, and Eric Zolov. Durham: Duke UP, 2001. 330–72.

————. "On Mexican Pro Wrestling: Sport as Melodrama." *Sportcult.* Ed. Randy Martin and Toby Miller. Minneapolis: U of Minnesota P, 1999. 173–88.

————. "Sport and Melodrama: The Case of Mexican Professional Wrestling." *Social Text* 50 (1997): 57–68. *JSTOR.* Accessed on 1 May 2008.

Madigan, Dan. *Mondo Lucha a Go-Go.* New York: Harper, 2007.

Mazer, Sharon. *Professional Wrestling: Sport and Spectacle.* Jackson: UP of Mississippi, 1998.

Méndez, Teresa. "Lucha! Behind the Mask." *Christian Science Monitor* 23 June 2006: 11. *LexisNexis.* Accessed on 27 May 2008.

Monsiváis, Carlos. "Notas Sobre Cultura Popular En Mexico." *Latin American Perspectives* 5.1 (1978): 98–118. *JSTOR.* Accessed on 1 May 2008.

Oppliger, Patrice A. *Wrestling and Hypermasculinity.* Jefferson: McFarland, 2004.

Rothstein, Simon. "El Hijo del Santo: Behind the Mask." *The Sun.* News Group Newspapers Ltd., 23 June 2008. Accessed on 9 July 2008. <http://www.thesun.co.uk/sol/homepage/sport/wrestling/article1330124.ece>.

Sullivan, Chris. "Wresting: Viva Lucha Libre!; This Week, a New Movie Takes Us into the Weird and Wonderful World of Mexico's Fabled Masked Wrestlers. The Plot May Sound Implausible the Truth is Stranger Than Any Fiction." *Independent* 5 Aug. 2006, final ed.: 19. *LexisNexis.* Accessed on 27 May 2008.

Webley, Irene A. "Professional Wrestling: The World of Roland Barthes Revisited." *Semiotica* 58 (1986): 59–81.

"Wrestling Titles." *Wrestling-Titles.com.* Puroeso Dojo, n.d. Accessed on 30 Aug. 2008. <http://www.wrestling-titles.com/mexico/>.

Notes

1. The WWE is one of the primary American professional wrestling organizations. Prior to 2002, it was known as the World Wrestling Federation (WWF), a name change prompted by a court decision in the United Kingdom brought forth by the World Wildlife Fund.

■ Part Three

How Elements of Sports and Games Are Taken up into Performance in the Wider Culture

■ Introduction

Sports and games are rarely simple phenomena. Performance in the ring, on the court, on the field often affects performances in the wider world. This is true not only for players and athletes but also for their fans. Part Three studies connections between performance in sports and games and performance in our everyday lives, in four chapters. K. Jeanine Congalton begins within the context of competitive eating, in which contestants at local fairs attempt to eat the greatest amount of food possible in a limited time. Note how she then connects this practice to wider practices of eating, linking her subject to cultural problems with obesity, to globalization, and to other issues. Kevin A. Johnson studies complex interrelationships among hip hop, NBA basketball, and street basketball. Performance styles are so widely shared across these three phenomena that it may be difficult to discern which is most fundamental.

But note the social and political effects created by the rhetorics of these borrowed performances. Timothy R. Steffensmeier keeps an actual game, college football, at the periphery of his study of fan spectatorship. How fans tailgate, how they view games, and how performances on the field are taken up into these fan performances are questions that illustrate the interconnectedness of sports and spectators. In our final chapter, Meredith Bagley studies the well-known incident in which radio talk show host Don Imus insulted the Rutgers University women's basketball team. Issues of class, race, and gender are key to Bagley's study. Note that Imus and the players alike engaged in a rhetoric of performance on many fronts.

10

■ Competitive Eating as Sport

A Simple Recipe for Everyone

□ **K. Jeanine Congalton**

For those of us raised in rural America, the county fair was an event. Amid the livestock judging and the ribbons awarded to amateur gardeners, was the often raucous but considerably less important "pie eating contest." Yet within the past few years, eating contests have been transformed from events at county fairs (where a champion earned a blue ribbon) to corporate-sponsored spectacles where contestants earn up to $50,000 in prize money. And with ESPN's coverage of the Nathan's Famous 4th of July International Hot Dog Eating Contest, competitive eating has moved into the national spotlight. The establishment of major competitions with big prize money has secured this "sport" as a significant artifact in popular culture. The form and structure, the language, and the spectacle of competitive eating not only enhance the drama of competition but also enable the identification of this sport with more traditional sports and explain why fans flock to see their favorite competitive eaters perform their feats. A closer reading of the competition's dramatic storyline reveals a masking of issues of sexism and health, issues that present an inherent paradox in the sport of competitive eating.

■ The Significance of Competitive Eating

The significance of competitive eating in our culture is demonstrated at a number of levels. Nerz claims that since classical times, "excessive eating" has been a part of culture (55). And references to competitive eating can be found in ancient myths (Fagone 16; Suddath). Today, competitive eating is considered "one of the fastest growing 'sports' in America" (Wilson 1D). Regardless of the origins of eating contests, it is in the past few years that competitive eating has emerged as what its promoters and its competitors deem a legitimate, professional sport.

Various forms of media have played an important role in moving competitive eating into the national spotlight. In recent years, documentaries, books, and even a discussion in a scientific journal have all contributed to the increasing interest in this sport. Storylines that resemble the drama of Nathan's hot dog eating competition have found their way into the animated series *King of the Hill,* and into the situation comedy *According to Jim.* The reality program *Hurl!* is based on competitors' abilities to ingest great amounts of food, followed by such activities as a roller coaster ride or an appointment with a mechanical bull.

Less daring persons have the option of virtual participation in the sport. Prior to the 2008 Krystal Square Off World Hamburger Eating Championship, fans were invited to create or to join a competitive eating fantasy league. Through their fantasy teams, fans of competitive eating could "go for the glory" at the world championship (Home page, Krystal). Or fans might choose to purchase Wii's Major League Eating: The Game. Just as fans assume their favorite professional football, baseball, and basketball players, video gamers can become avatars and choose one of the profession's top competitors ("Preview"). As they monitor their stomach capacities, Wii enthusiasts can also choose what foods they want to tackle. And if the game should end in a tie, a winner can be determined by a "burp off" (Red).

Whether in a traditional or in a "new media" format, when media attention focuses on any pinnacle sporting event, those who participate garner national attention. And although there is regional media coverage of eating contests, no one contest can command national attention like the Nathan's Famous 4th of July International Hot Dog Eating Contest. Not only do beat reporters cover the event, in recent years, ESPN has carried even live broadcasts of this 4th of July spectacle. In 2006, for example, a reported 1.5 million viewers watched ESPN's coverage of the historic 4th of July competition (Hoffman). Given a recent contract extension with ESPN, fans can be assured of access to Nathan's contest through 2012 ("Nathan's Famous"). With the assurance of future ESPN coverage of this historic contest, competitive eating can continue to claim its status as a sport.[1]

Nathan's, as well as numerous other eating events, fall under the purview of the International Federation of Competitive Eating. The IFOCE maintains an official Web site complete with rankings, video links, and the opportunity for visitors to purchase IFOCE-sanctioned products.[2] Fans of the competitive eaters can check the official rankings, link to video replays, and read all of the recent news related to individual contests and to IFOCE competitors. As the major promoter of competitive eating, the IFOCE has catapulted competitive eating to the status of one of America's newest pastimes.

■ The Functions of Form and Structure

The IFOCE serves as the governing body of several major competitive eating contests and as the overseer of a number of competitive eaters. The IFOCE's taking of the form and structure of other professional sports associations enables its resemblance to other legitimate sports. That mimicking of and identification with other professional sports structures creates the perception of competitive eating as legitimate sport.

Form and structure are also important elements in the development of a dramatic storyline; so too do the form and the structure of the IFOCE add to the drama of eating competitions. It is through the use of a form and structure, that the IFOCE becomes both the producer and the director of the spectacle of competitive eating. It is through the form and structure that the competition is promoted, heightened, and sustained. And it is through the form and structure of the IFOCE that rhetorical strategies, which promote identification, are sustained.[3] This form and structure are reflected in the IFOCE's development of official rules for governing competition, its establishment of a ranking system, and the maintenance of competitive eating records.

Similar to other professional sports organizations, the IFOCE has established or produced rules for each of its sanctioned contests. Judges (and medical personnel) must be on hand at every contest. Much like competitors in MLB, the NBA, the NFL, and the NHL, participants must abide by the decisions of umpires and/or referees, the outcome of competitive eating contests are determined by the judges. As with other professional sports organizations, despite the rules established for each contest, competitive eating judges make subjective "calls," calls that can often change the outcome of a competition and thus decide the fate of the contestants. For example, judgment calls must be made as to how many or how much of the food has been consumed in regulation time. Wing eating contests can result in disputations arising over concerns as to whether a wing was "clean" or whether too much meat was left on the bone. Jason Fagone's coverage of Wing Bowl 13 reflected some of the potential problems with judges' decisions. In the first round, Tim Janus (Eater X) was eliminated. Fagone reports that in a telephone call to him, Janus claimed that, "'Wing Bowl is a fucking joke…It's rigged and there's not a guy here'—meaning the other IFOCE eaters—'who doesn't think the same things'" (Fagone 197). Fagone also reports that Sonya Thomas (the Black Widow) was unhappy with the judging (203) and that even a "longtime Wing Bowl judge and tabulator" was not able to make a "categorical statement" that the Wing Bowl "was not fixed" (204).

Judgment calls about whether a competitor has a "reversal of fortune," a game moment that includes acts that range from food spewing out of one's mouth to vomiting, are very important decisions. For competitors, a "reversal" is an act that results in automatic disqualification. At the 2007 Nathan's contest, for example, there was a question as to whether Takeru Kobayashi had suffered the fate of such a reversal. In this particular match, "Kobayashi appeared to spew hot dog out of his mouth at the end, but caught it in the air and clamped his hands to his mouth" (Sederstrom and Lisberg 3). As fans anxiously awaited the final decision, ESPN commentators heightened the drama of the moment noting that "It's the judges' decision" and reminding the audience of the potential ramifications, "If they don't full on DQ him, they're gonna deduct for those hot dogs" (2007 Nathan's). Ultimately, since Kobayashi "did not expel effluvia," he was not disqualified (Sandomir D6). And yet, even though the reversal call favored him, Kobayashi was not credited with another hot dog when judges ruled that the hot dog was "in the air but not in his mouth and under his control" (Sederstrom and Lisberg 3). The suspense created by waiting for the judges' call and heightened by the sportscasters' debate over the potential outcome of the competition was reminiscent of the drama of any major sporting competition, whose outcome is determined by the "final call."

Legitimacy and drama are also reflected in the IFOCE's maintaining an official ranking system for its sanctioned competitors ("Rankings"). In the professional sporting world, ranking systems serve to provide notice as to who is the very best in a respective sport. Fans participate in conversations focused on "who really should be #1" by joining coaches, competitors, and sportscasters as they debate the merits of various ranking systems. These debates, in and of themselves, help sustain interest in the sport and in the competitors. And it is through these debates that fans can join competitive eaters as a part of the sports performance; they become a part of the competitive drama and help to create it.

The IFOCE's ranking system, a system seemingly not bound to a specific statistical analysis, provides greater room for interpretation and in turn creates a greater space for debate. The IFOCE home page, for example, does not explain whether emerging as the victor in an asparagus-eating contest is weighted more than earning first place eating pulled pork sandwiches. Yet, as with any major sport, the IFOCE's ranking system is continually updated. And the results of any one high-profile eating contest can easily change the ranks of competitors. Therefore, it should come as no surprise that in addition to the fans, sanctioned eaters, especially those eaters who hope to attain top professional status, have been known to dispute these rankings, rankings that can influence an eater's competitive and financial destiny. It is after all, the top-ranked eaters who are "encouraged" or invited to attend various contests, thus increasing the opportunities for earnings. These same competitors are also more likely to receive reimbursement for travel expenses. In short, regardless of how the rankings are calculated, top eaters gain more face time, which translates into enhanced financial rewards.

The recording of official records for the various categories of eating also serves to provide legitimacy and drama to the sport. As eaters continue to challenge their limits, they chew away at these records. Like in other professional sports, record holders gain the respect not only of their fans but of the other competitors as well; that respect often transcends time. Until Hank Aaron, Babe Ruth's home run record, a record that stood for decades, seemed insurmountable. The central drama of the 2008 Summer Olympics focused on whether Michael Phelps could break Mark Spitz's seemingly untouchable seven gold medal record. To the average person, competitive eating records would also appear unbreakable. But in 2007, a reported twenty-four records were broken ("Year in Review"). Patrick Bertoletti, for example, set ten new records, including eating 10.63 pounds of corned beef and cabbage and 11.1 pounds of Shoo-Fly pie. Two-time Nathan's champion Joey Chestnut set and then broke his record of sixty-six hot dogs in the infamous 4th of July competition. Additional records for Chestnut include his consuming 8.6 pounds of tempura deep-fried asparagus spears in ten minutes and 103 Krystal hamburgers in eight minutes. Tim Janus established a record for eating 10.5 pounds of ramen noodles in eight minutes. Competitive eaters, then, continue their quest to set new records by surmounting a record three pounds and three ounces of whole pickled beef tongue, 9.75 pounds of deep-fried okra, or six pounds of Spam ("Records"). Winning is a thrill, but holding a record bestows an honor that transcends time.

Given the variety of contests, competitive eating provides a number of opportunities for record-breaking performances. As with other sports professionals, competitive eaters earn status and command respect by winning a number of titles. In baseball, we come to know players by their titles as well (e.g., MVP, Cy Young Award winner, all-time home run leader), this holds good for competitive eating too (e.g., six-time Nathan's hot dog champion). The fact that multiple contests are held, which results in multiple winners, allows for the possibility of broader fan support. Fans can identify with any number of competitive eaters, many of whom will become champions in at least one contest. And competitors can bask in the honor of being record holders as their names are announced, for example, to the Nathan's cheering crowd. The information used for introducing eaters mimics the introductions of professionals in other sports; eaters are introduced by height, weight, and, perhaps most important, references to their titles. In the 2007 contest, for example, we learned that we had a "Burrito Specialist," a "former Bologna Eating Champion of the World," the "World's Fry Bread Eating Champion," "a former Shoe Fly Pie Eating Champion of the World," and the "undisputed Pig's Feet Champion of the World" (Nathan's 2007). The announcements delivering names of top competitors, who hold multiple titles, are made with a cadence and crescendo that sends the crowd into a frenzied state and elevates the status of the individual competitors.

The IFOCE's taking the form and structure of more traditional sports provides a sense of legitimacy to competitive eating as sport and fosters a link to and a sense of identification with traditional professional sports. The judges' interpretation of a rule or IFOCE's reordering of the official rankings provides the opportunity for competitors and fans to become further entrenched in the drama of competition as they debate questionable "calls" or argue which competitive eater truly is "#1." And it is these discussions that aid in the promotion of competitive eating as sport.

■ Language: The Tie That Binds Fans

As with most professions, in addition to taking on the structural form of sports, the discourse of the sport provides a means to both distinguishing the unique features of a sport and providing a common rhetoric for a variety of sports enthusiasts. Within the realm of competitive eating, organizers, competitors, and those describing competitive eating have converged to produce a specialized language. As with other sports, competitive eating uses its technical rhetoric to describe various elements of the sport. Basketball players are referred to as cagers; competitive eaters are gurgitators. Labels have also been assigned to various techniques and strategies. In hot dog eating contests, eating the bun separately from the hot dog has been dubbed the "Japanese method." A contestant who uses the Japanese method, but with two hot dogs, is using a "Double Japanese." Kobayashi's method of tearing the hot dog in half is known as the Solomon method. Chestnut has been described as one of the best "chipmunkers" on the circuit and his signature "Chestnut shake" (2007 Nathan's) is said to help him force the food down creating more room. Violations of the rules have also been named. An inability to keep one's food down is called a "reversal of fortune." Much like the second technical foul in basketball, a "reversal of fortune" results in the disqualification of that competitor.

Fans, however, do not need to be concerned with learning an entirely new vocabulary to understand the essence of competitive eating. Competitive eating relies also on the use of more common sports language. Regardless of their favorite sport, the use of sports discourse provides a means of identification for sports enthusiasts. Borrowing an identifiable vocabulary of more recognizable sports provides easy access for fans. Fans and casual viewers need not learn a new set of terms to understand this "new" sport; they need to only rely on their previous knowledge of sports. That use of traditional sports discourse is apparent in the language used by the IFOCE, the language used by competitors, and the language used by the commentators.

The IFOCE, the governing body of MLE (Major League Eating), for example, has established a sanctioned competitive "circuit" from which will emerge its annual "Rookie of the Year." The organization has increased the number of "qualifiers" for the Nathan's 4th of July contest. As a result, "wild card" berths for that contest were eliminated. And the winner of the Nathan's contest wins the coveted crown jewel of eating, the "Mustard Belt." NASCAR or rodeo fans would be familiar with "circuits." Baseball, football, basketball, and hockey fans understand the excitement of being named Rookie of the Year. Wild card berths provide last chance opportunities for baseball and football teams to contend for the World Series and the Super Bowl. And to earn "the belt" is to own the crown jewel of boxing or professional wrestling. The IFOCE's use of conventional sports discourse provides fans a rhetorical entrée into the world of competitive eating.

Competitors, too, have adopted the vernacular of other professional athletes. Again, the use of conventional sporting terms provides a means for competitive eaters to present and indeed frame themselves as sports professionals. Borrowing the language of marathon runners, competitive eaters often discuss the concept of "hitting the wall" during a competition. By making reference to the plight of marathoners, the competitive eater enables fans to understand that the competitive eater is at that point in the competition where she feels like giving up but must push herself, indeed use every force in her body, to complete the competition.

In order to perform their best, competitors in virtually all professional sports maintain rigorous training schedules. Without training, a competitor often fails to perform to his potential. Two-time Nathan's champion Joey Chestnut frames his preparation for competition by comparing his routine to that of any marathon runner (Berton, "Eating"). Like a marathoner, he must "find [his] rhythm: Bite, bite, swallow. Bite, bite, swallow…. Like a marathoner, my rhythm is everything. My first hot dog should be as easy as my last" (Berton, "Joey Chestnut" E1). Crazy Legs Conti and Eater X have expanded their training repertoire to include yoga (Ravn F1). And some competitors admit to using sports psychology (and sports psychologists) to give them a competitive edge. Be it drinking a gallon of water to stretch the stomach or engaging in practice sessions designed to strengthen jaw muscles, rhetoric related to training is now a routine part of competitive eating discussions.

Discussions of rigorous training are but one means competitive eaters use to frame themselves as sports professionals. Prior to the 2007 Nathan's 4th of July competition, when Takeru Kobayashi claimed to have an "arthritic jaw," charges that he was doing nothing more than trying to "psyche out" or "wage psychological warfare" on his opponents abounded (Ramirez 3). Responding to questions about Kobayashi's alleged jaw injury, Dale Boone had these comments: "You must wake up on game day because you're dealing with the body…because you are dealing with that you must keep yourself in check 100%" (2007 Nathan's). Crazy Legs Conti noted that a "sign of the greatest athletes in the history of sports have been people who performed with great injuries. I look at Willis Reed or Curt Schilling and now I think, Kobayashi" (2007 Nathan's). And much as a batter might try to steal a glance back at the catcher, competitive eaters, too, have been known to "glance" at their competitors.

As with professionals in other sports, competitive eaters further their presentation of the self as competitor and attempt to carve out a unique place in competitive eating through the use of nicknames. Fans love to use the nicknames of professional sports stars. In sports, nicknames tend to reveal the unique characteristics of the athlete and connote a sense of an athlete's or a particular group's status in the sport. Fans might not remember an athlete's given name (e.g., George Herman Ruth), but they will remember a nickname (the Babe), a nickname representing a persona that fans can enjoy and remember. The Babe was followed by Hammerin' Hank who was followed by Big Mac. Basketball has its "Magic," its "Clyde the Glide," and its "Earl the Pearl." Football was graced by the Four Horsemen and the Steel Curtain. Even professional wrestling, which suffers from accusations of being pure performance and not a true sport, is best known by its competitors, who have adopted nicknames and the accompanying personae. Thus, for several decades, fans have been drawn by characters such as Andre the Giant, the Hulk, and the Undertaker. In sports, the unique nature of nicknames is that even "outsiders" of a sport can associate the nickname to the corresponding sport.

Competitive eaters, too, have adopted or have been given nicknames. And reminiscent of professional wrestlers, many competitive eaters enact the accompanying competitive personae. Whether it is Eater X, the Black Widow, Crazy Legs Conti, or El Wingadore, many competitive eaters have transformed themselves (or have been transformed) into various roles for competition. And it is in these roles that the competitors perform. Eater X (Tim Janus) face paints for competition, Patrick Bertoletti sports a brightly dyed Mohawk, and Crazy Legs Conti is recognizable to any eating fan by his trademark hat and dreadlocks. Even Joey Chestnut, who resists any showboating, has been "given" the nickname "Jaws" by the IFOCE.

Sportscasters who cover competitive eating events also have adopted the discourse of traditional sports.[4] Those assigned to cover the Nathan's competition, for example, routinely perform scripts that are easily identified with coverage of major sports competition. For example, ESPN'S coverage of the 2007 Nathan's contest featured "late breaking news regarding Kobayashi's jaw arthritis," and sportscasters wondered whether Kobayashi was "in the house." Once the contest was "under way," sportscasters used color commentary to describe the action. Calls of "Chestnut jumps out with 4" and "Kobayashi is bringing it" let viewers know that "we're on a record pace." The combination of baseball, basketball, and horse racing references provided several links to professional sports. A remark that one competitive eater "seems trapped.... a little bit like Stephan Marbury and Ed Currie. They're great ballers, but will they win a title?" was later followed by a query as to whether Kobayshi was "Schillingesque," The contest between Kobyashi and Chestnut was described as being "jaw to jaw," when eventually Kobayashi "began to pick up the pace" and "close on Chestnut." In the final minutes of the contest, Chestnut was "still out in front" and then "Kobayashi pull(ed) even with Chestnut." In a "cheek to cheek, jaw to jaw finish," a "photo finish," the thousands attending the event and the million plus viewers waited for the announcement of the winner.

Coverage of the 2008 Nathan's International 4th of July competition heightened the drama of the competition with phrases such as "Chestnut in the lead," "it could be an upset," there is a "2 dog difference," and, of course, the call of the infamous "photo finish." The tie that resulted from the 2008 competition necessitated the first ever "dog off." During this same contest, the potential battle between the top two competitors was compared to that of Ali and Frazier.

The use of language to describe the sport, the competitors, and the competition creates a means for fans and viewers to identify with and thus understand the world of competitive eating much as they would traditional sports. A casual fan would understand that the chanting of a nickname or a fan response to a competitor "in character" is indicative of that competitor's status (or at the very least that competitor's relationship) with the fans. Sportscasters who use parts of conventional scripts to call a competitive eating event certainly make that event increasingly accessible for fans of traditional sports. The crafting of characters and scripts provides a means for competitive eating to perform as a legitimate, professional sport.

■ The Spectacle, the Plot, and the Characters

Certainly, the adoption of the language of traditional, established sports is one means to argue that a sport is "legitimate." And in order to perform as a legitimate, professional sport, competitive eating has adopted the organizational form and discourse of a professional sport. But to truly attain sports status, to keep the fans interested in the game and the sponsors inclined to make investments, a sport must have its dramatic storyline. Unlike any other competitive eating event, Nathan's 4th of July contest, the most historic and revered event in competitive eating, captured America's attention through sheer drama. The spectacle of Nathan's is so great, that one author has dubbed the contest "the big daddy of them all" (Nerz 210). To understand the Nathan's event as a spectacle is to understand the plot and the characters that are integral to it.

Berger explains that "one of the ways people become tied more strongly to their social groups, subcultures, and cultures is through participation in spectacles" (*The Agent* 29). If Berger is correct in his assessment that spectacles not only provide a source of entertainment but also "reinforce our connection with American culture and society and its values and beliefs," then an analysis of the Nathan's International 4th of July Hot Dog Eating Contest further reveals how competitive eating performs as a dramatic sporting event that provides the opportunity for a predominately American crowd to demonstrate its nationalism (*The Agent* 29). And who better to lead the American charge to victory than a good, old-fashioned American hero, a typical hero whom Berger describes as being "good," "rescuing damsels in distress," having "extraordinary talents and skills," and winning (*Cultural* 126). It is the plot and the characters that reveal why so many "audience members" are caught up in the excitement of a hot dog eating contest.

The Nathan's contest, which lives up to the expectations of any sporting spectacle, has been described as the "Super Bowl of competitive eating" and to win it is "like winning the green jacket at Augusta" (Collins 25). And much like the Super Bowl or the Master's PGA tournament, the Nathan's hot dog eating spectacle gains the attention of people ranging from the die hard fans carrying signs supporting a favorite gurgitator, to those who rarely attend sporting events of any kind but are drawn to the uniqueness and the hype of the event. In competitive eating, the drama of the Nathan's 4th of July contest—a uniquely American event, taking place on an American holiday, featuring what is claimed to be an "All American" food—cannot be surpassed.

It was at the 2006 contest that for the sixth time Japanese competitor Takeru Kobayashi retained his title of the "undefeated champion of the World Cup of wieners" (Lucadamo 13). But it was also during this contest that rivalry, one of the oldest and most dramatic storylines in sports, unfolded once again. In 2006, a potential new rivalry, one that pitted champion against newcomer and nation against nation, emerged. During ESPN's coverage of the 2006 event, Chestnut was not even recognized as a threat to Kobayashi; the sportscasters did not list him as a top contender. But Chestnut, who is described as having "trained with the seriousness of any semi-pro athlete" (Glionna A1), has a reputation for his work ethic (Berton A1). Despite Chestnut having what was described as a commanding two-dog lead, Kobayashi, the reigning champion, "came from behind with just four minutes to go to clinch the title," his sixth. Chestnut was left to claim, "I feel like I could have prepared better.... I could have pushed myself harder" (Berton, "Eating" A1).

The drama of the 2007 Nathan's contest promoted a rivalry equal to that of any storyline (real or fictional) in the sporting world. Chestnut noted that his rival, Kobayashi, changed the sport. At 131 pounds, Kobayashi would not appear to be the typical "big eater." Rumors of his having a second set of teeth or even a second stomach hovered over the six-time Nathan's champion. Yet despite such rumors, Kobayashi's technique seemed to have given him an edge. Kobayashi had been dubbed by many as the Babe Ruth of competitive eating. The question for the 2007 contest was whether "the Babe" could win the Mustard Belt for a seventh time.

Adding to the drama of the 2007 contest were reports that Kobayashi was suffering from an arthritic jaw. Speculation arose as to whether the jaw injury was real or was it simply conjured up as a means to wage psychological warfare on the other contestants. But as Chestnut noted, "even if his jaw is wired shut, I wouldn't take him lightly" (Goldiner 15). As Kobayashi announced that he would make "a game day decision," Chestnut suggested that he would "love to bring [the title] back to America on the Fourth of July" (Zambito and Lucadamo 4). Chestnut, "the country's best hope for taking back the coveted mustard belt," became recognized as America's "red-white-and blue hope" (Derakhshani). Chestnut emerged as a potential American hero, one who would hopefully prevent a non-national from winning what millions consider a distinctly American contest.

This use of sports metaphors heightened the drama for the 2007 re-match. These sports metaphors advanced the competitive storyline, enhanced the characterizations of the competitors, and, in turn, heightened the spectacle of the Nathan's competition. Ultimately, the contest described as a "one-game World Series" (Ramirez B3), in which the top two contenders were described as being like McGwire and Sosa, lived up to its expectations (Zambito and Lucadamo 4). The battle between Kobayashi and Chestnut was described as having the excitement of a match between Ali and Frazier ("Dr. Remote"). It was an epic battle. The contest played out like "a script that could have been out of a 'Rocky' movie, with an upstart trying to fell the champion"—in this case, an upstart American trying to beat a Japanese champion (Belson, "Teeth" 2). Throughout the sportscast, several references were made to Chestnut as the new "American hero." At one point, he was compared to "Abe Lincoln, Neil Armstrong," and, yes, even American Idol winner "Taylor Hicks." In the midst of the competition, viewers were told that this would be the "greatest moment in the history of American sports if Chestnut can bring the belt home to Coney Island" (2007 Nathan's). With "plenty of patriots in the crowd cheering for an American to win the belt" and amidst chants of "U.S.A.," Joey Chestnut reclaimed the Mustard Belt for America by eating sixty-six of an American favorite on America's Independence Day (Belson, "The Winner" B5).

Performing as any national hero, Chestnut, after being declared the winner, held up an American flag and said, "It feels great...it's about time it comes back to America on the 4th of July" (2007 Nathan's). Chestnut, claimed to be "inspired by the thoughts of the 'Fourth of July'—and bringing the title back" (Sederstrom and Lisberg 3). Chestnut's 2007 win was heralded as a "great day for America" and as a triumph of American patriotism (2007 Nathan's). If Berger is correct that spectacles, even hot dog eating contests, reinforce our connection with cultural beliefs and values, then Americans certainly could identify with an American triumphing over a Japanese competitor; it was as if America was repeating a historic triumph over Japan.

Chestnut's superior performance in the 2008 Nathan's contest resulted in his retaining his status as the Nathan's 4th of July champion. Perhaps because an American had reclaimed the title in 2007, or perhaps because there were no rumors of injured jaws, the pre-contest media coverage for the 2008 competition was decidedly low key. Although the contest featured a rematch between Chestnut and Kobayashi, the rivalry and the contest could not match the drama of 2007. The only pre-event issue focused on the change in the regulation time limit from twelve minutes to ten (Associated Press; McShane). Still, "35,000 fans" attended the event and "an estimated million more" watched it on television (Wiedeman). At the conclusion of regulation time, the contest was ruled a tie, resulting in the contest's first ever "dog off," thus creating a potentially new storyline for future contests. And once again, it was Chestnut who won the dog off, retaining the Mustard Belt for America. Chestnut maintained his heroic status and guaranteed another year of American dominance.

Chestnut certainly meets many of the characteristics associated with a mythical hero. Reclaiming the Mustard Belt for America is just one reason why Chestnut appeared (and still appears) to be a model American sports hero. Despite his rise to prominence in competitive eating, and despite his embodiment of the American Dream, Chestnut appears to be nothing more than the "average guy," an average guy with whom many fans can identify.

Chestnut performs his heroic role with much humility. He has not been caught up in the theatrical hype that is reflected by so many competitive eaters. Instead of calling attention to himself through dress or actions, Chestnut, as described by many, has the "pleasant demeanor of a guy who sits in the back of class, and wears a simple uniform of cargo shorts, sneakers and a T-shirt" (Berton, "Eating Contest" A1). Yet, by winning the 2007 Nathan's contest, the good, hardworking, average college student had metaphorically rescued his damsel (America) in distress. And by repeating the feat in 2008, Chestnut has continued as a symbol of American dominance on an all-American day. Americans once again celebrated an unassuming hero bringing a happy ending to the most important story in competitive eating.

■ The Subtext of the Story

Although the 2007 and 2008 Nathan's dramas resulted in happy endings for American fans, the world of competitive eating is not without its antagonists. In this case, the antagonists take the form of issues related to the role of women in a masculinized sports culture and the inherent paradox of eating as sport. These issues, which relate to broader concerns of obesity and food security, raise questions as to whether the spectacle, the plot, and the performance fail to embrace the more serious themes of sexism and health.

■ The Issue of Sex

Within the world of competitive eating, there are no true damsels in distress, but there are damsels. As with other traditional sports, official cheerleaders (of sorts) have found their way into competitive eating. The Bunnettes, trademarked by the IFOCE, are described as "more beautiful than Miss America, hotter than a Cowboys Cheerleader and more talented than Vanna White" ("Bunnette Videos"). Bunnettes, who dress in short shorts and wear red, white, and blue vests, keep track of competitive eaters' numbers. The Bunnettes performance is directed toward those who choose to participate in the male gaze. At first glance, they are the "props" and can be understood as a part of the set decoration for the competition. As the Bunnettes hoist the numbers of hot dogs consumed by each Nathan's competitor, the association to ring card girls cannot be shaken.

Although IFOCE co-founder George Shea claims that he wants to attract women to the sport, the IFOCE Web page does not target female eaters, it instead focuses only on prospective Bunnettes. It is as if the Bunnettes, and not the female competitive eaters, who are auditioning for the starring roles. "The Fallen Bunnette," a parody of a supposedly failed Bunnette, recounts the story of Danielle, described as the "physical embodiment of what it is to be a Bunnette" ("Bunnette Videos"). The storyline takes the viewer from the rise of a Bunnette, whose presence assured any gurgitator "hot dog gold," to her fall from grace that resulted in her being reduced to working in "underground Lesbian piñata parties." Other Bunnette videos are not as dramatic but do include statements as to why each woman "wants to be a Bunnette." The IFOCE will continue to promote the "Bunnettes." By highlighting the Bunnettes, the IFOCE intimates that perhaps this role is the most open and acceptable space for women to participate and perform in the sport.

Those women who do choose to compete are also sexualized. In a tongue and cheek interview with IFOCE co-founder George Shea, Sonya Thomas is asked whether she enjoys beating a male companion, embarrassing him, dominating him, and getting a thrill out of winning over a man. She is also asked, "Does it disturb you that some of the eaters are dreaming about you?" Although exhibiting signs of embarrassment at the questions, Thomas does attempt to refocus the discussion on her desire to win ("Featured Videos"). Despite the lightheartedness of the interview, the tone of this brief interview takes on a decidedly sexist tone.

The overt sexualization of women in competitive eating leads to the question of whether competitive women in this "professional sport" play secondary roles not only to their male counterparts but also to the Bunnettes.

As with other professional sports, competitive eating is a male-dominated sport.[5] Yet it should be noted that, with the exception of maintaining "women's" and "men's" records in the Nathan's contest, there is no formal codification of essentialism in competitive eating. However, the emergence of women in the sport might is perceived as an anomaly; presently, there are only two women among the top ranked competitors. By virtue of her numerous records, Sonya Thomas, the Black Widow, has earned recognition as a major contender; she is consistently one of the IFOCE's top ranked eaters. Perhaps her determination and winning ways can be attributed to her competitive attitude of "thinking...like a man" (Salamone 35). And yet one might question whether her masculine way of thinking explains why she is one of the few female competitors on the circuit. Given the recent retirement of Carla LeFever, "the lovely Janet Lee" is the only other top ranked female competitor.

As with other professional sports, the masculine ideology of "competition" is embedded in competitive eating. Whether the IFOCE chooses to recognize and then work to resolve sexism in the sport will have implications for determining what space is available for women's participation in it.

■ A Polarization of Paradoxes

Unlike basketball, baseball, and soccer, where the ability to put a ball through a hoop, to catch a ball, to hit a ball, or even to kick a ball is not a necessary behavior for sustaining life, eating is necessary. But the IFOCE and MLE have taken a process that is necessary to sustain life and transformed it into a competitive spectacle. To sustain life, food (the product) and eating (the process) are necessary. Food, the product, fuels the body. In competitive eating, food, the product (and its brand name), fuels the competition. Without sponsorship, any competition can unfold. But it is sponsorship that brings publicity and increased prize money to the corporate sponsor, which in turn provides the financial backing for the competitive eating performances.

Corporate sponsors are certainly aware of the natural link between the geographic location of the venue and the type of food that is consumed. In essence, the food becomes a natural link to the scene of the competitive performance. For example, sanctioned jalapeño eating contests are held in Arizona and Texas while sweet potato casserole is consumed at the North Carolina State Fair. And there is little doubt that overt product placement is a major part of competitive eating. Stagg Chile is listed as the brand for chile eating; Krystal Hamburgers, of course, are the choice for the Krystal Hamburger World Championship Square Off; Entenmann's pumpkin pies are listed as the brand of pie used in the IFOCE-sanctioned pumpkin pie eating contest

("Records"). Such alignments provide not only the source of the competition but also publicity for the corporate sponsors. Although all professional sports rely on sponsors, several eating contests feature their sponsors in a manner unlike how any other professional sport would—through consumption.

It is this consumption or the process of eating that reveals inherent contradictions in this sport. These contradictions, which can be framed as a polarization of paradoxes, are reflected in two significant issues: obesity and food security. These issues are rooted in the very nature of the competition. The act of eating as much food as possible within a very short time limit results in antagonistic forces that create conflict within the storyline of competitive eating.

The first paradox centers on the issue of obesity. The Centers for Disease Control (CDC) continues to identify obesity as a disease and notes that it "continues to be a health concern for adults, children and adolescents in the United States" ("Overweight"). The CDC also reports that in 2005–2006, just over one-third of men and one-third of women in the United States were categorized as being obese ("Overweight"). Dr. Goutham Rao of the Children's Hospital of Pittsburgh notes that "childhood obesity has become so severe that diseases that once affected only adults are now appearing in children" (Rao 56). These diseases, which range from hypertension to diabetes, have resulted in the grave prediction that "this may be the first generation ever to have a shorter lifespan than their parents" ("Fat" 32). In addition, the CDC reports that the direct and indirect costs related to obesity total billions of dollars ("Overweight"). Given the nation's concern with obesity, it is ironic that only three days following the 2008 Nathan's contest, in response to the growing number of obese children, the American Pediatric Association suggested that cholesterol medication should be considered for some children. There is little doubt that obesity is one of the fastest growing diseases in society.

Not only are an increasing number of people in American society being labeled as obese, but also, on the opposite end of the spectrum, a second paradox concerns the estimated "35 million Americans" who experience "food insecurity" (Gerson A15). "Food security means having access, at all times, to enough food for an active, healthy life without resorting to using emergency food supplies, begging, stealing, or scavenging for food" (Holben and Pheley). In order to help reduce food insecurity, Feeding America (formerly Second Harvest) reports that its food banks distribute over two billion pounds of food to America's hungry ("About Us"). Unfortunately, factors such as the instability of the economy, a surge in the prices of essential consumer goods such as food items, and an economic slowdown are often cited as reasons for the shortages in contributions to food banks. Although many Americans struggle to "have access" to food, top ranked competitive eaters earn prize money for ingesting pounds of food in just a few minutes.

This disjunction of food-related issues, then, falls into the categories of having too much (obesity) or too little (a lack of food security). The question then relates to how in a society plagued by both obesity and hunger can the performances of competitive eaters be deemed as acceptable? That is, how does the world of competitive eating respond to these conflicts in what appears to be an otherwise successful sporting drama? The responses to these issues also are polarized and thus, are targeted to the individual problems.

In response to the obesity epidemic, the IFOCE clearly states (and promotes) that it does not advise using home-training methods that include excessive eating and "discourages younger individuals from eating for speech or quantity under any circumstances" ("Safety Standards"). Moreover, since Kobayashi burst onto the competitive eating scene, many "average"-size competitive eaters have risen in the ranks. Sonya Thomas and Janet Lee are both known for their diminutive physical statures. Joey Chestnut, Tim Janus, Patrick Bertoletti, and Rich LeFevre are known for their skill, not for their size. As mentioned earlier, many gurgitators report that in between contests, they maintain healthy diets and exercise regularly. Although people of size compete in the event, physical bulk is not a requirement for success.

The IFOCE has also taken a more active stance in response to food security. For example, the IFOCE has established "ifoceGIVES," a program established to collect and then donate money to such causes as Second Harvest (now Feeding America) and the American Red Cross. Fans who peruse the MLE Web site will observe posted requests for donations to a variety of charitable organizations ranging from the Grameen Foundation to China Relief. Moreover, the IFOCE now employs a director of philanthropy who "will expand the reach of IFOCE hunger-related efforts, increasing volunteering at food banks and food kitchens and seeking donations of food and resources to support charities" ("ifoceGIVES"). The IFOCE also reported that in conjunction with the annual hot dog eating contest, Nathan's would donate 100,000 hot dogs to various New York City food banks. And both Kobayashi and Chestnut are reported to "frequently donate all or part of their winnings to charity" (Tan).

Despite the IFOCE's and its competitors' responses to these food-related issues, the tension between competitive eating and food-related issues will not disappear. As problems related to obesity and food security persist, the IFOCE and its competitors must fulfill roles similar to their sports counterparts; the superstars must highlight their contributions to alleviating health problems directly related to eating. Whether society continues to sanction contests that fly in the face of such health problems can be answered only with time.

■ The Finale?

Whether competitive eating continues to maintain its status as a cultural artifact is yet to be determined. There is no doubt that the drama of whether an American can retain the Mustard Belt will continue through 2009. But in order for competitive eating to maintain its status with the American public, old rivalries will need to be sustained or new rivalries will need to emerge.

Additionally, through the IFOCE, Major League Eating is now expanding to the international arena. On July 27, 2008, Singapore became host to MLE's first contest in Asia ("Japanese Man Wins"). As the IFOCE continues to expand internationally and perhaps works to meet its mandate of encouraging "the development of new categories of competitive eating," innovation will perhaps continue to retain its current fan base and attract new fans to the sport (Mandate).

Whether people are intrigued or repulsed by professional eating, the gurgitators, who consider themselves as serious athletes, continue to train and continue to set new world records. The IFOCE continues to promote sanctioned contests as it expands the realm of professional competitive eating into the virtual and international arenas. Although the IFCOE and MLE must grapple with various issues inherent in any professional sport, the alignment with more traditional sports enables fans to identify with the sport and promotes the drama of rivalry as more competitive eating events move from mere contest to spectacle. The debate about whether competitive eating is a true sport will continue, but until that debate is resolved, competitive eating will continue its performance as sport.

Works Cited

"About Us." *Feeding America*. Feeding America, n.d. Accessed on 26 Sept. 2008. <http://feedingamerica.org/about-us.aspx>.

Associated Press. "Celebrating, Indifferent Ways: The Contest; Trying to be Top Dog Again." *Newsday* 4 July 2008: A02. *LexisNexis*. Accessed on 8 July 2008.

Belson, Ken. "Teeth Don't Fail Me Now: Upstart Seizes Hot-Dog Title." *International Herald Tribune* 6 July 2007: 2. *LexisNexis*. Accessed on 14 June 2008.

———. "The Winner and New Champion, with 66 Hot Dogs." *New York Times* 5 July 2007, final ed.: B5. *LexisNexis*. Accessed on 18 Oct. 2007.

Berger, Arthur Asa. *The Agent in the Agency: Media, Popular Culture, and Everyday Life in America*. Cresskill: Hampton, 2003.

———. *Cultural Criticism: A Primer of Key Concepts*. Thousand Oaks: Sage, 1995.

Berton, Justin. "Eating Contest Is Dogged by Controversy." *San Francisco Chronicle* 5 July 2006, final ed.: A1. *LexisNexis*. Accessed on 14 Feb. 2007.

————. "Joey Chestnut Hopes to be the New Face of Speed Eating – First, He Has Some Cramming to Do." *San Francisco Chronicle* 27 May 2006, final ed.: E1. *LexisNexis*. Accessed on 14 Feb. 2007.

"Bunnette Videos." *Major League Eating*. N.p., n.d. Accessed on 30 July 2008. <http://www.majorleagueeating.com/>.

Burke, Kenneth. *A Rhetoric of Motives*. Berkeley: U of California P, 1969.

Collins, Clayton. "Eating as Sport and Spectacle." *Christian Science Monitor* 25 Nov. 2005: 25. *LexisNexis*. Accessed on 14 June 2008.

Derakhshani, Tirad. "From Wing Bowl to Top Dog." *Philadelphia Inquirer* 5 July 2007: E02. *LexisNexis*. Accessed on 14 June 2008.

"Dr. Remote." *St. Petersburg Times* 4 July 2007: 2C. *LexisNexis*. Accessed on 14 June 2008.

Fagone, Jason. *Horsemen of the Esophagus: Competitive Eating and the Big Fat American Dream*. New York: Three Rivers, 2006.

"Fat and Getting Fatter." *Economist* 25 Aug. 2007: 32. *EBSCO*. Accessed on 29 July 2008.

"Featured Videos." *Major League Eating*. N.p., n.d. Accessed on 25 July 2008. <http://www.majorleagueeating.com/>.

Fuller, Linda K., ed. *Sports, Rhetoric, and Gender: Historical Perspectives and Media Representations*. New York: Palgrave, 2006.

Gerson, Michael. "A Week of Hunger." *Washington Post* 9 July 2008, regional ed.: A15. *LexisNexis*. Accessed on 30 July 2008.

Glionna, John M. "Enjoying the Fill of Victory; Joey Chestnut Is a Top 'Gurgitator' on the Power-Eating Circuit." *Los Angeles Times* 4 Sept. 2006: A1. *LexisNexis*. Accessed on 4 Sept. 2007.

Goldiner, Dave. "Ailing Champ Still Yearns for Coney." *Daily News* 27 June 2007, final ed.: 15. *LexisNexis*. Accessed on 14 June 2008.

Hoffman, Benjamin. "The More He Devours, the More Fans Eat It Up." *New York Times* 1 July 2007, late ed.: SP9. *LexisNexis*. Accessed on 4 Sept. 2007.

Holben, David H., and Pheley, Alfred M. "Diabetes Risk and Obesity in Food-Insecure Households in Rural Appalachian Ohio." *Preventing Chronic Disease* (July 2006): n. page. Accessed on 29 July 2008. <http://www.cdc.gov/pcd/issues/2006/jul/05_0127.htm>.

Home page. *International Federation of Competitive Eating*. IFOCE, n.d. Accessed on 30 July 2008. <http://www.ifoce.com/home.php>.

Home page. *Krystal Square Off World Hamburger Eating Championship*. Krystal Company, n.d. Accessed on 26 Sept. 2008. <http://www.krystalsquareoff.com/>.

"ifoceGIVES." *International Federation of Competitive Eating*. IFOCE, n.d. Accessed on 30 July 2008. <http://www.ifoce.com/ifocegives.php>.

"Japanese Man Wins Eating Competition." *CHINAdaily.com.cn*. China Daily Information Co., 29 July 2008. Accessed on 29 July 2008. <http://www.chinadaily.com.cn/cndy/2008-07/29/content_6884120.htm>.

Lucadamo, Kathleen. "Wiener and Still Champion. Hot Shot 6-time Victor Is Top Dog at Nathan's." *Daily News* 5 July 2006, final ed.: 13. *LexisNexis.* Accessed on 14 June 2008.

"Mandate." *International Federation of Competitive Eating.* IFOCE, n.d. Accessed on 30 July 2008. <http://www.ifoce.com/about-mandate.php>.

McShane, Larry. "Ex-hot Dog King: Won't Choke in '08." *Daily News* 3 July 2008: 18*LexisNexis.* Accessed on 8 July 2008.

"Nathan's Famous to Donate 100,000 Hot Dogs." *International Federation of Competitive Eating.* IFOCE, 24 June 2008. Accessed on 30 July 2008. <http://www.ifoce.com/news.php?action=detail&sn=609>.

Nerz, Ryan. *Eat this Book: A Year of Gorging and Glory on the Competitive Eating Circuit.* New York: St. Martin's, 2006.

"Overweight and Obesity: Introduction." *Centers for Disease Control and Prevention.* U.S. Government, n.d. Accessed on 29 July 2008. <http://www.cdc.gov/nccdphp/dnpa/obesity/>.

"Preview: Major League Eating." *GamePro.* IDG Entertainment, 16 Apr. 2008. Accessed on 8 July 2008. <http://www.gamepro.com/article/previews/177168/major-league-eating/>.

Ramirez Anthony. "Hot Dog Champ and Upstart Set for July Fourth Face-Off." *New York Times* 28 July 2007, late ed.: B3. *LexisNexis.* Accessed on 4 Sept. 2007.

"Rankings." *International Federation of Competitive Eating.* IFOCE, n.d. Accessed on 30 July 2008. <http://www.ifoce.com/rankings.php>.

Rao, Goutham. "Childhood Obesity: Highlights of AMA Expert Committee Recommendations." *American Family Physician* 78.1 (2008): 56–63. *Google Scholar.* Accessed on 29 July 2008.

Ravn, Karen. "Speed Eaters Push the Limits." *Los Angeles Times* 5 May 2008: F1. *LexisNexis.* Accessed on 14 June 2008.

"Records." *International Federation of Competitive Eating.* IFOCE, n.d. Accessed on 30 July 2008. <http://www.ifoce.com/records.php>.

Red, Carmine "Cai" M. "Major League Eating: The Game." *NintendoWorldReport.com.* Nintendo World Report, 15 Apr. 2008. Accessed on 8 July 2008. <http://www.nintendoworldreport.com/impressionsArt.cfm?artid=15757>.

"Safety Standards." *International Federation of Competitive Eating.* IFOCE, n.d. Accessed on 30 July 2008. <http://www.ifoce.com/safety.php>.

Salamone, Gina. "Hungry Women: They're Taking a Bite Out of Male-Dominated Competitive Eating Contests." *Daily News* 25 June 2006, final ed.: 35. *LexisNexis.* Accessed on 4 Sept. 2007.

Sandomir, Richard. "The Hideous Masters of Gluttony." *New York Times* 6 July 2007, late ed.: D6. *LexisNexis.* Accessed on 21 July 2008.

Sederstrom, Jotham, and Adam Lisberg. "I Was Bun in the U.S.A. After 6 Yrs., American Wins Nathan's Hot Dog Crown by Chomping Down 66." *Daily News* 5 July 2007, final ed.: 3. *LexisNexis.* Accessed on 14 June 2008.

Suddath, Claire. "A Brief History of Competitive Eating." *Time* 3 July 2008: n. pag. *Time.com.* Accessed on 8 July 2008. <http://www.time.com/time/nation/article/0,8599,1820052,00.html>.

Tan, Rebecca Lynne. "Eating Champs Donate Wins; Big Names in Eating Competitions say They Give to Charity in the Face of Criticism of Gluttony Events." *The Straits Times (Singapore)* 29 July 2008: n. pag. *LexisNexis*. Accessed on 30 July 2008.

2006 Nathan's Famous Hot Dog Eating Contest. ESPN. 4 July 2006.

2007 Nathan's Famous Hot Dog Eating Contest. ESPN. 4 July 2007.

2008 Nathan's Famous Hot Dog Eating Contest. ESPN. 4 July 2008.

Wiedeman, Reeves. "Crowds Flock to Nathan's, but Once Is Enough." *Si.com*. Time Inc., 4 July 2008. Accessed on 25 July 2008. <http://sportsillustrated.cnn.com/2008/more/07/04/hot.dog.contest.2008/index.html>.

Wilson, Craig. "On July 4th, 66 Hot Dogs Is Par for the Course." *USA Today* 2 July 2008, final ed.: 1D. *LexisNexis*. Accessed on 3 July 2008.

"Year in Review: 2007." *International Federation of Competitive Eating*. IFOCE, 1 Jan. 2008. Accessed on 25 July 2008. <http://www.ifoce.com/news.php?action=detail&sn=574>.

Zambito, Thomas, and Kathleen Lucadamo. "Frank Exchanges in Coney Dog Fight." *Daily News*. 4 July 2007, final ed.: 4. *LexisNexis*. Accessed on 14 June 2008.

Notes

1. This analysis focuses on the International Federation of Competitive Eating (IFOCE), IFOCE competitive eaters, and the IFOCE sanctioned Nathan's Famous 4th of July International Hot Dog Eating Contest. This analysis includes only a cursory examination of, for example, the Wing Bowl. The Wing Bowl is held in Philadelphia's Wachovia Center and draws twenty thousand fans a year.

2. The IFOCE is the most visible of professional eating organizations. Nerz discusses the origin and development of the IFOCE (16). It is important to note the existence of one other eating organization, the Association of Independent Competitive Eaters (AICE), a more loosely structured organization. Both Nerz and Fagone discuss the goals of the AICE.

3. Assumptions of the concept of identification are based on the work of Kenneth Burke, who includes discussions of identification in several of his treatises. See, for example, *A Rhetoric of Motives* (Burke).

4. ESPN coverage of the Nathan's Hot Dog Eating Contests is admittedly humorous. Sportscasters themselves admit to the use of humor, exaggeration, and hyperbole. Generally, throughout the broadcasts, visual and verbal references focused on the great records or the great rivalries of traditional sports are advanced. Information pertaining to competitive eaters, of course, finds its way into those comparisons.

5. There are several discussions pertaining to gender and sports. Many of these discussions focus on revealing the masculine privilege in the performance and presentation of sports. See, for example, *Sport, Rhetoric, and Gender: Historical Perspectives and Media Representations* (Fuller).

11

■ Hip-Hop, the NBA, and Street Basketball

The Rhetorical Dimensions
of Performance at the Intersection
of Class, Race, and Popular Culture

☐ Kevin A. Johnson

There is a circulation of signs between the culture of hip-hop and the professional ranks of basketball. In the NBA, players such as Shaquille O'Neal (Shaq),
Ron Artest, and Allen Iverson (AI) have ventured into making their own rap
albums as a sign of their connection with hip-hop culture. One of the earliest
signs of hip-hop culture's connection with professional basketball occurred
in commercials promoting Nike where Michael Jordan "appeared alongside
Spike Lee, who also connected to Public Enemy and the hip-hop culture"
(Smith). According to Jeffrey Williams, "the league's liaison with hip-hop
culture is an excellent illustration of the complex commercial ventures typical
of the league. Consider a recent advertisement on NBA.com featuring Allen
Iverson alongside 50 Cent." AI is a prime example of the way the NBA has
marketed hip-hop culture. Thomas Oates pointed out that AI has become
one of the league's most marketable players. He enjoys a lifetime contract
with Reebok, which sells his endorsed shoe "The Answer" by positioning

the player as a rebel in the hip-hop tradition. The NBA licensed and produced a special DVD profiling him, and his image is now being used to promote the league worldwide. (378)

By the year 2000, "both hip-hop and the NBA had billions of fans worldwide, many of whom looked to Iverson as one to emulate if you desired to be either hip-hop or a basketball player" (Smith). The connection between the performance of NBA athletes and hip-hop aesthetics may be found in several other places including video games, halftime entertainment, All-Star Game festivities, and several other commercial ventures. These interconnections show how signs of hip-hop culture are performed within the NBA basketball league and extended into the sports industry, the sports apparel industry, and the hip-hop cultural industry.

Many scholars have articulated the way NBA athletes perform the cultural signs of hip-hop and how such signs are circulated within larger cultural industries. For example, Boyd examined the way basketball and hip-hop changes the signs of the "American Dream from the perspective of the young, Black, rich and famous" (15). Nonetheless, scholars have largely ignored an important aspect of the circulation of signs in basketball performances. The glaring omission is the way streetball circulates signs to the NBA performers, and, perhaps more importantly, which signs are denied circulation into NBA performance. Streetball is a form of basketball that exists outside the dominant organizational structure of basketball games and is largely associated with the type of basketball that you might find on playgrounds across the world rather than with the type of basketball that is played inside arenas. One of the minor points that this chapter will posit is that streetball offers a very different reaction to the "American Dream" than the pursuit of basketball at the NBA level. In making this minor point, I will demonstrate that the NBA wants hip-hop without hip-hop, and that this idea is necessary to sustain its commercial vitality.

The central argument of this chapter is that there is an important bank of signs within sports that reflects the intersectional performance of race, class, and hip-hop culture and that these signs have important rhetorical effects as they circulate within the popular consumption of culture. In advancing this argument, this chapter will move back and forth between the formal characteristics of hip-hop culture in professional basketball and analyze the implications for the popular cultural consumption of basketball as performance. Thus, this chapter will articulate the dynamic tensions involved in the clash between athletic performance in the game of basketball and artistic signs found in hip-hop culture. In the end, we will be able to learn valuable insights into larger struggles between economic classes and the cultural performance of class, race, and gender in sports and popular culture.

Street basketball was perhaps made most famous with the rise in popularity of the Harlem Globetrotters, which grew out from the playgrounds on the South Side of Chicago in the 1920s. Since then, street basketball has increasingly garnered popularity. Rucker Park in Harlem, New York, has seen many popular basketball legends such as Wilt Chamberlain, Julius Erving, and Kareem Abdul-Jabbar. Recently, many popular NBA legends, including AI, Lebron James, and Vince Carter, have played at Rucker and Kobe Bryant, Magic Johnson, and Baron Davis have played at Venice Beach in Los Angeles to show that they can play with those on the street. Most recently, streetball has reached unprecedented levels of success with the popularity of AND1.

AND1 is the most popular form of streetball in America. AND1 began in 1993 as a school project by three students at the University of Pennsylvania's Wharton Business School. After AND1 received footage of Rafer Alston (AKA, Skip to My Lou), they introduced a Mix Tape series (streetball highlight set to rap music) and a worldwide streetball tour and soon became "synonymous around the world with a new style of 'streetball' that transformed basketball" (Vecsey). AND1 has garnered its success by riding the coattails of hip-hop. AND1's mixtapes "have been a major feature of promoting the hip-hop influenced streetball aesthetic" (Oates 380). In terms of apparel in the NBA, AND1 is garnering increasing popularity amongst players. According to Alexander Wolff, "Nike still has slightly more than half of all NBA players under contract, but AND1 now services 21% of the league, more than Adidas, Reebok, or Converse." According to Oates, "These efforts have played an important, perhaps even central, role in the sudden profitability of basketball's emerging hip-hop aesthetic" (380). While AND1 is indeed a corporate institution, AND1 gains its niche market based on its claims to streetball authenticity. Thus, weaving between the constraints of the consumer base of AND1 and the NBA will prove productive in highlighting some of the major differences and tensions between sport performance in the NBA and streetball. This chapter will primarily discuss the NBA, while occasionally using streetball (i.e., AND1) as an example of the limitations placed on the performance of NBA athletes.

Specifically, this chapter is organized into five sections. The first section explains the role of market racism and its effect on Black male hip-hop performance in the NBA. Section two explains the formal characteristics of hip-hop performance. Section three provides an analysis of the way class is performed in the signs of hip-hop in the NBA. Section four analyzes the various aesthetic dimensions of professional and street basketball in order to articulate the performative restrictions placed on the NBA athlete. Finally, section five will look into some of the implications of the popular cultural consumption of hip-hop aesthetics in the sport of basketball.

■ Market Racism and Black Male Hip-Hop Performance in the NBA

The existence of hip-hop signs that are found in the performance of athletes in the NBA cannot be understood outside the consumer base of the NBA market that manages the range of tolerable hip-hop signs that are able to appear in the league. The battle over which hip-hop signs the NBA athlete may use to perform as a basketball player may best be understood by examining the larger popular cultural consumption of the NBA player and the hip-hop young Black male body. According to David Leonard, such an examination requires an interrogation of the popular cultural "demonization of hip-hop in general and young Black males and societal efforts to reform, discipline, and punish those 'othered' deviant bodies who persistently threaten the (NBA) status quo" (164). Racism in the NBA is manifest in at least two significant ways: (1) "market racism" occurs as the result of a fundamentally racist fantasy lying behind a popular cultural consumption that dominates a significant part of the market that the NBA relies upon for its profit margins and (2) more overt forms of racism in data concerning the economic disparities between White and Black players in the NBA.

"Market racism" may be defined as a type of racism that occurs when capitalist interests are upheld even when they have racist implications. For instance, when the NBA caters to fans who make complaints based on the race of the players in the NBA, the NBA is implementing a form of market racism. Important to note is that "middle-class whites form a significant chunk of the revenue base behind the hip-hop industry" and also the NBA (Williams). According to Williams, "a large majority of hip-hop artists are black and hip-hop contains musical and lyrical connections with black culture. The actual contours of the rap market are lost on consumers disinterested in the music products or personalities. An aversive audience sees only the frightening similarity; differences are lost." Many players in the NBA perform the artistic dimensions of basketball with similar implication. The actual contours of the hip-hop basketball art form are lost on consumers. An aversive audience sees only the frightening similarity between the various elements of hip-hop culture; differences are lost. This tension between an aversion to hip-hop culture and the simultaneous consumption of the performance of hip-hop culture in the NBA is the precise tension that the hip-hop NBA baller must continually be in the position of managing.

There are numerous symptoms of the racist fantasies that are found in popular cultural narratives about the use of hip-hop signs in the performance of NBA athletes that are symptomatic of a paranoia of the Black hip-hop basketball player or, at the very least, a paranoia about the hip-hop aesthetic. For example, the NBA cracked down on the types of clothing and apparel that their players were allowed to wear after many fans wrongly conflated the hip-hop aesthetic with the aesthetic of gang membership. One "fan" wrote in favor of the dress code: "No one is taking away your cultural identity. You're being told to wear dress pants and to stop looking like a thug" (Carter 11C). Allusions to hip-hop aesthetics being "thug" aesthetics are found in many editorials and reactions specifically talking about the NBA dress code. The inaccuracy of this conflation shows clearly how dominant popular culture does not understand the complexities of hip-hop culture.

In this case, gang aesthetics are much more varied than a universal hip-hop aesthetic form. The cultural performance of hip-hop is made up of three distinct formal characteristics: flow, layering, and rupture. I will discuss these characteristics much more in section four of this chapter. For now, it is important to note that, in terms of the performance of gang aesthetics, there are many biker gangs, mafia gangs, and the like that do not ascribe to a hip-hop aesthetic. Certain gangs may have chosen to express themselves with a hip-hop aesthetic, but that is a far cry from hip-hop aesthetics being the same as gang aesthetics. This is not to mention the type of gangster aesthetic that dresses the same way that the NBA dress code mandates ("business" attire). Thus, in a perverse way, if we treat all gangs equally, the dominant popular culture chooses to single out the gangster aesthetic that the fantasy identifies with Black gangs. So, at its perverse core, the popular cultural demand for a dress code in the NBA is racist by singling out the images of the Black gang (or, as popular culture would identify, as "looking like a thug") for regulation while looking like White gangsters who ascribe to a "business" aesthetic by wearing suits is privileged.

Regardless of the racial implications in dominant popular cultural narratives, the NBA decided to crack down on the attire that constitutes a "proper" performance aesthetic of an athlete by instituting a dress code to explicitly ban certain hip-hop aesthetic clothing and accessories that are signs of hip-hop culture. Thus, because of the dominant popular cultural consumption, many Black athletes who identify with hip-hop as being bound to their own cultural identity/expression (Black or not) were forced to leave their cultural identity closeted at home if they were to continue having access to public space in the NBA. At the most, this is market racism. At the very least this is a product of cultural imperialism.

This cultural imperialism is part of a larger popular cultural fantasy that seeks to control, discipline, and ultimately disarm Black bodies. This fantasy is reflected in America in the growth of "prison populations, shrinking social welfare budgets, and overzealous police, prosecutors, and judges ready to throw children into jail just as teachers, principals, and school administrators increasingly expel students (of color) for even the smallest infraction" (Leonard 163). As long as the NBA concerns itself with catering to the dominant popular cultural fantasies of its market base, they will continue to be highly susceptible to the racist impulses of segments of their fans. Thus far, the NBA does not appear to be intending to move away from such fantasies since, aside from the dress code, the NBA's catering to racist fantasies may be found reflected in other areas such as the existence of a wage gap between White and Black players in the NBA favoring Whites by anywhere from 11 to 25% (Shropshire) and the fact that "white players have a 36 percent lower risk of being cut than black players,...translating into an expected career length of 7.5 seasons for an apparently similar player who is white and 5.5 seasons for the same player who is black" (Hoang and Rascher 69).

The control over the signs of hip-hop and the disciplining of the bodies that attempt to use such signs as part of their performance as basketball players are brought into an even more vivid light in the context of the mandating of the minimum age for players in the NBA and the instituting of a rookie salary scale.

In response to the NBA's requirement that players be at least one year out of high school before playing in the league, Jermaine O'Neal (an NBA athlete) said, "As a black guy you kind of think (race is) the reason why it's coming up. You don't hear about it in baseball or hockey. To say you have to be 20, 21 to get in the league, it's unconstitutional. If I can go to the U.S. Army and fight the war at 18, why can't you play basketball for 48 minutes and then go home?" (qtd. in "Pacers'"). You can certainly see where O'Neal is coming from when you know that "hundreds of anonymous, White young men leave high school each year to make $650 per month to play minor league baseball," coupled with the fact that eighteen-year-old men are entrusted with rifles on the battlefield (Shropshire). So why was the dress code instituted?

Along with the inscription of the "White man's burden," NBA Ccommissioner David Stern emphasized that the age limit was important for "winning back fans" and that "the league's motivation emanated from business concerns, their effort to placate fan concerns, and the increasing discomfort of many NBA executives with scouting teenagers" (Leonard 170). The age limit in the NBA "embodies a long history of the 'White man's burden' in which White men have presumed to know what is best for people of color" (Leonard 171). The narrative that such a fantasy supports is found in the popular cultural discourse that argues that "an age restriction will not save those players who are not ready for the league by forcing them to college to receive an 'education' or greater athletic development, but will serve as a deterrent for thousands of young Black males by creating role models who go to college rather than to the league" (Leonard 171). Thus, the fantasy of the White man's burden teaches popular culture how to desire a "seasoned" and "domesticated" Black male and teaches the Black male how to "perform" culture in such a way as to cater to this White man's burden.

What demonstrates that the NBA is, in fact, catering to the popular cultural fantasy is that in every "negative" category (from the perspective of the fantasy) NBA players who enter straight from high school are empirically more "well-behaved" (or "per-form" better) than those who attend college for up to four years. For example, "according to a study of recently arrested NBA players, NBA players who attended college for four years represent a disproportionately high percentage of arrested NBA players, while those who did not attend college represent a disproportionately low percentage" (McCann). Therefore, the NBA's decision to mark an age limit must be strictly to conform to a public fantasy that functions to establish/craft authority for a managerial role "model" for a particular aesthetic. Those who are able to take to the NBA stage to perform their craft must now fit into a certain age group.

Another mode for the paternalistic crafting of the managerial aesthetic is the creation of a sense of "obligation" to the interests of the ownership. This obligation is important because it is an explicit strategy for controlling the performance of hip-hop signs in the NBA. One of the ways the obligation is created in the NBA is through the rookie wage scale that was established as part of the 1995 collective bargaining agreement signed between the league and the player's union. After this agreement, "rookies could no longer negotiate their earnings over their first three seasons, and thus the earning power of top draft picks would plummet. Not surprisingly,…veteran players would now receive larger portions of their teams' salary caps" (McCann). Rookies do not get a seat at the collective bargaining table, so their interests are often not represented in collective bargaining agreements. This structure is intended to create a hierarchical scheme whereby the NBA may instill in players a sense of obligation. For instance, Phoenix Suns executive Cotton Fitzsimmons explicitly stated in relation to the wage scale, "We need to make young players feel an obligation to the game, to pay some dues" (qtd. in McCann). Taken together, then, we can see how the NBA clearly is embedded in a paternalistic fantasy as a means toward the end of creating a "proper" manager that both regulates their own self and serves to "manage" the arena where dominant popular cultural fantasies that are paranoid about hip-hop clash with hip-hop culture.

Aside from paternalism, another area of marginalization occurs with exploitation and the experience of alienation. For the NBA, as long as owners are able to exploit and alienate the athlete from the labor of their performance, the owners will also be able to control the signs of hip-hop that are used in the athletic performance itself. According to Leonard, the NBA wants to "push future players into conditions and spaces that will ultimately produce a commodifiable yet controllable installment of today's hip-hop baller" (175). This is perfectly consistent with the January 30, 1995 cover of *Sports Illustrated* that warned the NBA about a new generation of disrespectful players, raised on the culture of hip-hop, who were "like a cancer" in need of surgical removal to ensure the league's survival (Taylor 20). Though the NBA has removed a few players from the league by refusing to tend contracts (for whatever reason), they have most explicitly preferred to remove certain aspects from the hip-hop aesthetic from their players' appearances in the league. In order to maintain its vision of creating a controllable hip-hop baller as a commodity, the NBA hires popular hip-hop athletes to ensure the NBA's commercial vitality. Then, the NBA performs the function of molding the hip-hop baller as per the form of the controllable commodity. In this way, there is a performance from both the NBA and the hip-hop NBA baller—they both fit a proper form to perform.

Aside from banning certain hip-hop expressions in its dress code while continuing to market other hip-hop aesthetics, a prime example of the NBA's strategy to control the performance of hip-hop signs while simultaneously commodifying its hip-hop baller is the hiring of Rafer Alston (AKA, Skip to My Lou). Skip to My Lou was made famous worldwide by AND1. After signing with the NBA, Alston performed the controllable hip-hop baller role through many of his interviews comparing and contrasting the NBA with streetball. For instance, he has stressed that streetball ought to "play within the rules," when he criticized the newer mix tapes for featuring "more and more illegal moves and globetrotterish japery" (Wolff). Specifically, Alston stated, "Everything I did on Volume One was legal. O.K., maybe a palming violation or two—but 98 percent of the players in the NBA palm to get from one place to another. Now the Tapes are more about trying to do tricks" (qtd. in Wolff). Moreover, with Alston's "street credibility" the NBA is able to benefit by rhetorically crafting AND1 as a minor league of the NBA where players lack "proper" basketball fundamentals. Speaking about what accounts for AND1's popularity both as a league and on the streets, Alston stated, "A lot of it is that the people who enjoy it and gravitate to it are looking to see who can be the next guy from street ball to make it to the NBA. The other thing is creativity. It's something other than an ordinary basketball game" (qtd. in Nance 5C). He also stated, "One thing [streetball's] going to do is make sure [the players] can handle the ball. But the fundamentals won't be there...that come with being a successful player" (qtd. in Nance 12C). This is a clever statement (potentially much deeper than Alston had intended) since it privileges the NBA style of basketball by labeling the ability to play in the NBA as the ultimate "success" that any basketball player should want to achieve while at the same time privileging the fundamentals that are necessary for the NBA game at the expense of the fundamentals of the street game.

Exploitation is difficult to measure amongst NBA players because their share of the wealth is so much higher than that of other employees who are necessary for the NBA's functioning (e.g., the employees who clean the arenas after games). However, by championing itself as the "American Dream" for millions of basketball players throughout the world, those who are seeking to "make it" in the NBA are alienated from their labor. AND1 is a perfect example of the way players are exploited. According to Wolff, AND1 "counts 165 employees and $180 million in annual revenue, and sells products in 125 countries." In addition, it is specifically streetball that has "become AND1's meal ticket." Even though streetball represents the most significant profits for AND1, each of its streetball players (between ten and twenty-one players each year) earns an annual amount ranging from $35,000 on the low end to just over $100,000 on the high end ("How Much"; Vecsey). Even if the roster averaged $100,000 per year, AND1 still would average profits of at least $178 million per year. If the rest of the 145 or so employees earned $100,000 per year, the owners of AND1 would still profit $163,500,000 annually. Karl Marx defined the "rate of exploitation" as "the proportion of unpaid, surplus labour a worker performs for their employer to the necessary labour workers perform, producing the value equivalent of the wage they are paid" ("Exploitation"). Thus, for AND1, the rate of exploitation is roughly $163,500,000 (you can give or take a million dollars or eight if you'd like). Recently, as a result of such exploitation and AND1 being sold to American Sporting Goods, several players began their own company named Ball4Real so that they could have a share of the ownership of their labor. AND1 was able to retain ten players on its roster and will continue to market its street basketball. All of this does not even take into account the unpaid labor involved in the hours of training and equipping athletes who are the future of AND1, the NBA, and other professional basketball leagues.

The rift between the players of AND1 and the newly established Ball4Real is indicative of the importance of the battle over sport performance in the game of basketball. The battle over the regulation of performative dimensions of basketball is a site of contestation over the battle between cultures. How this battle is fought and mediated has much to teach us about the way contrary cultural forces mediate tensions and at the same time is indicative of the relation between performance and class exploitation.

■ Formal Characteristics of Hip-Hop Performance

The performance of hip-hop is distinct in its characteristics. The contestation over the way hip-hop is performed in basketball has much to do with hip-hop's rootedness in Black culture. In order to understand this contestation over the way hip-hop signs are circulated between the culture of hip-hop and the professional ranks of basketball, this section will lay out the foundational features of the hip-hop form. Tricia Rose credited Arthur Jafa with the explanation that hip-hop is constituted in a formal sense by flow, layering, and ruptures in line. According to Rose, "In hip-hop, visual, physical, musical, and lyrical lines are set in motion, broken abruptly with sharp angular breaks, yet they sustain motion and energy through fluidity and flow" (38). She continued by arguing that flow, layering, and rupture "create and sustain rhythmic motion, continuity, and circularity via flow; accumulate, reinforce, and embellish this continuity through layering; and manage threats to these narratives by building in ruptures that highlight the continuity as it momentarily challenges it" (39). In terms of style and aesthetics, these three features make up the ordering of the hip-hop cultural art form.

For example, if you listen to a rap song you will find all of these elements. You will commonly hear MCs give "shout outs" to previous MCs either by explicitly mentioning their name or by quoting a line from them that is so famous that you don't even need to say who said it. This is part of the layering process in rap music whereby the MC pays homage to other MCs while layering it into their own new contribution. In the same song, you will hear breaks in the rhythm that are built in at the same time that the music flows together. So, for instance, you hear the layering occur in Lil' Kim's "Hold It Now" where she uses beats from the Beastie Boys. You also hear the rupture with the "hold it now" lyrics when the record scratches, and you hear how the music continues to flow together with the ruptures.

Important in the formal characteristics of the hip-hop performance is the role of the audience who consumes such performance. Specifically, the main questions that this chapter asks in terms of the popular cultural consumption and commodification of hip-hop are as follows: For which popular culture is the fantasy of a hip-hop art form staged? Specifically, which popular culture is the restriction of hip-hop signs in the NBA catering to? Furthermore, this chapter asks which narrative of the hip-hop NBA baller is privileged in the larger popular cultural arena?

Important to note is that the hip-hop performance art emerged from the radical loss of meaning for Black culture throughout history. This radical loss of meaning is referred to as "nihilism" whereby there is absolutely no purpose to anything—hip-hop exists for the sake of hip-hop. In African American history, "The slide towards nihilism began with the disintegration of the Black family, the absence of Black fathers, and the subsequent loss of eldership authority. Thus one of the core values which had sustained Afrikans in America since the end of The Holocaust of Afrikan Enslavement was lost" (Makheru). Hip-hop was one of the elements that filled this void for many Black youths. Whenever asked to compromise an element of hip-hop culture, those in hip-hop culture often battle for hip-hop since the loss of hip-hop means the return to the void of oppressive conditions. Therefore, it is no surprise that there are dynamic tensions at play when hip-hop youth are asked to perform class in a way that compromises the culture that has given them meaning for so long.

■ Performing Class in Hip-Hop and the NBA

Hip-hop has been a means of cultural expression toward the end of attempting to create meaning out of oppressive conditions. According to Rose, "Hip-hop is a cultural form that attempts to negotiate the experiences of marginalization, brutally truncated opportunity, and oppression within the cultural imperatives of African-American and Caribbean history, identity, and community" (21). This is not to get into the problematic of an authentically Black culture, but rather to explain that hip-hop grew out of the attempt to negotiate experiences of marginalization in general. Mumia Abu-Jamal wrote that hip-hop "arises from a generation that feels with some justice that they have been betrayed by those who came before them. That they are at best tolerated in schools, feared on the streets, and almost inevitably destined for the hell holes of prison." The roots of hip-hop come from a generation that "grew up hungry, hated and unloved. And this is the psychic fuel that seems to generate the anger that seems endemic in much of the music and poetry. One senses very little hope above the personal goals of wealth and the climb above the pit of poverty" (Abu-Jamal).

The collision of hip-hop with sport as popular culture is interesting because of the way the formal characteristics of hip-hop are found in the performance of athletes who have experienced the ability to climb above the "pit of poverty" and achieve the "personal goals of wealth," while at the same time struggling to negotiate the web of class relations and racial and cultural identities found in the popular culture that pays their salaries. This web of tension is typical of what Marx called the "petite bourgeoisie." For Marx, the petite bourgeoisie is a fancy name for what amounts to a managerial class. The managerial class must perform a delicate balancing act, and such performance is often confusing.

According to Marx, "the major classes of capitalistic society (the bourgeoisie and the proletariat) meet and become blurred—the petite bourgeoisie is located between these two classes in terms of interests as well as social situation" ("Petite Bourgeoisie"). Although there is no definitive bright line to establish the precise border of inclusion and exclusion from the transitional class of the petite bourgeoisie, we can see how this managerial class functions in the commodification of hip-hop. According to Rose, what is important about "the shift in hip-hop's orientation is not its movement from precommodity to commodity but the shift in control over the scope and direction of the profit-making process, out of the hands of local black and Hispanic entrepreneurs and into the hands of larger white-owned, multinational businesses" (40). The NBA (to a greater extent) and AND1 (to a lesser extent) are in the same tradition by purchasing a share in the hip-hop generation and (by extension) by purchasing a share in the negotiating of the fantasy constructions that result from the experiences of marginalization that are at the root of hip-hop culture.

Rose extensively documented that, "Rap music is fundamentally linked to larger social constructions of black culture as an internal threat to dominant American culture and social order. Rap's capacity as a form of testimony, as an articulation of a young black urban critical voice of social protest has profound potential as a basis for a language of liberation" (144). As a result, big business is smart to hire a managerial class in order to manage the threat of social constructions of Black culture as an internal threat to dominant American culture and social order. More specifically, "the politics of rap music involves the contestation over public space, the meanings, interpretations, and value of the lyrics and music, and the investment of cultural capital" (Rose 124). As such, there is a "complex web of institutional policing to which all rappers are subjected, especially in large public space contexts" (Rose 124). In the largest public space of basketball (the NBA), players are subject to the rules and regulations of the league whereby the players are expected to "manage" (in the petite bourgeoisie tradition) the clash between hip-hop culture and the dominant popular cultural consumption of the hip-hop signs.

In order to get the proper managerial training to be equipped to handle this challenge and to provide an adequate performance as a manager, dominant institutions and dominant popular culture advocates to whom players go "appropriate" trainers who will teach the players "proper" managerial aesthetics. Leonard documented the dominant advocacy noting descriptions of adult players as "too young" and "long legged freaks" while demanding that the

NBA's future stars be forced to go to college so that they may gain "experience away from the court" (167–68). While in college, the players will be subject to the discipline of great trainers such as Roy Williams, "Coach K," and others so that the players may "grow, to remove the pimples from their face, to become men on the court and gentlemen" off the court (167–68). If the Black athletes can subject themselves to the paternalism of proper "trainers" and "keep their nose clean" while managing their shop in the NBA in an effective manner, they might even be allowed to be "promoted" to a larger shop: Shane Battier "never even raised his voice. All Memphians hope he plays here for twelve years and then runs for mayor or governor" (Dan 12C).

■ Aesthetic Dimensions of Professional and Street Basketball

The contestation over aesthetics can never be fully understood outside the context of the political and economic conditions of popular culture. As the politics and economics of the NBA and streetball demonstrate, the battles over the performative dimensions of the sport are the products of a larger cultural politics and the economic decisions of owners who commodify athletic performance. Having already looked into some of the politics of performance involved in catering to dominant popular cultural expectations, we can now turn to several of the specific manifestations of the differences and similarities between the NBA and streetball and how these two forms of basketball have negotiated with hip-hop identity. Speaking about his experience, Alston said that the streetball "style of play is not tolerated (in the NBA). You have to win games. You have to play hard-nosed, straight-up basketball" (qtd. in Nance 5C). Interestingly, streetball also emphasizes winning. What is "hard-nosed" and what is "not tolerated," therefore, are a cultural politics and, therefore, the restrictions of cultural performance in professional basketball are useful to interrogate, since such interrogation will highlight the corporate investment in negotiating the popular cultural consumption of experiences of marginalization.

The Slam Dunk. The performance of the slam dunk differs in both the NBA and streetball. In streetball, it is not uncommon for players to warm-up by practicing the art of the slam dunk in an extravagant manner. The NBA players, on the other hand, warm up for their games with a series of lay-ups mixed in with the occasional garden variety dunk. The second difference in the two styles is that a streetball player on a fast break (assuming he is capable) must dunk the ball in extraordinary fashion or the crowd will boo the player. In the NBA, a fast break is cheered regardless of the style of the dunk because the points are scored. The art of the dunk in the NBA's slam dunk contest is similar to that of the art of hip-hop. The dunkers are expected to flow in their overall motion, layer by incorporating the styles of previous dunkers and pushing them forward, and rupture by incorporating elements such as the "double-pump" that break from the immediacy of the dunk. In the actual games, streetball players may take rupture to another level by putting their feet on the backboard while they hold onto the rim, and by throwing the ball into the stands after their dunk, thus rupturing the flow of the game; whereas in the NBA such "extravagances" are penalized.

Tattoos. In street ball, there are never any issues with players openly displaying their tattoos. In the NBA, there have been multiple cases of restrictions on players displaying their tattoos. For instance, the NBA has airbrushed out AI's tattoos on the cover of magazines (along with his cornrows). Although tattooing is certainly not unique to Black or hip-hop culture, the outcries about the hip-hop baller are often complemented with complaints about their tattoos and thus they become a sign of the performance of a hip-hop aesthetic. For instance, one editorialist wrote about the hip-hop style baggy shorts and the NBA dress code, "I know players are larger, and sometimes looser-fitting garments feel better, but let's get real—baggy bloomer shorts are a joke. And what about all the body art? That also needs to go, even if they have to be surgically removed" (Barry 11C). The NBA's willingness to cater to such demands through "surgically" airbrushing the tattoos reveals an intricate link it has with the cultural imperialism discussed in the previous section—there is no such catering in streetball.

Rubber Bands. In its dress code, the NBA specifically outlawed the ability for players to perform the role of an NBA player while wearing rubber bands. NBA players would often wear rubber bands around their wrists during basketball games. AND1 allows players to wear rubber bands. Rubber bands are popular in hip-hop culture as exemplified by the numerous people who wear rubber bands and rapper TI's hit song "Rubber Band Man." Rubber bands are important to hip-hop culture because they signify the struggle. Rubber bands are flexible and mostly return to shape after they have been stretched; this is metaphorical to the struggle because many who identify with hip-hop culture feel as though they are stretched by the system and yet they themselves stay true to their roots. So, it is not uncommon for wealthy hip-hop artists/athletes to wear rubber bands or use rubber bands instead of money clips in order to be constantly reminded of their roots as they are stretched in all different directions by forces around them (the political and economic forces outlined in the previous sections).

Do-rags. Do-rags are one of those signs of hip-hop culture that were banned in the NBA dress code, although even before the dress code do-rags were unofficially banned and "selectively" enforced as unacceptable signs of hip-hop in athletic performance. A classic example of this was when the NBA "admonished Cuttino Mobley for conducting interviews while wearing a skullcap. Despite his headgear donning the insignia of the NBA, and that he was 'a good guy,' league officials took this moment to remind players about professionalism, values, and the league's new official, yet unofficial, policy concerning hip-hop" (Leonard 161). This is part of the league's policy to create a controllable and commodifiable form of hip-hop. That is, it demonstrates that the NBA wants hip-hop without hip-hop—only the semblance of hip-hop itself. If the athlete is too much hip-hop, they must be subjected to "order." At the very least, the restrictions on rubber bands and do-rags demonstrate the NBA's culturally imperialist policy toward the hip-hop baller. The opposite of the NBA is AND1 and streetball where players are allowed to wear do-rags not only when interacting with fans and media but also while they are playing.

Names. In the NBA, players are mostly called by their legal names and approved nicknames ("Magic" Johnson, Shaq, "King" James, etc.). In streetball, it is not uncommon for players to be called by their street names. The street names sound more like hip-hop MC names than anything else and thus are signs associated with hip-hop performance. Famous street ballers such as Skip to My Lou, Hot Sauce, the Professor, Main Event, Spyda, and AO are referred to by these names on and off the court. According to Rose, "As in many African and Afrodiasporic cultural forms, hip-hop's prolific self-naming is a form of reinvention and self definition.... Taking on new names and identities offers 'prestige from below' in the face of limited access to legitimate forms of status attainment" (36). The NBA, unlike streetball, silences this cultural expression that is found in a long line of African and Afrodiasporic cultural tradition.

Repetition. Though differently manifested, both the NBA and streetballers get enjoyment out of repetition. In both AND1 and the NBA, players are wowed by buzzer beaters, alley oops, and fancy dribbling even though they happen over and over and over again—they never get old. In streetball, the emphasis is also on the repetition of making other people look foolish via crossover dribbles, hitting their opponent in the head with the ball while maintaining the dribble, and creatively getting assists (aka, "dimes"). In streetball, players may make a nasty crossover and be able to pass a player for an easy score, but rather than just score they will choose to perform a rupture in the game by coming back to where they started and dancing to upset the flow of the game. They will then continue back into the flow of the game. This type of making people look foolish is repeated over and over again. In psychoanalytic terms, this is called a "repetition compulsion" where certain acts get repeated again and again in order to get the return to the excesses of enjoyment (i.e., jouissance). The physical manifestation of this is when all of the "oooooooohs!," "ahhhhhhhhhs!," chest bumping, and high fives start flying all over the place. In doing so, the players and fans of streetball and the NBA are able to transform the problems of the self into being able to enjoy through the other (the baller enjoying through the fan and vice-versa).

Authenticity. Both AND1 and the NBA attempt to stake a claim in hip-hop authenticity. In studying a wide variety of texts from a variety of hip-hop artists, Kembrew McLeod found that being authentic consistently meant "staying true to yourself, representing the underground and the street, and remembering hip-hop's legacy, which is the old school" (145). Hip-hop artists perform authenticity claims as a "direct and conscious reaction to the threat of assimilation and the colonization of this self-identified, resistive subculture" (McLeod 145). Many players in the NBA feel the need to play streetball, as evidenced by the street appearances at the famous Rucker Park in New York by players such as Vince Carter, AI, Steve Francis, and Kobe Bryant. Carter said about playing at Rucker that "the best streetball players to ever play come out there, even the best NBA players and all that. You got a lot of tradition out there" (qtd. in "Exclusive"). Many people are of the opinion that streetball is not basketball at all. For instance, Jack Ramsay wrote, "hip-hop lessens the image of the NBA. It lends to associating the NBA with street ball—which really isn't basketball." This is akin to the perception that rap is not music. Such statements "clearly support Eurocentric notions of the terms of cultural progress and link them to music" (Rose 81). As applied to the notions about "inauthentic basketball," saying that streetball is not basketball clearly supports Eurocentric notions of the terms of cultural progress. Moreover, such statements are simply inaccurate given that NBA players are no better than many streetballers when they play them on the street (throughout history this has been true—the Harlem Globetrotters would regularly beat the then NBA Champion Minneapolis Lakers and many streetballers outplay NBA players in the contemporary era).

Announcers. The announcers in the NBA game sit behind the announcer's table the entire time, whereas announcers in the streetball game move around the players and are on the court. NBA announcers are more reserved, whereas streetball announcers will talk trash to the players in the middle of the game by saying things like "You just got schooled by the Professor!" It is not uncommon for announcers such as AND1's Tango (former Rucker Park MC) to weave "in and out of the action with a cordless mike, goading, upbraiding, sometimes even calling for a clear out so two guys can settle some issue one-on-one" (Wolff). The performative form of such trashtalking is a sign of hip-hop since battle rappers often perform such trashtalking through their lyrics. In the NBA, referees and the league typically "settle issues" through penalizing technical fouls and/or fines and/or suspensions. The "clear out" that announcers call for in street basketball is parallel to the battle rap that is in the African American tradition of "woofin.'" Woofin' refers to highly performative verbal sparring and/or performative physical displays as a substitute for physical violence in order to help preserve life and maintain peace and order. In streetball, the announcer is likely to allow woofin' as a way to substitute for physical violence, whereas in the NBA the settlement of issues is taken out of the hands of players and placed into the hands of league officials. Thus, the NBA, more than streetball, strips the players of the agency to decide how to best settle issues.

The Audience. In streetball, members of the audience will oftentimes come onto the court to watch (but still stay out of the way of play), to celebrate with players during the game, and to talk trash with players. In the NBA, fans on the court are subject to fines and jail time. These two different interactions reflect a stark differential in the performance of streetball and the NBA. In AND1, the audience can actually be in the game since tryouts are held a few days before each of the big games throughout the season so players have multiple chances to play in big games. In the NBA, players have to either prove their market worth as college or high school players or they have to try out in the beginning of the season for the entire season. Moreover, the audience is typically more active in their watching of the streetball game and they rarely sit down. At intermissions, you are likely to see breakdancing competitions between crews and freestyle rap sessions amongst crowd members.

Taunting and Celebrations. In streetball, performers commonly engage in taunting and celebrations. Oftentimes, these serve as ruptures in the game when players celebrate by throwing the basketball into the crowd. In the NBA, players are given technical fouls for taunting and excessive celebrations. Alston (Skip to My Lou when not in the NBA) said that fans always want to see (moves made popular on the AND1 tour), and there are times when I want to give it to them.... At [the NBA level] people see that as showboating and taunting. I don't want them to see me as that type of player. I just show them that I can get the job done fundamentally with a hard work ethic and with a business-like approach. (qtd. in Nance 12C) Sportswriter Roscoe Nance reported, "That approach, particularly on defense, earned Van Gundy's trust" (12C). Thus, players are able to gain the "trust" of upper management in the NBA by stripping the taunting and celebrations. C. Richard King and Charles Fruehling Springwood wrote that "disciplinary mechanisms such as these limits on celebration and nineteenth-century prohibitions of Native American dance are informed by a fear that these racial others have impulses that demand a civilizing force in order to rein them in" (201). Restrictions on celebrations in the NBA are thus implicated in the dominant popular cultural consumption of athletes' performance and the maintenance of a managerial aesthetic.

Performance of Gender and Hip-Hop. There are at least two important ways that gender factors into the NBA and streetball performance. First, there is a proper form of celebration and encouragement whereby players give other players "ass slaps." There is a proper form to the ass slap in order not to be a signifier of sexual attraction. For instance, the hand should not be cupped, the hand should not stay on the buttocks for any more than a split second, and there should be no grabbing the buttocks. Or, the player can avoid the ass slap altogether and opt for the chest bump or the high-five. These unwritten rules are consistent with popular homophobic fantasies in both the NBA and AND1. Second, there are no cheerleaders in streetball whereas the NBA has cheerleaders. Apparently, the NBA is less concerned about the impression transmitted about women with the "dress code" for cheerleaders and their expected conduct than it is with the implications of how their players dress on their way to work. Cheerleaders in the NBA are required to dress scantily while maintaining a certain body type—again catering to the "market" of the popular culture that restricts the manageable signs of hip-hop in the NBA.

■ Implications

There are a few implications to the use of hip-hop signs in the athletic performance of basketball. First, the NBA strategy for maintaining its billions of dollars of revenue is consistent with a larger cultural imperialist fantasy that continually wants "the thing deprived of its substance"—or, the thing on its own terms. More specifically, the NBA, and by extension its consumers, want hip-hop without hip-hop—that is, hip-hop deprived of its substance. The

NBA and other shareholders in the hip-hop aesthetic have created the conditions to strip hip-hop of its sub-stance. The paradox, of course, is that hip-hop's substance is to negotiate the expression of marginalization. The NBA (to a greater extent) and AND1 (to a lesser extent) are thus part of a larger popular cultural desubstantialization of hip-hop toward the end of marginalizing the very expression of marginalization through its market regulation of hip-hop culture. In other words, the commodification of hip-hop is reflected in the larger popular culture by appropriating the flow, layering, and rupture as the form of hip-hop while simultaneously allowing the consumer to remain largely unexposed to the expression of marginalization as the substance of hip-hop.

Second, market racism and market (hetero)sexism are the unwritten rules that sustain the popular culture that consumes the performance of NBA athletes. The analysis in this chapter has demonstrated that the NBA's and the popular culture's restrictions are supported by a fantasy of market racism, or at the very least by cultural imperialism—conquest over hip-hop culture and perpetuation of (hetero)sexism. The league is afraid that if it lets hip-hop culture go unchecked then the NBA may cease to exist as the most popular and profitable professional basketball league. In short, if the NBA were to not cater to the dominant popular cultural consumption, the NBA would risk its own disintegration. The preferred alternative from the NBA's perspective is to integrate culture by carefully crafting official prohibitions while allowing the continuation of the unwritten rules that sustain popular cultural fantasy.

The third implication is that the NBA does not care about hip-hop or Black people. The NBA cares about Black people only insofar as they buy their products, play their games, provide a "positive image" for the league, and in some cases manage their teams. What fascinated the NBA so much was not the eruption of an authentic hip-hop culture, but the marginalized (Black) interest in the NBA. Although the NBA knew that its own idea of race is and was corrupted, out in popular culture there were still people who looked to the NBA for racial successes (Michael Jordan, Magic Johnson, among others) and who believed in the NBA as a symbol of racial advancement. What ultimately fascinated the economic classes, and even the wider public, about the NBA was its keen interest in hip-hop (or Black youth) culture. This is the structure of fantasy. And, it was not only the NBA that was fascinated with hip-hop (Black youth) culture; hip-hop (Black youth) culture too was fascinated with the NBA. So we have a double implication. The NBA is able to make billions of dollars from a controllable commodity of hip-hop culture while at the same time instilling a fantasy in hip-hop culture (Black youth) that serves to fulfill three purposes that reinforce each other in cyclical fashion to maintain the league's power: (1) to instill the NBA baller fantasy in the hip-hop baller so they can be purchased and "owned" by the league, (2) to "manage" NBA relations with hip-hop culture and the tensions between hip-hop and popular culture, and (3) to create a reliable consumer base that will continue to purchase NBA products. As long as this cycle is perpetuated the league will continue to expand its markets to find other cultures they can conquer (the European baller, the Chinese baller, etc.).

The fourth implication is that the popular cultural consumption of NBA athletes' performances and the pursuant market racism are part of a larger popular culture that still fears the Black male body on a daily basis. Popular cultural signifiers of the Black male body are found in the streetball aesthetic and are subject to regulation by NBA authorities. Thus, it is not surprising that these signifiers are found in other racial controversies from racial profiling to portrayals of race in Hollywood. Stoler explained, "Whether with public debates concerning the on- and off-court behavior of Black ballers or those regarding welfare or drug abuse, communities of color signify the pollution to which the state or the commissioner 'must constantly purify itself'" (59). Part of the purification is the ability to keep raced bodies at a distance and in a "controlled environment" via prisons and ghettos on the harsh end, and in the NBA and other petite bourgeoisie environments on the soft end. This fantasy materialized itself in the Palace Brawl when Artest (who signified much of the hip-hop aesthetic) was insulted and pelted with trash by White fans. Apparently, laying down on the scorer's table did not coincide with the "clean" fantasy of the fan (perhaps linked to the same sentiments of taunting and celebrations discussed above). The fan felt the need to attempt to purify such a fantasy by trashing Artest himself by literally throwing trash at him.

The ability to navigate the complex relationship between hip-hop and basketball depends on, at the very least, a rich comprehension of the aesthetic and material dimensions of the game. Rapper TI stated, "Rappers do rap about positive things…. Any business, I don't care if you are selling music, haircuts, cutting grass, selling clothes—any business is supply and demand…. If you create a different demand then there will be a different supply. It is up to you guys as the consumer" (qtd. in Muhammad). TI is only partially correct. To place responsibility on the consumer is to ignore the other part of the equation. Leagues such as the NBA and AND1 as well as the consumer are responsible. The NBA chooses to devote most of its time and energy in placating a problematic popular cultural consumption rather than attempting to cultivate a demand that is less problematic. The NBA must do so even though it risks losing racist, culturally imperialist, and (hetero)sexist dollars. The consumer must organize as a part of a larger collective to form ties with people concerned about unjust signification in popular culture, and the players union should implement a stronger strategy in defense of its players (e.g., calling out the NBA for exploiting hip-hop culture while banning players from engaging in that culture). In the end, the "don't hate the player, hate the game" mentality sustains the popular cultural fantasy that sustains the game and the structure of market racism. The game of basketball is in need of change.

Works Cited

Abu-Jamal, Mumia. "Homeland and Hip-Hop." *Revolutionary*, V.2. Artist Immortal Technique. Nature Sounds, 2003. CD.

Barry, Bob. "Editorial: NBA Dress Code: 'Time to Grow Up, Act Like Men.'" *USA Today* 25 Oct. 2005: 11C. LexisNexis. Accessed on 1 Aug. 2008.

Boyd, Todd. *Young, Black, Rich, and Famous: The Rise of the NBA, the Hip Hop Invasion, and the Transformation of American Culture*. Lincoln: Bison, 2008.

Carter, Rich. "Editorial: NBA Dress Code: 'Time to Grow Up, Act Like Men.'" *USA Today* 25 Oct. 2005: 11C. LexisNexis. Accessed on 1 Aug. 2008.

Dan, Ray. "Garnett, Duncan Role Model MVPs." Reporter David Dupree. *USA Today* 24 Feb. 2004: 12C. LexisNexis. Accessed on 1 Aug. 2008.

"Exclusive Interview with Vince Carter about Rucker Park." InsideHoops.com. InsideHoops.com. 30 Sept. 2002. Accessed on 1 Aug. 2008.

"Exploitation." Encyclopedia of Marxism. Marxists Internet Archive, n.d. Accessed on 1 Aug. 2008. <http://www.marxists.org/glossary/terms/e/x.htm>.

Hoang, Ha, and Daniel A. Rascher. "The NBA, Exit Discrimination, and Career Earnings." *Industrial Relations: A Journal of Economy and Society* 31.1 (1999): 69–91. Academic Search Premier. Accessed on 1 Aug. 2008.

"How Much Do Players on the AND1 Tour Earn?" WikiAnswers. Answers Corporation, n.d. Accessed on 7 July 2008. <http://wiki.answers.com/Q/How_much_do_players_on_the_And1_Tour_earn>.

King, C. Richard, and Charles Fruehling Springwood. "Body and Soul: Physicality, Disciplinarity, and the Overdetermination of Blackness." *Channeling Blackness: Studies on Television and Race in America*. Ed. Darnell N. Hunt. New York: Oxford UP, 2005. 185–206.

Leonard, David J. "The Real Color of Money: Controlling Black Bodies in the NBA." *Journal of Sport and Social Issues* 30.2 (2006): 158–79. *Academic Search Premier*. Accessed on 1 Aug. 2008.

Makheru. "Hip-Hop: A Window on Generational Nihilism." By Angela Onwuachi-Willig. *Blackprof.com*. N.p., 25 Mar. 2007. Accessed on 7 July 2008. <http://www.blackprof.com/?p=1763>.

McCann, Michael A. "The Reckless Pursuit of Dominion: A Situational Analysis of the NBA and Diminishing Player Autonomy." *University of Pennsylvania Journal of Labor and Employment Law* 8 (2006): n. pag. *LexisNexis*. Accessed on 7 July 2008.

McLeod, Kembrew. "Authenticity within Hip-Hop and Other Cultures Threatened with Assimilation." *Journal of Communication* 49.4 (1999): 134–50. *Academic Search Premier*. Accessed on 1 Aug. 2008.

Muhammad, Ashahed M. "Rappers, Athletes, Actors Seek to End Youth Violence." *FinalCall.com News.* FCN Publishing, 14 July 2008. Accessed on 31 July 2008. <http://www.finalcall.com/artman/publish/article_4972.shtml>.

Nance, Roscoe. "Street Baller's Legend Grows in NBA." *USA Today* 3 Dec. 2004: 5C. *LexisNexis.* Accessed on 1 Aug. 2008.

Oates, Thomas P. "Book Review: Young, Black, Rich and Famous: The Rise of the NBA, the Hip-Hop Invasion and the Transformation of American Culture." *Journal of Communication Inquiry* 29.4 (2005): 377–81. *Academic Search Premier.* Accessed on 1 Aug. 2008.

"Pacers' O'Neal Says NBA Draft Age Limit Smacks of Racism." *NBC Sports* 12 Apr. 2005: n. pag. *LexisNexis.* Accessed on 31 July 2008.

"Petite Bourgeoisie." *Oxford Dictionary of Sociology.* eNotes.com, n.d. Accessed on 7 July 2008. <http://www.enotes.com/oxsoc-encyclopedia/petite-bourgeoisie>.

Ramsay, Jack. "Good for the Game?" *ESPN Page* 3. ESPN Internet Ventures, 21 Aug. 2004. Accessed on 31 July 2008. <http://sports.espn.go.com/espn/page3/story?page=analysts/040820>.

Rose, Tricia. *Black Noise: Rap Music and Black Culture in Contemporary America.* Middletown: Wesleyan UP, 1994.

Shropshire, Kenneth L. "Beyond Sprewell: The New American Dream." *Journal of Gender, Race and Justice* 4.1 (2000): n. pag. *LexisNexis.* Accessed on 7 July 2008.

Smith, Andre L. "Other People's Property: Hip-Hop's Inherent Clashes with Property Laws and Its Ascendance as Global Counter Culture." *Virginia Sports and Entertainment Law Journal* (2007): n. pag. *LexisNexis.* Accessed on 7 July 2008.

Stoler, Ann Laura. *Race and the Education of Desire: Foucault's History of Sexuality and the Colonial Order of Things.* Durham: Duke UP, 1997.

Taylor, Phil. "Bad Actors." *Sports Illustrated* 1 Jan. 1995: 18+. *Academic Search Premier.* Accessed on 7 July 2008.

Vecsey, Joseph. "The End of the AND 1 Dynasty." *Bounce.* N.p., 14 June 2007. Accessed on 7 July 2008. <http://www.bouncemag.com/2007/06/14/the-end-of-the-and-1-dynasty/>.

Williams, Jeffrey A. "Flagrant Foul: Racism in 'The Ron Artest Fight.'" *UCLA Entertainment Law Review* (2005): n. pag. *LexisNexis.* Accessed on 7 July 2008.

Wolff, Alexander. "The Other Basketball." *Sports Illustrated* 13 June 2005: n. pag. *Academic Search Premier.* Accessed on 7 July 2008.

12

■ Sacred Saturdays

College Football and Local Identity

☐ Timothy R. Steffensmeier

> It's my belief that tailgating is the last great American neighborhood.... This is
> a day and age where we don't pick up the phone without checking caller ID.
> This is a day and age where we don't even call people anymore; we e-mail them.
> We don't have socialization in our neighborhoods, where we walk around and
> talk to total strangers. When you're tailgating, you get to walk through thousands
> of backyards with no privacy fences. You can say hello to people, they'll say
> hello back—and really mean it.—Joe Cahn (qtd. in "Tailgating")

Joe Cahn, the self-proclaimed Commissioner of Tailgating, speaks of the
cultural significance of college football for more than 48 million fans who
serve as spectators of this sport (NCAA 2008). On autumn Saturdays, fans
congregate long before and leave long after the actual football game to participate in "tailgating"—an elaborate (and sometimes raucous) social gathering
that typically occurs around football stadiums on autumn Saturdays. The
tailgating spectacle, marked by spirited ritual practices that inform fan identity,
derives much of its symbolic resources from the football game itself in an
aim to recreate the practices that constitute local neighborhood gatherings.

The contention here is that fan behavior reveals how the sport of football
creates a local identity for fans. This focus, primarily on fan performance, is
important because it reveals the significant influence collegiate football has
on the cultural practices of millions of people. By focusing on a fan's everyday

gestures (e.g., wearing team gear, grilling steak sandwiches, etc.), we learn about an orientation toward being in the world. We can think of *orientation* as a "sense of relationships" that affects a person's expectations (Burke, *Permanence* 18). Thus, tracking and plotting relationships—patterns of experience—reveals an orientation around which fans perform their identity. These symbolic associations, revealed in fan performances at college football games, take on sacred status, in that the rhetoric of college football spills into everyday interactions and popular culture. Here, the rhetoric works to constitute a local identity amongst fans who share attitudes, orientations, and patterns of experience.

College football receives generous amounts of media attention, an indicator of the sport's mammoth revenues, including the $44 million the University of Georgia Bulldogs profited in 2006 (Donahue). Despite economic success and widespread spectatorship, sparse attention has been given to college football's centrality in orienting people around a common set of communication practices that carry beyond the game-day setting. Admittedly, it is not uncommon to hear US football equated to a religion. With the decline of religiosity in the United States, sport offers an "appropriate vehicle for a kind of religious experience" (Butterworth, "Ritual" 108). The analogous relationship between religion and sport suggests that college football not only reflects culture, in this case fulfilling unmet needs churches aim to address, but also "functions ideologically to *produce* and *reproduce* culture, including political culture" (Butterworth, "Ritual" 112, original emphasis). Thus, it is useful to excavate beneath the religious analogy to better understand the symbolic resources college football provides for fans to create a local identity. This neighborly brand of identity, referenced by Cahn at the opening of this chapter, historically has been a defining characteristic of community and organizational life; we see this in narratives concerning agrarian life and grassroots organizing. While sport, particularly baseball, is cited as evidence of US national identity (Butterworth, "Purifying"), the extent to which spectators engage locally around sport has been addressed minimally.

Examining the performance of fans reveals a sacred orientation to the sport. Reading these practices as sacred, as opposed to profane, philosopher Mircea Eliade's thesis echoes that sacred space organizes people around a center point. In this way, the sacred/profane dichotomy operates as a tool to ascertain degrees of influence regarding one's commitment to an orientation. Tracking orientation along the lines of sacred/profane is important because it speaks to the depth of one's commitments. The more consistency and rigidity are displayed in everyday interactions, the more a fan is rooted in a sacred orientation; here, the fan's center point begins with the football game, circulates through the game-day rituals and practices of fans performing allegiance to their team, and then, with a directive sacred orientation, the game-day performances spill into one's everyday interactions, familial and work-related alike.

This chapter focuses on the social sphere, a space that, Kenneth Burke contends, involves both situations and acts (*Philosophy* 103). In the case of collegiate football fans, the game-day experience is filled with symbols and rituals mined from the actual sporting event. To witness fan behavior is to see performances that indicate a sacred orientation. In other words, a fan's complete game-day experience serves as an important center point that functions, in part, to create a sense of shared local identity with other fans.

Theoretically this chapter extends Kenneth Burke's concepts of orientation and piety into a performative space. Burke, an often-cited rhetorical critic, created numerous tools to better work with a wide spectrum of rhetorical artifacts. Although there is an impressive array of scholarly works that employ Burke's ideas, performative acts are seldom examined, this despite the fact that Burke remained convinced that life and drama are one (Hopper 182). Furthermore, Burke concedes that "nonverbal things, in their capacity as 'meanings' also take on the nature of words" (*Rhetoric* 186). If we stretch Burke's concepts into a space where life is performed, his work is helpful especially for the task of better understanding college football fans. The turn to performance reflects the increasingly popular practice of studying culture as rhetorical performances (Brummett; Gunn and Brummett). Thus, this chapter tests the assertion that Burke's rhetorical tools apply to "any kind of human expression" (Keith 139), in an effort to take up Joe Cahn's contention that tailgating is reinventing the local neighborhood—a phenomenon the rhetorical critic is equipped to dissect and illuminate.

This chapter proceeds by analyzing the everyday performance of fans at college football games. To offer a framework to understand fan rhetoric, a theory of orientation and piety is discussed as they relate to the creation of sacred space. This theoretical framework is used to establish a manner of understanding the performances of fans. The chapter will conclude with a reflection on the relationship between fan rituals and local identity. And here, at this cultural intersection where game-days constitute communal identity, we see the influence of college sports on the social and political acts of a community. For example, businesses latch onto the team's brand, ceremonial events take on symbolic qualities of the game, and gender orientation mimics the roles necessary for traditional game-day activities.

■ Understanding Performance: Form, Orientation, and Social Piety

Form, a central notion of Kenneth Burke's thinking, is described as "an arousing and fulfillment of desires" (Burke, *Counter-Statement* 124). For example, form is at work in a football game when certain symbols foretell or point a viewer in a given direction (i.e., a marching band begins to play). Form preps readers to anticipate and construct a map of possibilities; it prepares a reader for what is coming next. In the case of the football game, the band might mean more cheering is needed or that an extra point will follow. Whatever the specific case, a successful band arouses and fulfills a fan's desire. Understood in this manner, form is about the audience, more specifically, the psychology of the audience. Psychology, for Burke, refers to people's desires. In this way, form creates and satisfies an individual's appetite (Burke, *Counter-Statement* 31). Thus, an eloquent marching band is one that satisfies appetites; the perfection of form is eloquence.

Locating and describing form provides important structures for us to better understand everyday experiences. The assumption here is that experience is formal—patterns of experience emerge from the relationship between a person and his/her environment. Burke writes, "Any such specific environmental condition calls forth and stresses certain of the universal experiences as being more relevant to it, with a slighting of those less relevant. Such selections are patterns of experience" (*Counter-Statement* 151). People use a given pattern of experience to deal with environmental conditions. Thus, locating a pattern of experience in college football fans can tell us much about their general conditions of life, because patterns of experience reveal what one ought and ought-not to do. For example, fans living far apart commonly gather together with extended family on a game-day, a day when other familial ceremonies are strongly discouraged (or boycotted). If by colossal mistake a wedding is scheduled on game-day, attendance in that wedding ceremony declines and those who attend come prepared with multiple means of learning the score. Although an emphatic "YES, touchdown!" whispered loudly for most to hear during a church ceremony violates decorum, it is not uncommon on football Saturdays. This gathering, a pattern of experience, reveals the importance for families to come together with a shared commitment and goal. Burke discusses this awareness of what one ought to do by using the term orientation.

Orientation involves a wide grouping of judgments a person makes in relation to the past, present, and future states of reality. An orientation arises from stimuli; however, it simultaneously "calls forth affective states" (Burke,

Permanence 150). Thus, an orientation stems from the point at which stimuli and meaning merge, the intersection of body and mind. This primal connection, in part, explains why individual orientations vary in degree, but as a composite, the collective human orientation remains relatively constant. Burke states, "At the bottom the aims and genius of man have remained fundamentally the same, that temporal events may cause him to stray far from his sources but that he repeatedly struggles to restore, under new particularities, the same basic patterns of the 'good life'" (*Permanence* 163). Ultimately, people yearn for an associative or congregational state of being—a more cooperative way of life. This cooperative form is possible only when the communicative environment is equipped with the necessary resources.

Sustaining an ordered world that revolves around an orientation involves repeating patterns of experience. When a person establishes a given orientation he/she constructs an associational map of what belongs together. To describe this process, Burke looks to the realm of religion wherein he grabs the concept of piety. *Piety* is "the sense of what properly goes with what" (*Permanence* 74). Piety is what constructs a system of living, a system that guides one's expectations in a manner largely unconscious to the person neck-deep in the moment. Burke explains that "piety is the schema of orientations since it involves the putting together of experiences" (*Permanence* 76). It is important to note that these schemas are neither "good" nor "bad." Piety is not a judgment differentiated on the grounds of goodness or worth; it is a schema that guides and explains the consistency of one's interactions. In the realm of piety, the saint and the damned sit together for both actors carry out their orientation with devotion. The language of piety surfaces in terms of universal characteristics, moods, thoughts, or actions.

Piety is a term traditionally reserved for those acts directly connected with religion. However, Burke expands the concept to "a response which extends through all the texture of our lives but has been concealed from us" (*Permanence* 75). Piety is the concealed devotion to patterns of experience in our everyday acts. It functions as a rut that obfuscates one's view to consider something otherwise. For example, a fan learns from football contests that opponents are to be diminished and defeated; this sporting goal spills over and creates antagonistic and hostile opinions of one fan base toward another, evident especially at tailgating during rivalry games. The antagonism between rivals reproduces itself in the everyday interactions of fans at workplaces and family gatherings. Over time, these interactions inflict a crease that gradually becomes deep enough to delimit all experiences to the confines of the gorge. Fans adhere to generalizations about the miserable ethos (and politics, intelligence, driving skills, etc.) of those who support the opponent. In this example, piety explains the reasonableness of many a fan in ways that mimic an asylum patient. Burke writes, "The patient, with pious devotion, had erected a consistent network of appropriateness about the altar of his wretchedness" (*Permanence* 126). The pious are always in a process of serving an altar with consistency—an act that highlights the relationship between piety and propriety.

■ The Social Dimension of Pious Orientations

Burke speaks about piety in relation to an awareness of "appropriateness." Propriety—the appropriateness of a text—is a fundamental aspect of the rhetorical tradition. For Burke "standards of appropriate social behavior always rest upon some principle of order, and hence they are symptoms of piety" (Rosteck and Leff 328). Piety, when considered in relation to propriety, represents a "principle of symbolic order" (329). The propriety of a rhetor (i.e., fan) stems from a sense of order, a sense of piety.

Connecting piety with propriety opens up a space to better understand social behavior. Social piety implies that a certain degree of self-monitoring occurs in any public performance. In other words, the presentation and maintenance of a public self is a fundamental aspect of social piety. Thus, the presentation of self as it relates to propriety has much to do with the general social order. Hugh Duncan, a sociologist influenced by Burke, offers a method for interpreting public behavior. He contends that social order is generated from ultimate principles of order, in that every act is "beyond reason in the sense that no one before he acts can really prove that a specific end will follow from certain means" (110). Propriety comes from a culture's sense of belief that is derived from an ultimate principle of order. Our social forms—manners, etiquette, and play, for example—reveal this order (Duncan 212). Thus, studying the patterns of behavior involved in a communicative performance reveals the social order of a given culture. Whereas Burke is interested in symbolic hierarchies, Duncan's focus is on how these hierarchies are established and maintained in formal social interactions.

Although Burke and Duncan get us to the concept of social piety, they do not offer sufficient resources for explaining the variance involved in orientations. We are still in need of explaining why some social pieties are more difficult to modify or abandon than others. In the case of college football fans, the question remains: how do game-day performances constitute a local identity? We are in need of a construct that explains why some people's orientations are felt so deeply. We expect people to be amused by viewing sporting events, but what makes the game-day experience evoke such passionate performances? If we return to the contention that tailgating creates a public brought together in a neighborhood atmosphere, these fan performances are both politically and socially important. Sport is providing the symbolic resources for community development. Building community evokes spatial memes as is the case with physical and metaphorical public squares. These memes warrant a focus on the rhetorical construction of space. For assistance on this front, we turn to philosopher of religion Mircea Eliade's discussion of sacred space. Eliade fits well with Burke and Duncan; he too is primarily concerned with orientations. But his concern anchors social piety in a manner that helps to reveal the social and political significance of tailgating performances.

Social Piety and the Construction of Sacred Space

Social piety is a primary factor in Eliade's distinction between the sacred and the profane, as he uses historical examples of cultures, not individuals, to demonstrate sacred orientations. Eliade's project *The Sacred and the Profane: the Nature of Religion* locates a useful opposition between the manner in which people operate in sacred and profane environments. He explains the distinction in the following manner:

> Revelation of a sacred space makes it possible to obtain a fixed point and hence acquire orientation in the chaos of homogeneity, to "found the world" and to live in a real sense. The profane experience, on the contrary, maintains the homogeneity and hence relativity of space. No true orientation is now possible, for the fixed point no longer enjoys unique ontological status; it appears and disappears in accordance with the needs of the day. (23, original emphasis)

Two terms, "orientation" and "revelation," are especially significant to understanding the religious element involved in patterns of experience.

Eliade moves beyond Burke's discussion of piety when he dichotomizes orientation into the sacred and the profane. In the former situation, the fixed point, upon which orientation is guided, is revealed to a people. Revelation is what separates a true orientation (sacred) from another less stable orientation (profane). The revelation of an orientation can come in many forms; for instance, a bush that miraculously blooms fixes a center point (Eliade 27). In this case, the bush establishes the necessary point from which an orientation could be developed. Eliade describes this process of shaping disorder as hierophany. He explains, "Every sacred space implies a hierophany, an irruption of the sacred that results in detaching a territory from the surrounding cosmic milieu and making it qualitatively different" (26). The initial revelation irrupts and emerges as a distinct point of departure for a given people. The hierophany "makes orientation possible; hence it founds the world in the sense that it fixes the limits" (30). For example, the Achilpas, an Arunta tribe, believed that a divine transcended to heaven from a cosmic gum tree pole. The nomadic tribe carried this pole with them throughout their travels. The pole represented the Achilpas' cosmic axis—it provided order in the cosmic chaos. The tribe used the sacred pole as a compass by dictating the direction of their travels on the bend of the pole. When the pole finally broke, the Achilpas became disoriented. The story goes that the tribe roamed aimlessly for a few days before lying down to die. Their world, their orientation, had been uprooted in the most debilitating fashion (Eliade 33). True orientation or sacred experience, as illustrated in the case of the Achilpas, is a directional act revealed to people; whereas, profane experience lacks the revelation necessary to stabilize a fixed center point.

Although profane experiences involve orientations, they are adopted and discarded at will in accordance to the circumstances of the day, as is the current state of a secular postindustrial world. Yet, a highly secular world—one that dedicates so many human resources to collegiate football, for example—does not mean elements of a religious experience are entirely absent. A religious way of being is noticeable even in the most secular people attending a most secular sporting event. Eliade writes, "It must be added that such a profane existence is never found in the pure state. To whatever degree he may have desacralized the world, the man who has made his choice in favor of a profane life never succeeds in completely doing away with religious behavior" (23). The religious behavior is a carryover from a time when religious people operated around a revealed axis point. Eliade further describes this process:

To acquire a world of his own, he [secular person] has desacrilized the world in which his ancestors lived; but to do so he has been obliged to adopt an opposite of an earlier type of behavior, and that behavior is still emotionally present to him, in one form or another, ready to be reactualized in his deepest being. (204)

The affective baggage explains the tendency of secular people to participate in making sacred worlds. The festivities and rituals surrounding football games are one example of secular sacrilizing. Fans ritualize the secular sport in an effort to rejuvenate community space—to recreate sacred, interactive neighborhoods that diminished under a suburban ethos. In each fan's life a hierophany emerges, maybe a championship season or an unforgettable game-day experience, whereupon the football game-day becomes a fixed point around which orientations emerge.

Recall that Kenneth Burke also speaks about orientation in relation to its ability to call forth "affective states." Eliade's project grounds these affective states evoked by orientation in past acts and behaviors. The religious element witnessed in secular life stems from an age when orientations were revealed to religious people through totems such as the gum pole of the Achilpas. Eliade's contention that religious traces are wrapped into the deepest level of being illuminates Burke's contention that the basic orientation of humans has remained essentially unchanged throughout history. Contemporary US culture reflects this consistency in an array of forms. Whether it emerges as a family's dining room table, a national memorial, or a virtual space in Second Life, secular people are rhetorically constructing sacred spaces. The game-day tailgating too illustrates the creation of sacred space, in part, by the performative acts that sustain beliefs, taboos, and myths. These acts reveal that patterns of experience are guided by orientations formed while people huddle to make order from chaos.

To this point, this chapter has put forth the concept of social piety as it relates to the creation of sacred space. The integral concepts of this theory include form, orientation, piety, and sacred. These concepts are important to understanding spectator performances because they offer insight into the rhetorical influences that motivate and sustain these local fan communities.

Interpreting Sacred Saturdays

The performance of spectators on college football game-days are analyzed with attention given to patterns of experience. These patterns of experience fit within four primary activities: (1) Site-construction, (2) Dressing up, (3) Eating and Drinking, and (4) Competing and Interacting. The categories are not to be viewed as discreet activities or chronologically ordered acts, nor are they to be viewed as exhaustive or particularly meaningful in and of themselves. Rather, the categories stand in for routine patterns of experience that gain meaning for fans within the context of game-day. Football games provide the symbolic resources so that everyday acts—securing shelter, clothing, companionship, and nourishment—have the capacity to orient fans around a local identity.

The artifacts for this analysis were derived from tailgater testimony on social networking sites, game-day observations on three different NCAA division on campuses, and scholarly research on fan behavior. It is also important to note my active participation in these cultural performances over the past three decades. Like many of the fans described in this chapter, my connection to college football has pious roots in that they spill beyond sacred Saturdays.

The purpose of this analysis is to locate specific everyday gestures that point to the pious acts of football fans. Devoutly pious spectators of college football embody a sacred orientation to a given team—fans who devoutly perform the actions constituted by the football game. They are fans for whom the tailgating experience becomes an orientation that structures their performance of local identity.

Constructing the Site

The devoutly pious fan has a vested interest in each stage of the gameday experience; most significantly, they spearhead the planning and the set-up of the tailgating site. It is important to consider the public nature of tailgating, which in this regard is quite unlike private backyard barbecues or birthday parties. Tailgating, when performed by the devoutly pious, is a public-forming activity—it calls a community together that would otherwise not have formed. Here, the fan takes cues from the football game itself. For prosperous college football teams, it is standard for upwards of eighty thousand people to attend a given game and millions more to watch and listen via mass media. And as Bob Krizek muses, it is entirely plausible that more people engage sport on a given weekend than those how attend church or engage in sexual relations (104). There are many reasons attributed to the popularity of sport that go beyond the scope of this chapter. Yet, one important attribute is that unlike most religious (and sexual activities) that are practiced in more private spaces, sport is predominantly a public-making event. For college football that is signified by large open-air stadiums built on acres of lush property, spaces that transform into public tailgating grounds on game-day.

It is common for tailgating sites to be constructed around the perimeter of a football stadium. This is an important gesture that materially and symbolically represents the sacredness of tailgating. Unlike other public spaces (i.e., city parks or recreation fields), the college football stadium is sacred to the devoutly pious spectators who use them as dwelling places during home football games. Recall from Eliade's theory that sacred spaces orient people, in part, by clearly defining a center point. The field itself, encased with memories of past performances, serves as this sacred center point for tailgate planners. All patterns of experience for the devoutly pious point to and circulate through the one hundred yards of field-turf. The colloquial expression for the sacred nature of stadiums is "Our House." Many universities have capitalized on the sacred status assigned to stadiums by naming fields in honor of a great coach or community leader, for example, the University of Nebraska's turf is labeled "Tom Osborne Field" as a tribute to his guiding the Cornhuskers to three NCAA national championships. For the devoutly pious fan, game-day performances stem from and lead to the stadium.

A first-rate stadium calls for a first-rate tailgating space. Securing these prime spaces for a tailgate is extremely important for devout fans. These spaces ideally include electricity, access to restrooms, shade, and enough room to construct a game-day dwelling place. For many teams, these spaces are restricted to arrangements made by athletic department donors and rented at high premiums, spaces that surpass the game itself in terms of ticket prices. The point here is that it takes considerable material resources just to secure a space for a tailgate. For this reason, those fans who choose to dedicate resources attain a special status and locus of control.

We can get a better sense of a tailgate planner's perspective through a post by "Nick in Atlanta":

> For the 2005 Iron Bowl my father in-law and I rolled on to campus at 5:00 a.m. to get the grill started for the 12 whole chickens, 6lbs. of sausage and vat of brunswick stew we cooked for the 100 or so folks at our tailgate. The game was at 2:30 p.m. Needless to say we ran out of food. Fast forward to the 2006 Auburn Georgia game (The oldest rivalry in the South) and you have a recipe for a 4:00 a.m. grill start time—18 whole chickens, 4lbs. of sausage and sides you wouldn't believe. Again feeding about 100 people. This year we dumped the 36" TV for a 10'x10' screen and projector to watch the other games while we eat, drink and be merry. We also had an addition to almost all of our tailgates this year, it was our 9 month old daughter's first Auburn/Georgia game, she only missed two games all season. While the outcome was not in our favor the tailgating was top notch. After 14 hours of being on campus it was time to head back to the house. We're already planning for next season. WAR EAGLE! ("The Best")

Nick's story is telling about the game-day performance of the devoutly pious. The inclusion of family members spanning three (and sometimes four) generations coupled with fourteen-hour days that involve fans in planning, preparing, and constructing spaces suggests that hard work and long hours are integral ingredients for success in creating a tailgate site. These same ingredients make up the model of athletic success. Much is made in collegiate sports of the dedication and sacrifice of student-athletes who log regimented fourteen-hour days split between training and studying. The same meme constitutes coach life—the workaholic football coach who sleeps on the office couch during the season and is on the recruiting trail in the off-season. The model, hard work + long hours = success, motivates the devoutly pious fan, coach and athlete alike. In emphasizing fourteen-hour days and 365 days of planning we get a sense of Nick's sacred orientation.

While the symbolic connection between stadium and tailgate sites and between team and fan has been articulated, we still need to explicate the social and political importance of tailgating. Unlike a discarded Halloween mask, pious dispositions and acts are not simply shaken off upon leaving the stadium grounds. The symbolic resources of football games reproduced in tailgating construction spills into a fan's everyday interactions. These ingredients described for creating a first-rate tailgate are similarly employed in the design of sustainable communities. A motto of hard work and long hours, articulated by natural agricultural scientist Wes Jackson, assumes that place making is an ongoing process of constant refinement. In addition, the privileging of local methods and resources too signifies an important dimension of sustainable development.

■ Dressing Up

Dress and bodily ornament are another important symbolic resource for the fan performances. In football, to "dress" for the contest signifies that an athlete has been given a jersey with a number, meaning that the he has earned a spot on the roster to actively participate in the game. The devoutly pious fan too takes pride in "dressing" for the game. The range of fan apparel is diverse, but two qualities are common: heritage and consistency. The uniform must have a story that oozes with tradition and it must consistently reflect prominent symbolic resources displayed at the tailgate and throughout the stadium. These qualities are illustrated in another telling of tailgate drama, this time by Jason W. in Jackson Mississippi:

> The best tailgating in the country, pro or not, is at the University of Mississippi, affectionately known as Ole Miss. The Grove, the main tailgating spot, has been recognized by *Sports Illustrated* as the single best tailgating place in the country. Hundreds of large tents, some even with chandeliers hanging from the tops, fill The Grove under huge oak trees, except for marked off walkways. The party starts early, sometimes as early as 7am for 11am games. The male students, dressed in their finest coat and tie, have a "date" they bring to The Grove each game. The players walk through The Grove on The Walk of Champions two hours before game time. But, the band playing has to be one of the most incredible sights. Thousands of people (around 10,000 or more for big games) crowd as close as possible around The Pride of the South for the playing of fight songs.... As a fan, seeing and hearing thousands of people sing the Alma Mater...is bone-chilling.... There is no tailgating experience that can half-way compare to being in the Grove on Saturday afternoons. ("The Best")

In this description, Jason tells of student-fans "dressed in their finest coat and tie" as they peruse through the pregame celebration. The fine threads are consistent with large tents and chandeliers that decorate the Grove on gamedays. Although students who participate in this tradition are not typically devoutly pious fans (at least, not yet), the ritual of dressing-up points to a pious performance. The tradition of dressing-up signifies the propriety of football for this particular local culture.

At Kansas State University's football stadium, a place characteristic of Midwestern traditions, the ties and jackets are replaced with player-like jerseys, coach-like polo shirts, and fitted t-shirts. It is not uncommon for fans to strategically choose clothing on a superstitious basis. A uniform's heritage—a cap worn during the best season or a jersey signed by an all-American player—brings good luck to the team, but, more importantly, these costumes properly dress the fan to perform. Devoutly pious fans dress for games with careful consideration given to the meaning enveloped within the costume. Dressing up reflects a strong orientation to a local identity.

In treating the topic of dressing up, it would be remiss to not address the pervasive employment of team colors on game-day. At Kansas State University, the dominant hue is purple, an unmistakable color that paints the tailgating landscape with a broad brush. For the devoutly pious, the uniform color signifies "Purple Pride," an expression circulated throughout game-day promotional materials. Obviously team colors perform a necessary function for football players making snap decisions on who to clobber and who to protect. Likewise properly colored fan uniforms function as identity shorthand to quickly distinguish between friend and foe.

The emphasis on uniform dress on the football field and at tailgate gatherings indicates a heightened awareness of aesthetic style in contemporary living. We see this performed by homeowners in their detailed manicuring of personal property, which has been heightened further by popular home makeover shows. In addition, aesthetic style has never been so opaque. Popular social networking sites provide users ample resources to design and modify their presentation of self.

■ Food and Drink

Foods and drink, specifically grilled meats and alcoholic beverages, are native to tailgating performances. This trend is so pervasive that entire product lines (i.e., Freedom Grill and Booze Belly) exist to provide ease and functionality to tailgate dining and drinking. Furthermore, it is common to see homemade grills, some large enough to require a special trailer for towing purposes. Although overindulgence seems to take its cue from something other than football games, the tailgating events function much like teams. For starters, the mentality of devoutly pious fans is one of service to others.

Nick's narrative cited above is common tailgate propriety. He takes great pride in feeding many, and although it is not explicitly addressed, the food most likely is served free of charge. To serve well in all phases of the game-day experience, from the construction of the site to the preparation and serving of the food, planning with others in mind is necessary. One must plan and perform with a public in mind. Take for example, the Big Red Meat Wagon, a well-known tailgate at the University of Nebraska, Lincoln. The meat wagon, formerly an ambulance, is a customized tailgater's oasis. In this excerpt, the owners describe its features:

> Unique, great storage, built in keg cooler, functioning light bars, sirens, spotlights, electrical outlets, & a freaking PA system. What more could the well-rounded tailgater need? Um, apparently a bunch!…Was pine wood tongue and groove flooring with a replica of Memorial Stadium (College Football Mecca to the uninformed) necessary? No, but they did it anyway. Were 30" tall Husker & Blackshirt stickers needed? No, but they're on the rig now. Does a tailgate party really need a keg cooler? Wait, YES on that one and it is there. Does a tailgate party really need Satellite TV, surround sound, DVD, CD player, and a 6 foot inflatable Lil' Red doll? Nope, but they have it all. ("The Birth")

The symbolic consistency of this creation suggests the work of devoutly pious fans who clearly operate from an orientation rooted in game-day events. But even more revealing is the number of people the Meat Wagon serves every game-day, many of whom are strangers or friends of friends of friends. In a recent game-day blog, Meat Wagon owners brag of setting a record of polishing off eight barrels of beer (in a record time of twenty-three minutes). They also express their desire to purchase a $3,000 mobile grill and smoker to pull behind the meat wagon. Clearly, these fans are performing a brand of social piety as they accommodate hundreds of other fans every week.

Although not every tailgate is as extravagant as the meat wagon, core components and goals are shared amongst tailgaters. This commonality can be reduced to the mantra: indulge with many! The societal and political implications of such acts point to a communitarian cord held together by the thread of team unity. Although traditional gender roles, class-based divisions, and other identity markers remain, Sacred Saturdays bring forth a quasi-neighborhood for people to interact. Food and drink function to invite and perpetuate conversation once reserved for front porches and sidewalks. This is not to say that the tailgating trend will ultimately inspire a retro move to intimate physical neighborhoods, but it does reveal that people desire communal exchange especially when connected by an orientation made sacred by external forces, in this case the college football game.

■ Competing and Interacting

Another important aspect of the game-day atmosphere is the competitive climate that frames most interactions. For example, it is becoming more common for fans to add digital display systems to a satellite to broadcast a complete slate of collegiate football games. In addition to serving as status symbols, television allows fans to track how their team measures up in relation to other teams. Becoming knowledgeable about the entire spectrum of college football helps fans better understand the enemy(s). It also helps better define a unique local identity that sets apart my team from all others. Like the coach poring over game film in search of the next opponent, the devoutly pious fan needs to consume as much football as possible to scout future foes.

Another important part of tailgating is the interaction fans have with official actors in the game (e.g., players, coaches, band members, etc.). When official members become available, thousands of people huddle together "as close as possible" to sing "fight songs" that are emblematic of the scheduled contest that pits a beloved home team against a strange visitor. The collective singing reproduces the team's historical lineage, in a way that circulates local rhetorical resources to constitute fan identity. When the band performs and the football players parade through the crowd within arms reach at The Grove, a pattern of experience loaded with significance is on display. On an affective level, the ritual—a goose-bump moment for Jason cited earlier—provides the ultimate sensory experience. On an existential level, the experience of intermingling with the "real" players in this dramatic performance further affirms fans' beliefs that they are an integral part of this dramatic performance. It is appropriate to call these "live events" because their organic nature reaffirms the very local orientation of devoutly pious fans. In both cases, the football team provides the rhetorical resources necessary for a local identity to shape.

In this way, football provides symbolic resources for fans to perform a local identity. "Nick in Atlanta" divulges how the "oldest rivalry in the south" adds extra incentive to perform, in this case through grilling in an exceptional manner. Because the on-field competition has increased over time, tailgating too gets ratcheted up to the extent that grown men wake up in the middle of the night to fire up the grill. Although not explicit in his post, a contest of sorts takes place at tailgating sites that mimics what happens inside the stadium. An impressive spread of food, highlighted by quality grilled meat with ample supplies of cold beer, is but one of many ways fans compete during game-days.

Although competition is firmly embedded in US social and political culture, the tailgate further reinforces a worldview dichotomized by friend and foe. The rivalries between fan bases can become very intense and sometimes violent, especially when a multi-billion dollar market is driving the hostility. The controversies played out on the field, later mimicked in parking lots, adhere to confrontation as the preferred conflict resolution method. This hyper-competitive form of public discourse is performed daily in popular culture versions of political communication or message board exchanges.

■ Conclusion

This chapter examines the way college football games provide the rhetorical resources necessary for fans to create local identity. The performative acts involved in this process were analyzed with Burke's notion of form, orientation, and piety serving as theoretical underpinnings. In an effort to analyze public and collective commitments such as those made by football fans, social piety and Eliade's notion of sacred space were introduced. Eliade's work is especially important because it highlights the social and political significance of one's rhetorical construction of space. In the case of college football fans, devoutly pious spectators recreate the stadium's sacred space in their tailgating designs and this orientation spills into their everyday acts.

This chapter points to specific patterns of experience that constitute a spectator's relationship with a sport. What was revealed in this analysis is that devoutly pious fans, like athletes and coaches, put in hard work and long hours into game-day performances. In addition, the tailgate environment offers a place for fans to perform a local identity—one that operates like an ideal neighborhood, wherein people visit on front porches and borrow cups of sugar. This means that through performance identity emerges.

This local identity is constituted through a rigid "us vs. them" dichotomy that is fueled by a hyper-competitive environment. Although Sacred Saturday offers a place for fans of a given team to transcend typically divisive identity markers, the neighborly ethos is premised on an element of exclusionary politics, namely, the opposing team. Here, sport is a public-making activity composed of various factions, which reminds us that these are sites of social and political struggle.

Assuming Joe Cahn is right about the deterioration of American neighborhoods, college game-day offers a site where people can gather as neighbors to perform a local identity. And these would-be neighbors are connected by a center point that guides their patterns of experience in meaningful ways. For the pious fan, college football mysteriously has always been more than just a game; it is an orientation. The popular culture performed on Sacred Saturdays is life, in that these performances constitute social and political actions in places far removed from university stadiums and meat wagons.

Works Cited

"The Best Tailgating Experiences Sent to Us by Tailgaters across America." *Tailgating. com*. N.p., n.d. Accessed on 23 July 2008. <http://www.tailgating.com/TalesFive. htm>.

"The Birth of the Big Red Meat Wagon." *Big Red Meat Wagon*. N.p., n.d. Accessed on 28 Sept. 2008. <http://www.bigredmeatwagon.com/history.htm>.

Brummett, Barry. *Rhetorical Dimensions of Popular Culture*. Tuscaloosa: U of Alabama P, 1991.

Burke, Kenneth. *Counter-Statement*. 3rd ed. Berkeley: U of California P, 1931.

———. *Permanence and Change: An Anatomy of Purpose*. 3rd ed. Berkeley: U of California P, 1935.

———. *The Philosophy of Literary Form*. 3rd ed. Berkeley: U of California P, 1941.

———. *A Rhetoric of Motives*. Berkeley: U of California P, 1969.

Butterworth, Michael L. "Purifying the Body Politic: Steroids, Rafael Palmeiro, and the Rhetorical Cleansing of Baseball." *Western Journal of Communication* 72.2 (2008):145–61.

———. "Ritual in the 'Church of Baseball': Suppressing the Discourse of Democracy after 9/11." *Communication and Critical/Cultural Studies* 2.2 (2005): 107–29.

Donahue, Kevin. "Ranking the Top College Football Revenue Programs." *fanblogs.com*. N.p., 7 Nov. 2007. Accessed on 10 July 2008. <http://www.fanblogs.com/ncaa/007263.php>.

Duncan, Hugh D. *Symbols and Society*. New York: Oxford UP, 1968.

Eliade, Mircea. *The Sacred and Profane: The Nature of Religion*. Trans. Willard Trask. New York: Harcourt, 1959.

Gunn, Joshua, and Barry Brummett. "Popular Culture after Globalization." *Journal of Communication* 54 (2006): 705–21.

Hopper, Robert. "Conversational Dramatism and Everyday Life Performance." *Text and Performance Quarterly* 13.2 (1993): 181–83.

Jackson, Wes. *Becoming Native to This Place*. Lexington: UP of Kentucky, 1994.

Keith, Philip M. "Burkeian Invention, from Pentad to Dialectic." *Rhetoric Society Quarterly* 9.3 (1979): 137–41.

Krizek, Bob. "Introduction: Communication and the Community of Sport." *Western Journal of Communication* 72.2 (2008): 103–06.

Rosteck, Thomas, and Michael Leff. "Piety, Propriety, and Perspective: An Interpretation and Application of Key Terms in Kenneth Burke's Permanence and Change." *Western Journal of Speech Communication* 53.4 (1989): 327–41.

"Tailgating as Good as the Game." *NBC Sports*. NBC Universal, 20 Aug. 2004. Accessed on 21 July 2008. <http://nbcsports.msnbc.com/id/5739112/>.

13

■ Performing Social Class

The Case of Rutgers Basketball
versus Don Imus

☐ Meredith M. Bagley

Imagine playing in the national championship game of your college sport, with all the pressure and expectations of that event weighing on your shoulders. You play your heart out, you lose, you endure the dreary locker room. Imagine now that the next day you wake up to national headlines about comments made not about your basketball skill, your game plan, offensive strategy, or clock management, but about your personal appearance. Instead of your jump shot or zone defense, the whole country is talking about your hairdo and your teammate's tattoos.

You have just put yourself in the shoes of the 2007 Rutgers University women's basketball team. On April 4, the day after they lost to the University of Tennessee in the national final, the nation was abuzz over these comments made by well-known radio personality Don Imus and his co-host Bernard McGuirk:

> IMUS: "So I watched the basketball game last night between, a little bit between Rutgers and Tennessee...the women's final?"

MCGUIRK: "Yeah, Tennessee won, I-Man. Pat Summit's seventh national title, they beat Rutgers by 13 points."

IMUS: "There's some rough girls from Rutgers, man...they got tattoos and...

MCGUIRK: "That's some hard core ho's..."

IMUS: "That's some nappy-headed ho's there I'm gonna tell you that much. Man, that's some...oohf! And ah, the girls from Tennessee, they all looked cute, you know? So, like, kind of like, I don't know, a Spike Lee thing.

MCGUIRK: "Jiggaboos versus Wannabees?"

IMUS: "Yeah"

MCGUIRK: "That movie he had?"

IMUS: "That was a tough-"

MCGUIRK: "*Do the Right Thing*, yeah, yeah."

IMUS: "I don't know if I'd a wanted to beat Rutgers or not, but they did, right?"

MCGUIRK: "Yeah, you look at Rutgers and they look exactly like the Toronto Raptors."[1]

Notice how little Imus and his co-host discussed the actual game, focusing instead on the appearance and style of the Rutgers and Tennessee teams. The Rutgers women were playing their guts out for the chance to be national champions; the attention to aesthetic aspects of their performance suggests more was at stake than the national title. Indeed, Imus's interest in the aesthetic elements of the basketball players underscores how female athletes are viewed in ways that marginalize their athletic skill. From Imus's outburst we also learn that this performance, however marginalized, threatens established notions of gender, race, and sexuality. Further, Imus's targeting of the Rutgers team exposes how standards for competitive behavior in women rely on judgments of social class. By dissecting Imus's hateful comments we see the complex construction and meaning associated with sport performances. This chapter argues that women's sport are often contained within discourses like Imus's, and those of others, in an effort to preserve existing hierarchies of race, gender, class, and sexuality.

To support this claim, this chapter proceeds in four sections: first, we will explore the concept of performance and review scholarly literature about its application to women's college basketball. Placing the 2007 national championship game in this context reveals a perplexing aspect of the Imus versus Rutgers incident. Namely, why did Imus focus his disparaging remarks on the Scarlet Knights and not the Lady Volunteers? Both teams were made up of strong, skilled African American women, so what was it about the Rutgers' team that drew his focus? A rhetorical analysis of Imus's comments suggests that the Rutgers' team performed an unacceptable level of competitiveness that violated class-based norms for femininity—that is, Imus characterized the Rutgers team members as urban, aggressive threats as opposed to "cute" Tennessee players based on a reading of their socioeconomic class. Once again, performance and style guided his reading.

The second section of the chapter addresses another perplexing element of Imus's comments. In his apologies and follow-up interviews, Imus attempted to recast his words—particularly "ho" and "nappy"—as complimentary to the Rutgers team. To pursue this reframing, Imus drew upon other aesthetic forms, namely hip hop and film. These allusions suggest that sport, rather than providing escape from other cultural discourses or functioning as an isolated realm of organized contest, interacts with other major aesthetic, cultural influences in shaping our notions of race, class, gender, and sexuality. As a result, when women compete at sports their efforts do not exist in a vacuum—they are interpreted in conjunction with messages about appropriate behavior and appearance for women in other major cultural forums.

In the third section, we will shift gears and assess the reaction of those who defended the Rutgers team from Imus's comments. These allies grew in number as the Imus controversy persisted. However, it is vital that as rhetorical critics we examine these "allies" of women's basketball as closely as we do its enemies. This section will ask how performances of women's basketball are mined for signs and symbols that support interests or agendas that may be far removed from the players' best interests. Indeed, this chapter will argue that both Imus and his critics used Rutgers' basketball performance to advance ongoing debates over the place of Black women in American society.

Finally, the showdown between Imus and the Rutgers team allows us to pursue two questions related to the study of social class: what are the performative elements of socioeconomic class, and what are the implications of defining class as performance? Class is often defined as an objective status position that we all hold in society—how much money we make, how much control we have over our labor, what freedoms and opportunities we have based on that position. However, the Rutgers episode clearly shows us that our understanding of class is based in part on elements of style, or the performance of acting "classy." This chapter argues, however, that an understanding of social class that rests too heavily on performative qualities risks doing more damage than good. That is, while we rely on visible characteristics to literally "read" class in America, it is dangerous to reverse this equation and promote performances that have little chance of improving structural economic inequality.

As we move through these four sections, we will discuss recent scholarship in sports sociology and communication that addresses this fundamental question about class. Cultural studies show us that we perform class and rely on these stylized performances to understand each other. However, college sport has become a multi-million dollar business with very material consequences for athletes, schools, coaches, and sponsors. To trace these questions and arguments about race, gender, class, and sexuality in sport performances, we will consider Imus and McGuirk's on-air exchange as well as forty newspaper articles related to the game and the scandal.[2] Twenty articles published before the game allow us to see how the Rutgers team was described before Imus's inflammatory comments. Twenty articles published after Imus's comments demonstrate how the performance of women's college basketball came to signify wider tensions, particularly those related to working class African American women.

■ 1. Tip-Off: Women's Basketball as Performance

It may seem incongruous to point to a collection of real, moving, sweating athletic bodies and call them a performance. Indeed, using this concept to understand gender, race, and sexuality does not take away from the reality experienced by individuals and groups who are doing the performing. The concept allows us, however, to loosen the bounds between bodies and social constructions of gender in order to better see the politics that are attached to those social norms. Judith Butler is credited with bringing this concept to the forefront of gender studies, arguing that

> acts, gestures and desire produce the effect of an internal core or substance, but produce this on the *surface* of the body…. Such acts, gestures, enactments, generally construed, are *performative* in the sense that the essence or identity that they otherwise purport to express are *fabrications* manufactured and sustained through corporeal signs and other discursive means. (*Gender Trouble* 173, original emphasis)

Calling gender or race a performance means that there is no set, natural, automatic truth of gender or race that is already imprinted in our bodies when we are born. Instead, we learn social conventions and expectation as we grow up and then act out a certain combination of these norms as our performance of gender, race, or sexuality.

Recall, however, that theorizing identity as a performance should not take away from its realness or its concrete consequences. Being called "ho's" was not made less painful for the Rutgers team by thinking of themselves as performers. Butler acknowledges this, although she favors a version of identity and social change that concentrates on discourse or sets of vocabularies to make gender performances intelligible (see *Undoing Gender* 223). Imagine a cycle of social norms disciplining our bodies, literally shaping and changing them, in such a pervasive way that we think these rules are natural and normal, so we enact a particular type of femaleness or heterosexuality that is correctly perceived by the outside world. This performance then reinforces the rules, which in turn shape the next performance. Or, in some cases, a performance may alter or loosen the rules, allowing the next act to be slightly different. This cycle is ongoing for Butler and central to our daily existence. Many scholars are concerned that Butler did not do enough to keep her influential theory from steering us away from more instrumental methods of social change, be they anti-racist, anti-homophobic, or feminist. For instance, Walters warns that

> this performance trope becomes vacuous when it is decontextualized, and overblown when it is bandied about as the new hope for a confused world.... Without substantive engagement with complex sociopolitical realities, those performance tropes appear as an entertaining but ultimately depoliticized academic exercise. (250–51).

Rhetorical studies that use the concept of performance have a second motivation to heed Walters' words: rhetoric is concerned with the available means of persuasion in any given situation and thus should be especially attuned to the context of any performance. In Hart and Daughton's words, rhetoric at its best is "ordinary language done extraordinarily" (8).[3] In this examination of Rutgers basketball, key contextual factors include the historical struggle of women to play and compete at sports, the multi-million dollar industry surrounding college sports and sports talk radio, and the ways Black women have been oppressed throughout American history. Far from being fun or a casual performance of race, gender, and sexuality, what the African American women on the Rutgers team (and their White teammates, who are involved in this same historical context) put forth was a very meaningful and consequential performance in their national title game. Viewing their experience as a performance will, however, allow us to trace the way these female athletes were utilized as a source of signifying material for larger social practices and discourses. In the final section of this chapter, we will discuss how socioeconomic class is not a performative category in the same way that gender, race, or sexuality is, and the implications of this for the Rutgers-Imus episode.

Black female athletes are often treated differently by mainstream sports media. For example, Banet-Weiser observed that Black players in the Women's National Basketball Association (WNBA) are presented as women first and African American second. She argues that their performance as Black female athletes is consciously reshaped towards images of motherhood and morality to counter the threatening presence of young, wealthy African American men in its parent league, the men's National Basketball Association (see also Baroffio-Bota and Banet-Weiser). Shugart, in an analysis of the 1999 Women's World Cup soccer team, noted that the one African American member of the team, goalkeeper Brianna Scurry, received far less media attention than her White teammates despite making the key save that clinched the championship. She argues that the performance of elite athleticism by a Black woman was inconsistent with the meanings derived from that of her White teammates, namely that the World Cup team members were "girls next door" with pony tails and normative performances of gender, race, and sexuality. Schultz analyzed the wide array of responses to Brandi Chastain's infamous sports bra pose after her game-winning penalty kick in the 1999 World Cup tournament, perhaps the penultimate illustration of the role of style in sport. She concludes that "Ultimately, the sports bra representations sexualize, homogenize and normalize an ideal of femininity, allow achievement only through technological discipline of the female body, and reproduce the traditional gender order" (185). Sporting performances are clearly linked to wider norms of gender, race, and sexuality—the task for scholars is to trace ways that these athletic performances reinforce or reshape these norms.

Conceptualizing sport as performance does not mean the athletes themselves do not play a role in the performance. Meâns and Kassing interviewed professional women athletes to document the intricate maneuvering these women undergo to construct and maintain their identity as female athletes. Given that "athlete" was long associated solely with men, many scholars have noted that the very existence of female athletes is paradoxical and requires resolution (see Clasen; Peper). The maneuvering required of female athletes largely centers around gender but can entail race and social class variables as well. African American tennis stars Venus and Serena Williams are prime examples of this phenomenon; Ifekwunigwe argues that the sisters deploy a public performance of "Ghetto Cinderellas" by emphasizing their childhood years in the rough neighborhoods of Compton, California, before moving to Florida for elite training. In all these machinations, style and performance are important tools for female athletes, as well as markers by which they are judged.

The issue of competition in women's sport has traditionally been resolved through imposing upper- and middle class norms of femininity upon women athletes. Participation of women in sport was justified, first and with much struggle, as beneficial to women's ability to be mothers (see Cahn). Women pursuing their desire to win at the highest levels of sport pushed the envelope of social acceptance. Festle famously argued that female athletes put forth a "feminine apologetic" in which their elite competitive status is balanced by performances of traditional femininity and heterosexuality. Cahn and others demonstrate how the traditional has often translated to middle or upper class, often in a vocabulary of sportsmanship.[4] More recently, scholars have zeroed in on the actual phenomenon of competitive women athletes as an ongoing challenge to these multiple and overlapping hierarchies. Barrofio-Bota and Banet-Weiser note that "action shots of strong, sweaty female bodies, simply by their sheer corporeality, challenge dominant masculine conventions involving sport" (485). Similarly, Dworkin and Messner argue that "it is the very centrality of the body in sport in practice and ideology that provides an opportunity to examine critically and illuminate the social construction of gender" (342). These authors go on to say that "the very existence of skilled and strong women athletes demanding recognition and equal access to resources is a destabilizing tendency in the current gender order" (346).

Imus and McGuirk's on-air comments suggest that they noticed the competitive zeal of the Rutgers team. His suggestion that "I don't know if I'd wanted to beat Rutgers or not" indicates that the Scarlet Knights' intensity was intimidating to Imus. The support Imus provides for this conclusion, however, did not involve basketball statistics or analysis. Instead, Imus points to Rutgers players' tattoos, "rough" appearance, and "nappy" hair (a team photo run in *Sports Illustrated* after the scandal affords a glimpse of one player with lettering on her right shoulder. Two of the eight Black players have braided hair, while the other six wear long ponytails). McGuirk supported this depiction by calling Rutgers "hard core" and initiating the "ho's" discussion of the team. In a short exchange, male observers of elite women's sport describe competitive play in terms of aesthetic performance.

Readers of Imus's comments may claim that Imus was guilty only of using vulgar language to express what many others had noted about the Rutgers team: they were indeed a very tough opponent. Imus stated in his appearance on Rev. Al Sharpton's show that he had heard from a sportscaster that the Rutgers team was "tough" and this was the information that inspired him to make his initial comments. Indeed, the unlikely path Rutgers took to the national final lends some support to this argument. Thanks mostly to a frenetic style of defense, the Scarlet Knights had beaten perennial title contender Connecticut in their conference final, knocked off top-seeded Duke in the national tournament, and smothered Louisiana State in the semifinals, holding the vaunted Lady Tigers to a mere thirty-five total points of offense. Coverage of the team before the final game reflected this reputation (see Araton, "Competition"; Auman; Brennan, "Parker"; Patrick, "Rutgers Looks"; Patrick, "Tenn., Rutgers").

The flaw in this defense of Imus, however, is that the championship game showcased the toughness of Tennessee, not Rutgers, and nearly every other sports commentator in the nation focused on this in their post-game coverage. On the same morning that Imus opined about "nappy-headed ho's" who played rough with their tough tattoos, professional sports writers were using words such as "annihilated," "crushed," "tough, rugged," and "overmatched" to sum up Tennessee's decisive victory (qtd. in Araton, "Competition"; Aldridge; Brennan, "Parker"; May, "Tennessee Routs"). The *New York Times* said that "the taller Lady Vols dominated the offensive boards and defeated Rutgers at its own game—a hounding, trapping defense that disrupted the Scarlet Knights" (Longman, "Lady Vols"). *USA Today* noted that, although Rutgers had earned its defensive reputation, both squads were tough on this measure (Patrick, "Tenn., Rutgers"). Tennessee, after all, allowed only fifty points in its semifinal game with powerhouse North Carolina. These tightly-fought semi final games led one commentator to make a prescient and ironic observation about how elite women's basketball coaches often have to defend their teams from accusations that women's basketball can get "ugly" (Brennan, "Big Picture"). In her usage, "ugly" referred to the assumption by many fans that low-scoring games lack skill or execution. Coaches often defend these games and praise the value of good defense. In the context of Imus's comments, however, it is clear that "ugly" was taken to a new level for Rutgers versus Tennessee—both in the racial slurs uttered by Imus and in the aesthetic basis of his dismissal of the Rutgers team.

A game report in *USA Today* by Johnnie Whitehead presents the starkest contrast between Imus and the sports reporting that appeared in national news media that morning. The Rutgers team was characterized this way: "Despite having reached the championship game, Rutgers is a program of have-nots. The Scarlet Knights don't have a single star who shines brighter than the rest. They don't have swagger. They don't even boogaloo after they make a great play" ("No Stars"). If the twenty thousand spectators and thousands more television viewers that night got this impression of the two teams, on what basis did Imus make his outrageous remarks? His vitriol exposes the middle class norms of sportsmanship and style that govern women's sport, thus Rutgers was targeted for attack.

■ 2. Style Points: Hip Hop, Film, and Sport

Imus's emphasis on stylistic elements of the Rutgers team forces us to consider the ways sport operates as an aesthetic form. An appreciation for sport's aesthetic function stands in contrast to a more sociological, structural view of sport. Gruneau terms this the "industrial" account of sport that sees sport as a beneficial force on social life and a realm where athletes make rational, voluntary choices amidst occasional and temporary conflict (14–16). The Imus scandal suggests, however, that the actual events of the final contest were less important than the ways in which college women's basketball produces images and impressions of young Black women performing a particular combination of race, class, gender, and sexuality. In articulating these aesthetic messages, Imus borrowed from two other genres to capture this stylistic effect of sport: hip hop and film. That Imus adapted two more well-established genres to describe women's sport suggests that we have neither fully acknowledged the stylistic vocabulary of sport nor developed an adequate language for articulating its connections to other existing forms.

Hip hop is a significant influence on the sport of basketball, specifically as an aesthetic form with its own unique style of dress, personal appearance, and language (see Johnson in this volume). Indeed, scholars differ in characterizing hip hop as a cultural art form or a widespread social movement. Chang situates the rise of hip hop within the turbulence following protests over South African apartheid, the rise of Islamic leader Louis Farrakhan, racial violence in northern cities, and suburban segregation (228). Chang and others have dubbed its followers the "post-Civil Rights generation" to capture the different racial and class-based identifications and agendas of this cultural movement (Chang 228).

Ifekwunigwe contests Chang's narrative, arguing for the existence of meaningful continuities between the Civil Rights and hip hop generations (2). She, unlike Chang who relies on aesthetic qualities, bases her argument on material realities facing Black youth today. First, she argues, not all Black youth benefited socially, economically, or politically from Civil Rights reforms, suggesting that we still need a form of race-based activism. Second, Ifekwunigwe finds tactical resemblances between Civil Rights and hip hop activism, arguing that the polymorphism and fluidity associated with today's hip hop culture also existed within the Civil Rights movement.

However, assessing the impact of hip hop culture and style on women's sport has not been a central project for sport scholars. In many ways this reflects the struggles women face to be recognized or respected within hip hop and Civil Rights discourse. As part of cultures or movements primarily identified with racial politics, Black women have been challenged to express their racial solidarity while still making space for gender-based concerns that related to their racial status. As Ifekwunigwe puts it, there has been a similar "hyper-visible but yet still marginalized status of Black women" in hip hop as in Civil Rights activism (4). Sharpley-Whiting argues that "hip hop's commercial success [is] heavily dependent upon young black women," and thus is "helping to shape a new black gender politics" (11). However it is less clear how our understandings of hip hop as an aesthetic form affect perceptions of Black female athletes.

Assessing the degree to which hip hop influenced Imus's comments about Rutgers is difficult. Certainly the use of the word "ho" brings to mind the frequency with which that word is used in popular hip hop songs to reference women. Stephens found that hip hop culture has effectively created eight "sexual scripts" for understanding Black women: the Diva, Gold Digger, Freak, Dyke, Gangster Bitch, Sister Savior, Earth Mother, and Baby Mama. Miller-Young explores the way hip hop's "illicit erotic" may allow African Americans to engage, negotiate, and challenge traditional economies of desire that rejected Black bodies or defined them as "repugnant." However, Imus's using of "ho" as a powerful, rich, White man with access to mass media adds an important element of material power to the usage of this word. Indeed, scholars of sports talk radio emphasize "talk radio's central role in efforts to restore masculine prerogatives to where they were before the women's movement" (Douglas 286). Nylund, who identifies moments of social justice activism within some sports talk radio shows, concludes that shows like Imus's function as an "attractive venue for embattled white men seeking recreational repose and a nostalgic return to a prefeminist ideal" (2).

Imus escalated the discussion of hip hop and basketball in his appearance on Rev. Al Sharpton's radio program four days after his initial comments. In an attempt to defend himself, Imus asked, "Why isn't there that kind of outrage in the black community when rappers demean black women?" (qtd. in Fenner and Siemaszko, "I-Mess!"). Imus was not alone in this complaint: one columnist echoed Imus in stating that "Sharpton says he hates the hateful message of rap music, language about women and everything else. Does he think that the rappers should just be boycotted, or should they never be allowed to make another record?" (Lupica). Two other flamboyant, controversial "shock jocks" went further, calling Imus "the victim of a 'double standard' because rappers and some black radio hosts routinely make disparaging remarks about women" (Fenner and Siemaszko, "Hoopsters' Dignity"). Some commentators situated Imus in a free speech defense that includes hip hop. For instance, Tom Knott of the *Washington Times* stated that firing Imus for his words, "though it might feel good, runs counter to a nation that clings to its free speech beliefs, no matter how idiotic and offensive much of the speech is. That belief applies to the hip hop artists who pen far more vile words in their releases than anything Imus said." Other commentators saw vindication of hip hop in Imus's use of "ho." A *Philadelphia Inquirer* article began by stating that "The best thing about the idiotic and insensitive rant on Don Imus's show on Wednesday is that it shows the hip hop industry can't be blamed for all the misogyny that exists in this world" (Smith). Imus's claim of hypocrisy fails to acknowledge his own powerful position in contrast to the Black players of Rutgers or Tennessee. His application of hip hop terminology to elite athletic women, however, demonstrates that the aesthetic qualities of sport link up and interact with other established aesthetic forms.

A second form of mass media that Imus invoked in both his initial comments and apology attempts is film. On the air the day after Rutgers lost, Imus and McGuirk compared Rutgers and Tennessee to "jigaboo's and wannabe's" and mistakenly credited the Spike Lee film *Do the Right Thing* for these terms. In fact, the phrases appeared in Lee's 1988 film *School Daze*. The film reference is notable for both its original intent and the way Imus and McGuirk mistakenly reference it in connection to women's basketball. Film critic Roger Ebert called *School Daze* "the first movie in a long time where the black characters seem to be relating to one another, instead of to a hypothetical white audience…. With utter frankness it addresses two subjects that are taboo in most 'black movies': complexion and hair." The story takes place at a prestigious all-Black college in the south, where students, both men and women, argue over the proper avocations of college: sorority and fraternity membership, or anti-racist activism. In the first camp are the "wannabes" who sport straightened, longer hair and join sororities. In the latter are the "jigaboo" girls who are darker skinned and wear their hair shorter or in Afros. In an interview after McGuirk misidentified his film, Lee stated,

> I came up with the jigaboos and wannabes for something very specific about how African Americans view themselves based on hair color, complexion, etc. I was trying to show how crazy it was to do that, that black folks come in all different shapes, tones and sizes, etc., that one is not to be ridiculed over the other because we're all beautiful. (qtd. in Smith)

The way McGuirk and Imus distorted the film's use of these categories, casting Tennessee as the "wannabes" and Rutgers the "jigaboos," underscores the way performative elements of sport carry important social message. In this case, one reading of Imus and McGuirk's exchange is that the outcome of a collegiate women's basketball game reaffirms a racial hierarchy in which White men hold the top position. Even for Tennessee, who won the game and "wins" in the hierarchy of skin color, Imus's compliments remain based on appearance. The Lady Volunteers are characterized as "cute" and subjected to objectification and condescension. (It is worth noting at this point that none of the twenty articles that reported on and responded to Imus's gaffe remarked on this part of his comment. No reporter called Pat Summit for a comment about her national champions being portrayed as cute and no one interviewed national player of the year and finals MVP Candace Parker about the phrase.)

A second film reference occurred when Imus compared the basketball game to the famous play (and later movie) *West Side Story*. During his interview with Rev. Al Sharpton, on April 10, 2008, Imus stated that "at the time I said it I wasn't even thinking race. I was thinking West Side Story: one team is tough, one team is not so tough" (de Mores). The famous story depicts racial and class tension in New York City in a modern version of Romeo and Juliet's woes as star-crossed lovers. Imus turned to this familiar story in an attempt to clarify and redeem his comments. Translating through the language of this film, he is now complimenting Rutgers as a tough urban team while Tennessee is cast as the more privileged, clean-cut gang.

Imus was again sorely mistaken in his depiction of the teams. While Rutgers did boast four starters from the New York/New Jersey area, Tennessee too had two key players from the city. Indeed, the urban roots of Rutgers had been a major storyline in news media before the game. Rutgers' tournament narrative involved a group of tightly knit, highly talented players who had forged the bonds that carried them from urban blight to the sport's highest level. Epiphany Prince had once scored 113 points in a high school game (Ackert, "Knight's Prince") while leading her team to a national championship in 2004 and she earned a starting position at once for Rutgers (Hutchinson). Kia Vaughn, a six-foot forward built like an oak tree, was positioned into a familiar hoop-dreams narrative; one profile stated that Vaughn's "mother reasoned that Vaughn was tall and a kid coming out of the Webster Houses [housing project] had to take advantage of whatever she had" (Daly). By earning an athletic scholarship and playing in a national championship, Vaughn provided a feel-good story of personal sacrifice and achievement through sport. One commentator cautioned that "it would be an overstatement to say that Rutgers had no primary shooter. But in the Scarlet Knights' minds, they are classic blue-collar climbers and Tennessee is Summitt, the six-time champion, one last opponent to outwork and surmount" (Araton, "High School Foes"). Regardless of the actual backgrounds of these players, Imus's comments after the game drew upon the aesthetic elements of their performance, not a deep knowledge of their team program. McGuirk's comment that the women resembled the NBA's Toronto Raptors reinforces this superficial reading of the team. Toronto, in 2007, fielded a young team known for physical play bordering on thuggish aggression.

However, Imus's hasty characterization of Rutgers as big bad city girls overlooked the fact that two major players on the Lady Vols squad also hailed from the mean streets of New York City. Niki Anosike, 6'4" and from Staten Island, was a workhorse reserve forward for Tennessee, who had sixteen key rebounds in the final game. Diminutive Lady Vol point guard Shannon Bobbitt, all 5'2" of her hailing from the same Brooklyn high school as the high-scoring Prince, was described by Rutgers head coach C. Vivian Stringer as the player who broke the Scarlet Knights' back (Longman, "Lady Vols"). Not only did Bobbitt finish with thirteen points, almost all off deadly three-point shooting, she also played with the swagger and playground flash associated with the hip hop style that Imus seemed to invoke in his comments—about the other team.

Imus's characterization of the teams suggests that the performance of the Rutgers team, in combination with its location in northern New Jersey, communicated an inherent toughness in those players. The performance of the Tennessee team, hailing from a state that evokes more pastoral scenes, did not conjure such images for Imus. In addition to making hasty characterizations of each team, Imus's use of hip hop and film references demonstrates how women's sport is linked, through the style of its performers, to other powerful cultural vocabularies.

■ 3. Turnover: "Defending" Rutgers

Imus was not the only one to use the performance of Rutgers versus Tennessee to advance larger arguments; those who defended the teams from Imus had their own agendas. And if Imus is to be condemned for making his comments based on glances of tattoos, cornrows, and urban upbringings, it is equally notable how often those who rushed to support the Rutgers players pointed to the same aesthetic elements of their racial or gender performance. Dworkin and Messner express concern that the success of women's sports since the passage of Title IX legislation "proves the effectiveness of organizing politically and legally around the concept of 'woman.' Indeed, the relative success of post-Title IX liberal strategy of gender equity in sport was premised on the deployment of separate 'male' and 'female' sports" (345). The distinction between sexes, for Dworkin and Messner, is a key obstacle in ever escaping the trivializing and sexualizing discourse in which Imus traffics. Dave Zirin mounts a more radical critique of mainstream commercial sport, drawing our attention to the immense amount of public money spent on athletic stadiums at the expense of more vital measures of public welfare (Terrordome). Critiques such as these remind us to examine arguments in defense of sport as carefully as those more slanderous voices such as Imus's.

Defenders of the Rutgers team emerged at the local, state, and national levels. A New York City high school coach defended the Rutgers players with local roots as "well-kept ladies" who "speak eloquently and represent themselves well" (Lelinwalla and Gagne). This coach remained within a vocabulary of style to refute Imus's characterization, reinforcing the important ways aesthetics and performance inform our understanding of class, race, gender, and sexuality. It is only in his final comments that this coach noted that these incredibly talented athletes are "performing at the highest level" (Lelinwalla and Gagne). The lingering presence of expectations regarding personal appearance, even from social actors who support the Rutgers team, speaks to the powerful norms that continue to govern women's sport performances.

Similar comments were made by New Jersey governor John Corzine on the day the Rutgers players held their news conference. Corzine seemed to avoid a feminized ideal by stating that the team "embodies all that is great about New Jersey: intelligence, toughness, tenacity, leadership, and, most of all, class" (Moroz). However, Corzine undermined his message in the next sentence by calling the team the "Lady Knights." While several colleges continue to add the term "lady" before their school mascots to denote women's teams, Rutgers women's basketball team has been called the Scarlet Knights, same as the name for their men's team, since the day head coach C. Vivian Stringer took over the program. Indeed, several articles covering the scandal mentioned Stringer's strong stand on this very issue—highlighted by Tennessee's continued use of "Lady Vols" for their team. That Corzine would violate this powerful symbolic change by the highest-paid basketball coach at his state's flagship university demonstrates the power of the discourses of style that govern women's sport.

Female competitive athletes are constrained from freely expressing their intensity even within nationwide discourses that encourage women's sport. Comments of the WNBA league commissioner Donna Orender demonstrate this paradox. Rushing to defend the Rutgers team, Orender stated that "the women's game is all about bringing people together, no matter their religion, nationality or other differences. For 10 years, the WNBA has celebrated the grace, beauty, power, achievement and strength of women's basketball" (Ackert, "WNBA's Prez"). Orender's attention to religious freedom is commendable but not at all relevant to Imus's comments. Likewise, rather than directly discuss racial makeup of Rutgers players or their professional mentors, Orender uses "nationality" as a less charged stand-in term. Finally, like the high school coach who praised the personal hygiene of the Rutgers team,

Orender includes words such as "grace" and "beauty" in the positive attributes of women's basketball. The salience of stylistic elements remains strong for women's basketball; it is not enough to hit 80% of free throws or possess impeccable footwork on defense—women, especially Black women, must also perform the proper mix of these intangible aesthetic qualities.

■ 4. Jump Ball: "Classy Ladies" versus Social Class

Attention to beauty, grace, and other physical attributes was one pattern among those who defended Rutgers from Imus's attack. The second common theme was to praise the players—especially after their nationally televised press conference where they addressed Imus's words—as "classy." Rhetorical critics of sport, performance, and social class should take pause at the implications associated with defining socioeconomic class as acting "classy." Certainly the Rutgers team provided a dramatic demonstration that privileged individuals may display disrespectful behavior while less advantaged persons can possess attributes we deem worthy of esteem, but wealth and power disparities persist between social actors such as Imus and collegiate female basketball players. After looking at examples of how this phrase was used in regards to the Rutgers team, we will discuss more fully the dangers of allowing social class to be a performative category.

Rutgers head coach C. Vivian Stringer was the first to receive the appellation when she was described as "one of the classiest acts in all of sports" by one reporter for speaking out on behalf of her team (Sheridan). Stringer also used the term herself in reference to her players, stating in her official statement about Imus's post-game comments that "to serve as a joke of Mr. Imus in such an insensitive manner creates a wedge and makes light of these classy individuals, both as women and as women of color" (Singleton). Four articles used the term in their headlines after the player's press conference, as well as a *Sport Illustrated* column that appeared a week later (Kinkhabwala). *New York Times* reporter Selena Roberts concluded her column with the quip that "the Rutgers women ran the [press conference rebuking Imus] without abusing the privilege. Very ladylike of them." *USA Today* columnist Christine Brennan described the players' press conference behavior as "polite...complete, comprehensible" ("Rutgers Women Stand Tall"). Brennan went on to contrast Imus's evocation of nappy-headed ho's with Coach Stringer's description of "valedictorians, future doctors, musical prodigies, and yes, even Girl Scouts." Finally, Fenner portrayed the players as "dignified...carefully coiffed and looking sharp" ("Hoopsters' Dignity"). Those who lauded the Rutgers team's "classy" behavior were clearly not discussing only their socioeconomic status. These characterizations focus instead on the decorum of the women (refraining from ad hominem attacks on Imus), their public presentation (eloquence), and personal appearance. All accounts quoted here construct a standard of "classy" behavior that is predicated on style and explicitly attached to femininity.

There is a darker side to these compliments. If attributes, behaviors, personal appearance, and etiquette can determine class designations, we risk losing grasp of more material realities of economic inequality. This is the heart of what Karl Marx argued over a century ago: if our sense of self and our awareness of social conditions is internally based, through thoughts and feelings, then the remedy for social inequality is relegated to individual action and optimism. In reversing this equation, Marx argued that lived experiences, specifically of our position in the economic order, shape our sense of self and awareness of the world around us. This means that to reduce inequality or to improve our social status we must address material concerns of everyday life such as conditions of employment, social welfare, and basic needs.[5]

Marxist understandings of class define it as an objective, empirical relationship between laborer and product of their labor. Sport scholars have, to some degree, embraced a cultural studies approach that seeks to balance these concerns with an awareness of the role performance, pleasure, and even desire play in sports. Recognition of the role of performance in sport challenges Marxist critics. It asks that we remain open to theorizing culture as constitutive—that is, shaped by our actions, words, and feelings—and not just as determined by economic conditions or our position within economic stratification (Carrington 13). One way to balance these competing views is to recognize the power of cultural identity and performance, and to define culture as a "way of struggle" (Carrington 13).

These questions of class, performance, and struggle fit neatly into the experiences of African Americans in the United States and perhaps with Black athletes in particular. Sport performances remind us that class remains a difficult topic in American discourse. Patricia Hill Collins notes that the "actual ghettoization of poor and working-class African Americans" is obscured behind "hypervisible" representations of Black youth in hip hop discourse and images (4). Sport provides another substantial source of images of Black youth, thus it is vital to ask what vision of social class is presented in those images. Cultural scholar bell hooks has persuasively argued that we simply do not discuss class, opting instead for a racial vocabulary that stands in for class judgments. As a result of this tendency, she says, we build racial solidarity but mask class inequality that may cross racial lines (5). This insight complicates Chang's narrative about the rise of hip hop. The racial identification that is associated with the rise of hip hop is most likely transected by both crossracial class affiliation and interracial class inequality.

hooks's reminder also compels us to acknowledge the connection between racial identity, class, and style in the United States. Novelist Rita Mae Brown expressed a similar stance, stating that

> class is much more than Marx's definition of relationship to the means of production. Class involves your behavior, your basic assumptions, how you are taught to behave, what you expect from yourself and others, your concept of a future, how you understand problems and solve them, how you think, feel, act. (qtd in hooks 103).

Calling the Rutgers team "classy" based on stylistic factors may deflect attention from notions of class that entail structural inequality or persistent disadvantages that many African Americans confront in their daily lives. If Imus was reacting to the performance of social class supplied by the Rutgers team, praising their responses as "classy" relegates our understanding of class to performance only, and not as a complicated interaction of material conditions and cultural expression.

Of the articles examined here, three directly tackled class issues in a material sense. Stephen Smith noted that of the 324 varsity women's basketball programs in the nation, where 42% of the players are Black, only 8% of the coaches are African American. Similarly, William Rhoden noted that although African Americans make up significant percentages in football, basketball, and track events, they comprise only 2.5% of all collegiate soccer players and are "virtually absent" in the other sports. However, Rhoden drops class consciousness from the conclusion of his piece, noting instead that "sexism and racism are very much alive" in women's sport. Daly reported the impoverished upbringing of Rutgers star Kia Vaughn, casting basketball as her best chance to escape the Webster House projects of the Bronx.

The "classy" responses of the players were indeed intelligent articulations of how race, gender, and sexuality overlap in women's sport. For instance, it was Rutgers guard Essence Carson, not any professional sports reporter, who made clear that "it's more than about the Rutgers women's basketball team. As a society, we're trying to grow and get to the point where we don't classify women as ho's and we don't classify African American women as nappy-headed ho's" (Roberts). Similarly, forward Kia Vaughn stated at the team's press conference that "unless, in my case, 'ho' stands for achievement or something you're getting done and you know you're a wonderful person, then I'm not a 'ho.' I'm a woman. And, I'm someone's child" (Daly).

In sum, those who defended the Rutgers players extended a cycle of constraint that may ultimately restrict these athletes' well-being. The cycle begins with the tough, aggressive, skilled play required to win championships; this style of play violates gender norms of proper femininity, thus female athletes and their allies work to recuperate their status as women. Asserting female and feminine credentials is often especially fraught with dilemmas for Black women who face a racial barrier from inclusion into "proper" femininity. However, pursuing this "classy" response—which is nearly demanded by powerful sport institutions—stuffs female athletes back into a box of passive, ladylike norms for women's sport. Upon their next hard-fought victory (or defeat), the cycle will start all over again.

■ Conclusion

The goal of this chapter is not to defend Don Imus. He was rightly criticized for using his powerful platform to demean those less privileged and he has continually, tragically misunderstood the vast power differential between himself and his targets of mockery. However, it is crucial that we look closely at his comments, his attempts at explanation, and the reaction of other major media and political voices to his disastrous comments. A too-quick rejection of Imus as "merely" an ignorant racist misogynist risks losing an opportunity to glimpse deeper truths about power in the United States, and the role sports performances play in challenging or reconfirming these relationships.

In this chapter, we saw how women's basketball provides signs, images, actions, and symbols integral to the ongoing struggle of athlete women to assert their presence in American society. This challenge is often more complicated for African American women who exist within multiple, intersecting oppressions due to interactions of racism and sexism. For many athletes, and for most elite ones, earning acceptance is complicated by class inequalities that reify and reinforce these gender and racial norms. By competing at the game of basketball, women of all races perform a particular combination of race, class, gender, and sexuality. The task for rhetorical scholars is to trace how these athletic performances are interpreted, understood, and utilized within larger discourses. This chapter has argued that without attention to the class status of many of the Rutgers women and their NCAA peers, we risk perpetuating a discursive cycle that hamstrings female athletes from full expression, denies them true recognition for their physical feats, and dampens truly radical, powerful demands for justice from social forces ranging from Don Imus to the WNBA.

Works Cited

Ackert, Kristie. "Knights' Prince Sees Pal in Way of Crown." *Daily News* (New York) 3 Apr. 2007, Sports Final ed.: 65. *LexisNexis.* Accessed on 24 July 2008.

———. "WNBA's Prez Blasts Imus." *Daily News* (New York) 10 Apr. 2007, Sports Final ed.: 66. *LexisNexis.* Accessed on 24 July 2008.

Aldridge, David. "Rebounds: Vols Rule the Glass, 'Rocky Top' Grates on the Ears." *Philadelphia Inquirer* 4 Apr. 2007, City-C ed.: E1. *LexisNexis.* Accessed on 24 July 2008.

Araton, Harvey. "Competition Defines a Friendship." *New York Times* 4 Apr. 2007, late ed.—final: D3. *LexisNexis.* Accessed on 24 July 2008.

———. "High School Foes form a Family at Rutgers." *New York Times* 3 Apr. 2007, late ed.—final: D1. *LexisNexis.* Accessed on 24 July 2008.

Artz, Lee, Steve Macek, and Dana L. Cloud, eds. *Marxism and Communication Studies: The Point Is to Change It.* New York: Lang, 2006.

Auman, Greg. "Stringer's Path Back to Final Four a Very Long One." *St. Petersburg Times* (Florida) 3 Apr. 2007, South Pinellas ed.: 3C. *LexisNexis.* Accessed on 24 July 2008.

Banet-Weiser, Sarah. "Hoop Dreams: Professional Basketball and the Politics of Race and Gender." *Journal of Sport and Social Issues* 23.4 (1999): 403–20. *Academic Search Premier.* Accessed on 10 Apr. 2008.

Barrofio-Bota, Daniela, and Sarah Banet-Weiser. "Women, Team Sports, and the WNBA: Playing Like a Girl." *Handbook of Sports and Media.* Ed. Arthur A. Raney and Jennings Bryant. Mahwah: Erlbaum, 2006. 485–500.

Brennan, Christine. "Big Picture Rises above Ugly Play in Women's Game." *USA Today* 3 Apr. 2007, Sports Final ed.: 8C. *LexisNexis.* Accessed on 24 July 2008.

———. "Parker Defined as Champion." *USA Today* 4 Apr. 2007, Chase ed.: 2C. *LexisNexis.* Accessed on 24 July 2008.

———. "Rutgers Women Stand Tall in Class." *USA Today* 11 Apr. 2007, Sports Final ed.: 12C. *LexisNexis.* Accessed on 24 July 2008.

Brummett, Barry. *Reading Rhetorical Theory.* Fort Worthm: Harcourt, 2000.

Butler, Judith. *Gender Trouble: Feminism and the Subversion of Identity.* New York: Routledge, 1999.

———. *Undoing Gender.* New York: Routledge, 2004.

Butterworth, Michael L. "Purifying the Body Politic: Steroids, Rafael Palmeiro, and the Rhetorical Cleansing of Major League Baseball." *Western Journal of Communication* 72.2 (2008): 145–61. *Academic Search Premier.* Accessed on 10 Apr. 2008.

Cahn, Susan. *Coming on Strong: Gender and Sexuality in Twentieth-Century Women's Sport.* Cambridge: Harvard UP, 1994.

Carr, David. "Networks Condemn Remarks by Imus." *New York Times* 7 Apr. 2007, late ed.—final: B7. *LexisNexis.* Accessed on 24 July 2008.

Carrington, Ben. "Marxism, Cultural Studies and Sport: Mapping the Field." *Marxism, Cultural Studies and Sport.* Ed. Ben Carrington and Ian McDonald. London: Routledge, 2009. 1–23.

Chang, Jeff. *Can't Stop Won't Stop: A History of the Hip-Hop Generation.* New York: Picador/ St. Martin's, 2005.

Clasen, Patricia. "The Female Athlete: Dualisms and Paradox in Practice." *Women and Language* 24.2 (2001): 36–42. *Academic Search Premier.* Accessed on 1 Feb. 2005.

Collins, Patricia Hill. *From Black Power to Hip Hop: Racism, Nationalism, and Feminism.* Philadelphia: Temple UP, 2006.

Daly, Michael. "A Tower of Strength: Rutgers Center 6-ft Plus of Dignity." *Daily News* (New York) 12 Apr. 2007, Sports Final ed.: 22. *LexisNexis.* Accessed on 24 July 2008.

de Moraes, Lisa. "Don Imus Is Punished with Two Weeks of Radio Silence." *Washington Post* 10 Apr. 2007, Met 2 ed.: C1. *LexisNexis.* Accessed on 24 July 2008.

Deggans, Eric. "To Save Job, Imus in Full Apology Tour Mode." *St. Petersburg Times* (Florida) 10 Apr. 2007, South Pinellas ed.: 1A. *LexisNexis.* Accessed on 24 July 2008.

Douglas, Susan J. *Listening In: Radio and the American Imagination, from Amos 'n Andy and Edward R. Murrow to Wolfman Jack and Howard Stern.* New York: Times, 1999.

Dworkin, Shari, and Michael A. Messner. "Just Do . . . What? Sport, Bodies, Gender." *Revisioning Gender.* Ed. Myra Marx Ferree, Judith Lorber, and Beth B. Hess. Thousand Oaks: Sage, 1999. 341–61.

Ebert, Roger. Rev. of *School Daze,* by Spike Lee. *rogerebert.com.* Digital Chicago Inc., 12 Feb. 1988. Accessed on 15 July 2008. <http://rogerebert.suntimes.com/apps/pbcs. dll/article?AID=/19880212/REVIEWS/802120303/1023>.

Fenner, Austin, and Corky Siemaszko. "Hoopsters' Dignity and Class Slam Dunk Imus." *Daily News* (New York) 11 Apr. 2007, Sports Final ed.: 5. *LexisNexis.* Accessed on 24 July 2008.

———. "I-Mess! Don Is Booted for 2 Wks." *Daily News* (New York) 10 Apr. 2007, Sports Final ed.: 9. *LexisNexis.* Accessed on 24 July 2008.

Festle, Mary Jo. *Playing Nice: Politics and Apologies in Women's Sports.* New York: Columbia UP, 1996.

Greenberg, Mel. "Destiny Denied." *Philadelphia Inquirer* 4 Apr. 2007, City-C ed.: E1. *LexisNexis.* Accessed on 24 July 2008.

———. "Scarlet Knights Ready for Their Rendezvous." *Philadelphia Inquirer* 3 Apr. 2007, City-D ed.: E6. *LexisNexis.* Accessed on 24 July 2008.

Gruneau, Richard S. "Modernization or Hegemony: Two Views on Sport and Social Development." *Not Just a Game: Essays in Canadian Sport Sociology.* Ed. Jean Harvey and Hart Cantelon. Ottawa: U of Ottawa P, 1988. 9–32.

Guthrie, Marisa. "Imus Have Been Nuts: Apologizes for Calling Rutgers Women Hoopsters 'Nappy Headed Hos.'" *Daily News* (New York) 7 Apr. 2007, Sports Final ed.: 3. *LexisNexis.* Accessed on 24 July 2008.

Hart, Roderick P., and Suzanne Daughton. *Modern Rhetorical Criticism.* 3rd ed. Boston: Pearson, 2005.

Hefler, Jan. "At Rutgers, Lack of Hoopla for the Ladies." *Philadelphia Inquirer* 3 Apr. 2007, Jersey ed.: B1. *LexisNexis.* Accessed on 24 July 2008.

Heywood, Leslie, and Shari Dworkin. *Built to Win: The Female Athlete as Cultural Icon.* Minneapolis: U of Minnesota P, 2003.

hooks, bell. *Where We Stand: Class Matters.* New York: Routledge, 2000.

Hutchinson, Bill. "No Loss Clause: HS Coach has 1 Ex-player Win NCAA Title at Another's Expense." *Daily News* (New York) 4 Apr. 2007, Sports Final ed.: 2. *LexisNexis.* Accessed on 24 July 2008.

Ifekwunigwe, Jayne O. "Venus and Serena Are 'Doing it' for Themselves: Theorizing Sporting Celebrity, Class and Black Feminism for the Hip Hop Generation." *Marxism, Cultural Studies and Sport.* Ed. Ben Carrington and Ian McDonald. London: Routledge, 2009. 130–53.

Ifill, Gwen. "Trash Talk Radio." *New York Times* 10 Apr. 2007, late ed.—final: A21. *LexisNexis.* Accessed on 24 July 2008.

Johnson, Peter. "Critics Demand Imus Be Fired for Rutgers Remark." *USA Today* 9 Apr. 2007, Sports Final ed.: 3D. *LexisNexis.* Accessed on 24 July 2008.

King, Colin. "Race and Cultural Identity: Playing the Race Game Inside Football." *Leisure Studies* 23.1 (2004): 19–30. *Academic Search Premier.* Accessed on 15 July 2008.

Kinkhabwala, Anita. "The Righteous Scarlet Knights." *Sports Illustrated* 23 Apr. 2007: 16–18. *LexisNexis.* Accessed on 24 July 2008.

Knott, Tom. "Undoing of a Radio Ham." *Washington Times* 10 Apr. 2007, Sports: C1. *LexisNexis.* Accessed on 24 July 2008.

Lelinwalla, Mark, and Matt Gagne. "Prince: 'I Comb My Hair.'" *Daily News* (New York) 8 Apr. 2007, Sports Final ed.: 58. *LexisNexis.* Accessed on 24 July 2008.

Longman, Jere. "Lady Vols Re-establish a Legacy." *New York Times* 4 Apr. 2007, late ed.—final: D1. *LexisNexis.* Accessed on 24 July 2008.

———. "With Same Background, Stars Take Different Paths." *New York Times* 3 Apr. 2007, late ed.—final: D2. *LexisNexis.* Accessed on 24 July 2008.

Lupica, Mike. "Hoopsters' Dignity and Class Slam-Dunk Imus: Their Face of Grace Outshines Insult." *Daily News* (New York) 11 Apr. 2007, Sports Final ed.: 4. *LexisNexis.* Accessed on 24 July 2008.

May, Peter. "Strength in Volunteer Numbers." *Boston Globe* 3 Apr. 2007, Third ed.: C9. *LexisNexis.* Accessed on 24 July 2008.

———. "Tennessee Routs Rutgers to Earn the Women's Title." *Boston Globe* 4 Apr. 2007, First ed.: E1. *LexisNexis.* Accessed on 24 July 2008.

Meân, Lindsay J., and Jeffrey W. Kassing. "'I Would Just Like to Be Known as an Athlete': Managing Hegemony, Femininity, and Heterosexuality in Female Sport." *Western Journal of Communication* 72.2 (2008): 126–44. *Academic Search Premier.* Accessed on 15 July 2008.

Miller-Young, Mireille. "Hip-Hop Honeys and Da Hustlaz: Black Sexualities in the New Hip-Hop Pornography." *Meridians: Feminism, Race, Transnationalism* 8.1 (2008): 261–92. *Academic Search Premier.* Accessed on 16 July 2008.

Morgan, Joan, and Mark Anthony Neal. "A Brand-New Feminism." *Total Chaos: The Art and Aesthetics of Hip-Hop.* Ed. Jeff Chang. New York: Basic Civitas, 2006. 233–46.

Moroz, Jennifer. "Angry NJ Rallies in Defense of Its Wounded Heroes." *Philadelphia Inquirer* 10 Apr. 2007, Jersey ed.: A8. *LexisNexis.* Accessed on 24 July 2008.

Nylund, David. *Beer, Babes, and Balls: Masculinity and Sports Talk Radio*. Albany: SUNY UP, 2007.

Olson, Lisa. "Two Weeks? He Needs at Least a Summer Vacation." *Daily News* (New York) 10 Apr. 2007, Sports Final ed.: 58. *LexisNexis*. Accessed on 24 July 2008.

Patrick, Dick. "Rutgers Looks to Shut Down Yet Another Star." *USA Today* 3 Apr. 2007, Final ed.: 8C. *LexisNexis*. Accessed on 24 July 2008.

———. "Summit, Vols on Top Again." *USA Today* 4 Apr. 2007, Chase ed.: 1C. *LexisNexis*. Accessed on 24 July 2008.

———. "Tenn., Rutgers Stress Defense." *USA Today* 3 Apr. 2007, First ed.: 1C. *LexisNexis*. Accessed on 24 July 2008.

Peper, Karen. "Woman Athlete = Lesbian: Mythology of Gendex." *Queer Words, Queer Images: The Construction of Homosexuality in Communication*. Ed. R. J. Ringer. New York: New York UP, 1994. 193–208.

Rhoden, William C. "The Unpleasant Reality for Women in Sports." *New York Times* 9 Apr. 2007, late ed.—final: D7. *LexisNexis*. Accessed on 24 July 2008.

Roberts, Selena. "A First-class Response to a Second-class Put-down." *New York Times* 11 Apr. 2007, late ed.—final: D1. *LexisNexis*. Accessed on 24 July 2008.

Schultz, Jaime. "Discipline and Push-Up: Female Bodies, Femininity, and Sexuality in Popular Representations of Sports Bras." *Sociology of Sport Journal* 21.2 (2004): 185–205. *Academic Search Premier*. Accessed on 10 May 2008.

Sharpley-Whiting, T. Denean. *Pimps Up, Ho's Down: Hip Hop's Hold on Young Black Women*. New York: New York UP, 2007.

Sheridan, Phil. "When Hate Meets Ignorance on the Air." *Philadelphia Inquirer* 7 Apr. 2007, City-D Ed.:1. *LexisNexis*. Accessed on 24 July 2008.

Shugart, Helene A. "She Shoots, She Scores: Mediated Constructions of Contemporary Female Athletes in Coverage of the 1999 U.S. Women's Soccer Team." *Western Journal of Communication* 67.1 (2003): 1–31. *Academic Search Premier*. Accessed on 1 Feb. 2005.

Singleton, Don. "Imus Can't Dribble Around This Flagrant, Racist Foul." *Daily News* (New York) 8 Apr. 2007, Sports Final ed.: 7. *LexisNexis*. Accessed on 24 July 2008.

Smith, Stephen A. "Imus' Indecency Contaminates Airwaves." *Philadelphia Inquirer* 8 Apr. 2007, City-D ed.: E1. *LexisNexis*. Accessed on 24 July 2008.

Stephens, Dionne. "Hip Hop Honey or Video Ho: African American Preadolescents' Understanding of Female Sexual Scripts in Hip Hop Culture." *Sexuality and Culture* 11.4 (2007): 48–69. *Academic Search Premier*. Accessed on 16 July 2008.

Walters, Suzana Danuta. "Sex, Text, and Context: (In) Between Feminism and Cultural Studies." *Revisioning Gender*. Ed. Myra Marx Ferree, Judith Lorber, and Beth B. Hess. Thousand Oaks: Sage. 222–57.

Whitehead, Johnnie. "No Stars No Problem for Rutgers." *USA Today* 4 Apr. 2007, First ed.: 8C. *LexisNexis*. Accessed on 24 July 2008.

———. "Tennessee, Summitt Get Seventh Title." *USA Today* 4 Apr. 2007, Chase ed.: 1C. *LexisNexis*.

———. "Women's Changes Weighed." *USA Today* 4 Apr. 2007, First ed.: 1C. *LexisNexis*. Accessed on 24 July 2008.

Wushanley, Ying. *Playing Nice and Losing: The Struggle for Control of Women's Intercollegiate Athletics, 1960–2000.* Syracuse: Syracuse UP, 2004.

Zirin, Dave. *Welcome to the Terrordome: The Pain, Politics and Promise of Sports.* Chicago: Haymarket, 2007.

———. *What's My Name, Fool? Sports and Resistance in the United States.* Chicago: Haymarket, 2005.

Notes

1. Transcript produced by author based on recording accessed at http://sports.aol.com/fanhouse/category/ncaa-basketball-media-watch/2007/04/06/whos-worse-don-imus-or-billy-packer/.

2. Articles were identified through a search of the *Lexis-Nexis* database. Pre-Imus articles were identified using search terms "Rutgers women's basketball" in a full text search of major publications from April 3 to 4, 2007. Twenty of the thirty-nine articles were randomly selected for analysis. Post-Imus articles were identified using the same search terms from April 5 to 12. Twenty of sixty-nine articles were randomly selected for analysis. The larger date range for the post-Imus articles was designed to encompass events in the wake of the initial comments, particularly the players' press conference.

3. It is beyond the scope of this chapter to give a full discussion of rhetorical studies as a field and form of criticism. See Hart and Daughton for a thorough introduction, and Brummett for more attention to the classical roots of rhetorical study.

4. Many sports scholars argue that the entire amateur model of sport is based upon class privileges in which athletes who need to play for money are cast as opportunistic and a threat to the pure pursuit of excellence. For a gendered example of this, see Wushanley. Zirin (*What's My Name?*) focuses more on racial aspects of sport and their interaction with social class hierarchies.

5. This is an extremely short version of the Marxist position and his critique of Hegelian dialectics. For an introduction to these ideas, see Lee Artz, Steve Macek, and Dana L. Cloud.

◼ About the Contributors

Meredith M. Bagley is a doctoral candidate at the University of Texas at Austin. She earned her Master's degree at the University of Washington and wrote a thesis on public discourse in the Women's National Basketball Association. She is preparing a dissertation on Title IX and the rhetoric of competition.

Laura Barberena is currently pursuing a PhD in Communication Studies at the University of Texas at Austin. She holds a Masters in International Relations from St. Mary's University and a Bachelor of Science in Communication from the University of Texas at Austin. Ms. Barberena's research interests include pop culture, media, and politics as they relate to Latinos in the United States.

Barry Brummett is the Charles Sapp Centennial Professor in Communication and Chair of the Department of Communication Studies at the University of Texas at Austin. He received his PhD from the University of Minnesota and has taught at Purdue University and the University of Wisconsin-Milwaukee. Brummett is the author of several books including *A Rhetoric of Style* (Carbondale, IL: Southern Illinois University Press, 2008), *Rhetorical Homologies: Form, Culture, Experience* (Tuscaloosa: University of Alabama Press, 2004), and *The World and How We Describe It: Rhetorics of Reality, Representation, Simulation* (Westport, CT: Praeger, 2003).

Alexis Carreiro is a PhD student at the University of Texas at Austin in the department of Radio-TV-Film. Her dissertation examines film editors and collaborative authorship during the Hollywood Renaissance. Her interests include feminist media criticism, gender and production culture, and screenwriting. She is the former Co-Coordinating Editor of flowtv. org, an online TV and media studies journal.

Jay P. Childers is an Assistant Professor of Communication Studies at the University of Kansas. He received his PhD from the University of Texas at Austin in 2006. His work has appeared in a number of scholarly journals and collections including the *Quarterly Journal of Speech* and *Presidential Studies Quarterly.*

K. Jeanine Congalton is an Associate Professor in the Department of Human Communication Studies at California State University, Fullerton. Dr. Congalton earned her PhD from the University of Utah. Her academic interests include sports rhetoric and forensics education.

Roger Gatchet is a doctoral student in the Department of Communication Studies at the University of Texas at Austin. His research interests include the rhetoric of popular culture, popular music, and oral history. He published a chapter titled "A Hystery of Colonial Witchcraft: Witch-Hunt Tourism and Commemoration in Salem, Massachusetts" in the 2008 edited collection *Uncovering Hidden Rhetorics: Social Issues in Disguise.*

Carlnita P. Greene is an Assistant Professor of Communication and Rhetoric in the Department of English at Nazareth College in Rochester, New York. She received her PhD in Communication Studies from the University of Texas at Austin in 2006. Dr. Greene's research specialization is the rhetoric of popular culture and her publications include "Shopping for What Never Was: The Rhetoric of Food, Social Style, and Nostalgia," in *Food for Thought: Essays on Eating and Culture* (York, PA: Mcfarland Press, 2008), "The 'Domestic Goddess': Postfeminist Representation in the Televisual Kitchen: A Media Ecological Analysis of *Nigella Bites,*" in *Explorations in Media Ecology,* 4.3/4 (2005) and "Snap, Crackle, Pop Culture and Communication Curricula," in *Popular Culture Across the Curricula: Essays for Educators* (York, PA: Mcfarland Press, 2004).

Kevin A. Johnson is a Lecturer in the Department of Communication Studies at California State University, Long Beach. He received his PhD in Communication Studies from the University of Texas at Austin in 2007. He is the author of several essays focusing on the study of rhetoric, human motivation, and sociopolitical controversy.

Rachel Kraft is a master's student in both Communication Studies and Public Affairs at the University of Texas at Austin. She is interested in political communication, new media use and voting, and intersections of the media and sport.

Timothy R. Steffensmeier is Assistant Professor of Communication Studies at Kansas State University. He has co-published an argumentation textbook and essays focused on deliberative democracy and community development. Steffensmeier earned a PhD from the University of Texas at Austin in 2005.

Sunshine P. Webster studies and teaches at the University of Texas at Austin as a doctoral student and an Assistant Instructor. As an organizational rhetorician, she studies organizational culture, temporality, and the rhetoric of popular culture. Specifically, she is interested in the intersections between work and home life and the ways popular messages shape experiences within these realms. As a woman and an athlete, she is always intrigued by media influences on and portrayals of femininity and the female body.

Luke Winslow is a doctoral candidate and an Assistant Instructor at the University of Texas at Austin. He earned his BA from Azusa Pacific University and his MA from Cal State Fullerton (both in California) before moving to Texas. His research interests include contemporary rhetorical criticism, the rhetoric of popular culture, and critical/cultural studies. More specifically, he is fascinated by how we use language to regulate behavior. This fascination often positions Luke's research at the intersection between the highly traditional discipline of rhetoric and the expression of the voiceless and marginalized in popular culture. He currently lives in Heaven, also known as Austin, Texas.

Jaime Wright is an Assistant Professor of Rhetoric at St. John's University in Queens, NY. She received her BA from the University of Alabama, her MA from Wake Forest University, and her PhD from the University of Texas in Austin. Her work focuses on the rhetorical intersections between history, argument, and post-structuralist theories of culture.

■ Index